Unity 2017 2D Game Development Projects

Create three interactive and engaging 2D games with
Unity 2017

Lauren S. Ferro

Francesco Sapio

BIRMINGHAM - MUMBAI

Unity 2017 2D Game Development Projects

Commissioning Editor: Amarabha Banerjee
Acquisition Editor: Larissa Pinto
Content Development Editor: Mohammed Yusuf Imaratwale
Technical Editor: Shweta Jadhav
Copy Editor: Safis Editing
Project Coordinator: Hardik Bhinde
Proofreader: Safis Editing
Indexer: Tejal Daruwale Soni
Graphics: Jason Monterio
Production Coordinator: Aparna Bhagat

First published: January 2018

Production reference: 1180118

Published by Packt Publishing Ltd.
Livery Place
35 Livery Street
Birmingham
B3 2PB, UK.

ISBN 978-1-78646-027-1

www.packtpub.com

`mapt.io`

Mapt is an online digital library that gives you full access to over 5,000 books and videos, as well as industry leading tools to help you plan your personal development and advance your career. For more information, please visit our website.

Why subscribe?

- Spend less time learning and more time coding with practical eBooks and Videos from over 4,000 industry professionals

- Improve your learning with Skill Plans built especially for you

- Get a free eBook or video every month

- Mapt is fully searchable

- Copy and paste, print, and bookmark content

PacktPub.com

Did you know that Packt offers eBook versions of every book published, with PDF and ePub files available? You can upgrade to the eBook version at `www.PacktPub.com` and as a print book customer, you are entitled to a discount on the eBook copy. Get in touch with us at `service@packtpub.com` for more details.

At `www.PacktPub.com`, you can also read a collection of free technical articles, sign up for a range of free newsletters, and receive exclusive discounts and offers on Packt books and eBooks.

Contributors

About the authors

Lauren S. Ferro has a PhD in player modeling. She works as a gamification consultant and designer in many different industries. She is an active researcher in user-/player-centered design. Lauren runs game workshops that focus on designing user-centered gaming experiences. She is also the creator of a game design resource, Gamicards, which is a prototyping tool for game experiences. She is passionate about the future of games, their technologies, and their potential to improve people's lives.

> *Packt Publishing - For the opportunity to write this book and be a part of the authoring community.*
> *Francesco Sapio - For your help and guidance throughout this book.*
> *Andreas Oehlke - For your time, comments, and suggestions.*
> *My family - For their motivation and encouragement.*
> *You, the reader - I hope that this book takes you on marvelous and intrepid adventures.*

Francesco Sapio has a Master's of Science, *summa cum laude* in engineering with a focus on AI and Robotics. Now, he is a PhD researcher.

He is a Unity and Unreal expert. Among many projects, he has developed *Gea2 (Sapienza)* and *Sticker Book* (Dataware Games), and has consulted for *Prosperity – Italy 1434* (Entertainment Game Apps, Inc) and *Projekt I.D* (RMIT).

He is an active writer on game development, authoring *Getting Started with Unity 5.x 2D Game Development, Unity UI Cookbook,* and many other books.

Finally, Francesco loves math, philosophy, logic, puzzle solving, and, most importantly, creating video games.

> *I'm deeply thankful to my family for their enthusiasm and support throughout my life; they have always encouraged me to do better, using the Latin expressions "Ad maiora" and "Per aspera ad astra" as motivation.*
> *I'm glad to have worked with Lauren Ferro; it has been a pleasure.*
> *Finally, a huge thanks to all the special people around me whom I love, in particular to my girlfriend; I'm grateful for all of your help with everything.*

About the reviewer

Andreas Oehlke is a professional software engineer and computer scientist who feels very much at home on any Linux/UNIX machine. He holds a bachelor's degree in computer science and loves to assemble and disassemble both software and hardware. His trademark has always been his enthusiasm and affinity for electronics and computers. His hobbies include game and web development, programming in general (software design and new languages), programming embedded systems with microcontrollers, sports, and making music.

He currently works full-time as a senior software engineer for a German financial institution. Furthermore, and has worked as a consultant and game developer in San Francisco, CA. He is also the author of the book *Learning LibGDX Game Development*. In his spare time, he shares his expertise with a German start-up called Gamerald.

Packt is searching for authors like you

If you're interested in becoming an author for Packt, please visit `authors.packtpub.com` and apply today. We have worked with thousands of developers and tech professionals, just like you, to help them share their insight with the global tech community. You can make a general application, apply for a specific hot topic that we are recruiting an author for, or submit your own idea.

Table of Contents

Preface   1

Chapter 1: Press Start   7

  Atoms of games   8

  Different approaches to games   9

  The game design process   10

    Workflow   10

      Concept development   11

      Design and prototyping   12

      Implementation   13

      Testing   13

      Iteration   14

      Finalizing   14

    A-Team   14

  Developing 2D games   15

    X, Y, and Z-axis   16

      Full 3D   16

      Orthographic (3D)   17

      2D with 3D graphics, also known as 2.5D   18

      Full 2D   19

      2D with a perspective camera   21

  The Unity Engine   22

    Downloading Unity   22

  An overview of built-in features in Unity   25

    Creating a new 2D project in Unity   26

    A brief overview of the Unity User Interface (UI)   27

    The main components of the UI in Unity   28

      Hierarchy Window   28

      Scene View   30

      Game View   31

      Inspector window   31

      Console window   33

      Project Window   34

    Customizing the workspace   34

      Hotkeys to keep in mind   37

      Primitive and placeholder objects   38

      Images   39

      3D model files   40

      Meshes and animations   40

Audio files	41
Naming conventions for assets (and in general)	41
Importing into Unity	41
Special folders	41
Assets	42
Editor	43
Editor default resources	44
Plugins	44
Gizmos	45
Standard Assets	46
StreamingAssets folder	48
Resources	48
Hidden Assets	49
Preparing for the projects in this book	49
Project 1 - Angel Cakes	49
Project 2 - intergalactic shooter: Quark	50
Project 3 - RETROformer	50
Summary	50
Chapter 2: Working with Assets	51
An overview of collecting games	53
Key features of collecting in games and things to keep in mind	54
What will you learn in the remainder of this chapter?	54
Textures and Sprites	55
Sprite Render	56
Sprite Editor	56
How to use the Sprite Editor	56
Sprite Packer	59
Sprite Creator is your friend when you have no assets	60
Setting up the Angel Cakes project	65
Folder setup	67
Importing assets into the engine	67
Configuring assets for the game	68
9-slicing Sprites	77
Best practices	85
Textures	85
Maximizing the space that you have	86
Scaling	86
Naming	87
Summary	87
Chapter 3: Let's Make Some Prefabs	89

Basics of audio and sound FX in Unity   90
Importing audio   92
    Audio Listener   92
    Audio Source   93
    Choosing sounds for background and FX   94
        Happy   95
        Sad   95
        Retro   95
Integrating background music in our game   96
Creating the Angel and the PlayerController   97
A brief overview of Unity's physics system   98
    Rigidbody   98
    Colliders   99
Assembling the Angel   100
    Tagging the player   101
    Creating the Script   102
    Enforcing components   103
    Exposing variables in the inspector   104
    From the player input to a new position in the world   106
Moving the character to the new position   107
    Testing the PlayerController   108
Collectable system   108
    Setting up the Angel Cakes   108
    Enforcing components, again!   110
    Triggering cake   111
    Testing the cake collectable system so far   113
Prefabs for our Game Objects   114
    Creating the Prefab for the player and the cake   114
Building the Map   115
Summary   118

Chapter 4: It's about U and I   119
Overview of the UI   120
Designing the user interface   121
    Programming the user interface   122
Four types of UI   123
    Diegetic   124
    Non-diegetic   125
    Spatial   126
    Meta   126

Usability and function	127
UI is not UX	128
Designing UIs for games	128
Feedback	128
Be bold, not ambiguous	130
Keep it simple, consistent, and focused	132
Ergonomics: devices, hardware, and gestures	132
Multi-device design	132
Meaning and integrity	133
Goals	133
Enjoyment	133
Test	133
Introduction to the UI system in Unity	133
Building UIs in Angel Cakes	134
Scripting a UI and integrating with the collection systems	134
Setting up the UI	135
Programming the scoring system	138
Increasing the score when the player collects a cake	139
Creating a Game Over Screen	140
Scripting the Game Over Screen	141
Last tweaks	142
Testing	143
More kinds of cakes	143
Adding more levels	144
Adding animations	144
Devils	145
Summary	145
Chapter 5: Freeze! Creating an Intergalactic Shooter	147
An overview of game #2	148
Overview of shooting games	149
First-Person	149
Third-Person	150
Top-down	150
Designing game #2	151
Setting up the project for game #2	152
Importing assets for the space shooter	152
Organizing the project	153
Introduction to the animation system	154
Concepts of Sprite animations	155

Generating the animations from the sprites	158
Adding a state behavior for destroying the explosion	160
Saving the explosion as a prefab	163
Summary	163
Chapter 6: No One Is Alone Forever	**165**
Creating a shooting system	166
Player controller	166
Requirements of the player controller	166
Creating the script	167
Moving the player	168
It's time to shoot	170
That explosion was bad	171
Testing the explosion	172
Enemy controller	174
Requirements of the enemy controller	174
Creating the enemy controller	174
New variables for the enemy controller	175
Modifying the movement	175
Shooting deadly bullets	177
Alternative enemy controller	177
Creating the second enemy controller	178
Changing the aiming system	178
Shooting with passion	179
Creating a bullet prefab	180
Creating a bullet controller	181
Enforcing components	181
Exposing variables in the Inspector	181
Getting the reference to the rigidbody	182
Auto-destroying the bullet	183
Moving the bullet	183
Hit spaceships	184
Exercises	185
Summary	186
Chapter 7: Getting Serious About Gameplay	**187**
Building the UI	188
Setting up the UI	188
Creating the lives counter	190
Creating the star score counter	194
Building an infinite scrolling map	195

Repeating the background	195
Falling stars and planets	198
Rotating satellites	199
Creating the prefabs	200
Including power-ups	200
Spawning system	202
Coroutines	202
Creating spawning points	202
Scripting the spawning system	203
Testing the game	206
Exercises	206
Other things you could consider adding to the game	208
Timer	208
Increase the speed	208
Combos	208
Bosses and waves	208
Summary	209
Chapter 8: Building a Tilemap and Importing it into Unity	211
Platforming games	211
Side-scrolling	212
Infinite scrolling/endless runner	212
Overview of the project for game #3 - RETROformer	212
Creating tiles	213
Introduction to the program - Tiled and Tiled2Unity	213
Mini-map	226
Changing level properties	226
Adding colliders to our tiles	228
Importing tilesets into Unity with Tiled2Unity	229
Post-Tiled2Unity	232
Summary	233
Chapter 9: Look, It Moves	235
Advanced animations	236
A short recap of the animation system	236
Setting up the sprite sheet for the animations	238
Creating the animations from the sprite sheet	242
Building the Animation State Machine	243
Summary	250
Chapter 10: Let's Get Physical	251

Physics Material 2D   252
Building the panda hero   257
Moving the panda   264
  The control scheme   264
    The Movement Component   265
    Setting up the Movement Component   270
Player Controller   270
Summary   272

Chapter 11: Don't Forget to Save!   273
  Save and load systems   273
    Creating a save/load system in Unity   274
      PlayerPrefs   275
      PlayerPrefs functions   276
      Variables to save in RETROformer 277
    Building the save/load system for our game   278
    Refining the save and load system   281
  Jump pads   282
    Creating the Jump Pad   282
  Wrapping up gameplay   286
    Creating the user interface   286
    Water zones   287
    Winning zone   291
  Enhancing the environment   292
  Testing   294
  Summary   294

Chapter 12: The Nature of Export   295
  Implementing mobile input for the game   295
    MovingController   296
    JumpController   299
  Exporting the game   301
    For Android   303
      Preparing an Android Unity project   304
  Summary   311

Other Books You May Enjoy   313

Index   317

Preface

Welcome to the world of 2D game development in Unity. In this book, we will explore how to use the powerful 2D features of the Unity engine to create three amazing games. You will learn many different skills throughout this book. Not only will these skills be applied to the games within this book, but they will provide you with a foundation for developing your own games.

With this said, let's get started!

Who this book is for

This is a book for game developers interested in building stunning 2D games from scratch. You will need to have a basic familiarity with game development techniques to get the most out of this book. However, no prior knowledge of Unity is expected or required, although having some programming skills, especially with C#, is preferable.

What this book covers

Chapter 1, *Press Start*, is our first chapter and will provide you with a primer about what game design and development are involved. This chapter offers an overview of the three different games that will be made throughout the book.

Chapter 2, *Working with Assets*, will get you started with Unity. This chapter begins with our first game—*Angel's Cakes*—and continues by explaining the importation of assets so that you can set up the foundations of the game (and others) within the book.

Chapter 3, *Let's Make Some Prefabs*, continues the development of our first game by introducing fundamental concepts in Unity. It also explains how to start scripting with C# to create most of the gameplay of this first project.

Chapter 4, *It's about U and I*, wraps up the first game of the book, and will guide you through understanding User Interfaces (UIs) in Unity.

Chapter 5, *Freeze! Creating an Intergalactic Shooter*, marks the beginning of the second game of this book, which, as the title suggests, will take place in outer space. This chapter will also introduce the animation system of Unity.

Chapter 6, *No One Is Alone Forever*, is all about adding a bit more substance to our shooter by integrating AI enemies into the rest of the game.

Chapter 7, *Getting Serious About Gameplay*, further iterates on the second game by implementing other core game mechanics as well as various suggestions and explanations on how to improve it.

Chapter 8, *Building a Tilemap and Importing It into Unity*, introduces a third-party tool for creating tilesets. Furthermore, you will learn how to incorporate these tiles into Unity to build 2D worlds for your third game.

Chapter 9, *Look, It Moves*, starts the actual development of the third and last game of this book by expanding the concepts learned for animation state machines and extending them for the main hero animation system.

Chapter 10, *Let's Get Physical*, focuses on some concepts of Physics 2D in Unity, and how these can be helpful to finish up the gameplay of the third game, in particular, to create a movement system that will work on both desktop computers and mobile devices.

Chapter 11, *Don't Forget to Save!*, outlines how to permanently store the data of your games, and how to use these techniques to create a save/load system.

Chapter 12, *The Nature of Export*, dives into how to export the games you made, especially the third one, to be played either as a standalone (Windows, Linux, or Mac) or on mobile devices, such as Android.

To get the most out of this book

In order to get the most out of this book, it's preferable that you have had some experience with some programming languages (specifically C#). Although this book will teach you how to script in Unity, this is not a programming book. In saying that, this book does not assume that you have any prior knowledge of Unity, scripting, or the other free programs that we will use (in Chapter 8, *Building a Tilemap and Importing It into Unity*). As a result, I highly recommend that you jump into the first chapter and start exploring the book. In fact, you can always revise sections of this book once you have developed your skills and understanding.

Download the example code files

You can download the example code files for this book from your account at
`www.packtpub.com`. If you purchased this book elsewhere, you can visit
`www.packtpub.com/support` and register to have the files emailed directly to you.

You can download the code files by following these steps:

1. Log in or register at `www.packtpub.com`.
2. Select the **SUPPORT** tab.
3. Click on **Code Downloads & Errata**.
4. Enter the name of the book in the **Search** box and follow the onscreen instructions.

Once the file is downloaded, please make sure that you unzip or extract the folder using the latest version of:

- WinRAR/7-Zip for Windows
- Zipeg/iZip/UnRarX for Mac
- 7-Zip/PeaZip for Linux

The code bundle for the book is also hosted on GitHub at `https://github.com/PacktPublishing/Unity-2017-2D-Game-Development-Projects`. We also have other code bundles from our rich catalog of books and videos available at `https://github.com/PacktPublishing/`. Check them out!

Download the color images

We also provide a PDF file that has color images of the screenshots/diagrams used in this book. You can download it here: `http://www.packtpub.com/sites/default/files/downloads/Unity20172DGameDevelopmentProjects_ColorImages.pdf`.

Conventions used

There are a number of text conventions used throughout this book.

`CodeInText`: Indicates code words in text, database table names, folder names, filenames, file extensions, pathnames, dummy URLs, user input, and Twitter handles. Here is an example: "Increase the `cakesCollected` variable every time the player collects a cake."

A block of code is set as follows:

```
void FixedUpdate () {
        //Get the new position of our character
        var x = transform.position.x + Input.GetAxis("Horizontal") *
Time.deltaTime * speed;
        var y = transform.position.y + Input.GetAxis("Vertical") *
Time.deltaTime * speed;
    }
```

When we wish to draw your attention to a particular part of a code block, the relevant lines or items are set in bold:

```
void Start() {
        rigidBody = GetComponent<Rigidbody2D>();
    }
```

Bold: Indicates a new term, an important word, or words that you see onscreen. For example, words in menus or dialog boxes appear in the text like this. Here is an example: "Select **System info** from the **Administration** panel."

Warnings or important notes appear like this.

Tips and tricks appear like this.

Get in touch

Feedback from our readers is always welcome.

General feedback: Email feedback@packtpub.com and mention the book title in the subject of your message. If you have questions about any aspect of this book, please email us at questions@packtpub.com.

Errata: Although we have taken every care to ensure the accuracy of our content, mistakes do happen. If you have found a mistake in this book, we would be grateful if you would report this to us. Please visit www.packtpub.com/submit-errata, selecting your book, clicking on the Errata Submission Form link, and entering the details.

Piracy: If you come across any illegal copies of our works in any form on the Internet, we would be grateful if you would provide us with the location address or website name. Please contact us at copyright@packtpub.com with a link to the material.

If you are interested in becoming an author: If there is a topic that you have expertise in and you are interested in either writing or contributing to a book, please visit authors.packtpub.com.

Reviews

Please leave a review. Once you have read and used this book, why not leave a review on the site that you purchased it from? Potential readers can then see and use your unbiased opinion to make purchase decisions, we at Packt can understand what you think about our products, and our authors can see your feedback on their book. Thank you!

For more information about Packt, please visit packtpub.com.

1

Press Start

Welcome. You are at the beginning of your journey into the world of 2D game development. Throughout this book, we will explore many things that the world of 2D games can offer and how to design exciting adventures. This book not only explains what to do in Unity but also what is involved in the game design process. In this way, you will have a solid foundation in game design and development.

In some instances throughout this chapter and the rest of the book, there are various links to resources (such as Unity documentation). In many of these instances, both the link and a QR code are provided. The intention here is to save time entering the URL into your browser if you are reading a hard copy of this book. Now with that said, this is what we will cover in this chapter:

- Game design
- The game design process
- Developing 2D games
- Unity Engine
- Creating new projects in Unity
- Preparing for the projects in this book
- Key tips and best practices for 2D (and general) game development
- Additional game design exercises to develop your skills as a game designer

By the end of this chapter, you will have achieved the following:

- Have a general understanding of game design and the processes involved in making a game
- Know how to download and set up Unity

• Know how to configure Unity for a 2D game project

Now, let's begin our journey.

Game design is an exciting adventure that draws from many different disciplines, such as programming, art, design, audio, and creative writing. This may be overwhelming, especially if you're new to game design. You may think "but I am neither a programmer nor a creative writer, and I can't draw to save my life!" If you have a passion for games, then game design *is* possible. However, it is not for the weary. Game design will challenge you and it will test your patience. However, I promise you that the feeling you get from learning how to make your first character move with text in a script, to having that character collect coins, shoot enemies, and finish a level is an extremely rewarding experience.

This book does not assume that you know anything about creating games or any of the skills that are associated with game development. Over the course of the book, you will learn the basics of programming in C#, how to create three different types of 2D games in Unity, and a whole lot more about the game design process in general. Fear not about the art or the sound, as we will be using some free asset packages and sounds so that you can create something magical. Of course, if you dare to push yourself, I encourage you to dabble in these areas, as even a basic level of understanding goes a long way.

Atoms of games

We can think of game designers like chemists, except chemists that create mixtures of entertainment, emotionally driven narratives, and exciting experiences. If you think back to chemistry in high school, we all learned that some things make smoke, other things make bubbles, and a few things when combined make explosions; games work in a similar way, just with different substances (for example, game elements and mechanics).

When it comes to the distinction between these substances, namely game elements, and mechanics, there are many interpretations of what they are and what they are made up of. For the purpose of this book, when a player performs an action, they are likely to get something. This could range from a Badge, Point(s), Levels, or part of a Story. The "thing" that the player gets is what we will define as a "game element". Of course, there are many different examples of and perspectives on what game elements are, but for the purposes of this book, this will be our definition.

On the other hand, since game elements are the outcome, then the process of how we get them is what we will define as *game mechanics*. This could be anything from trading with other players, exploring mysterious worlds, and even Winning or Losing. Performing or engaging in these actions will result in obtaining game elements.

When you're playing games, think about things that you are receiving during gameplay and how you get them. By being a bit more conscious during your own experiences and reflecting on them, you not only develop an awareness of the "reactions" that certain game elements and mechanics afford, it also provides you with a way to consider implementing these into your own games. As a result, you will learn how different combinations create different outcomes.

Different approaches to games

Games are enjoyable to play, we play them to entertain ourselves and friends. Over many decades, as games have developed along with the technologies that make them available, the context of their uses has also evolved. For example, most games are created to entertain us (for example, *Assassin's Creed*). That is, there is no underlying intention, such as to supplement/support curriculum material or teach us about science (for example, *Ludwig*) all the way to operational health and safety. Finally, there are games that have been developed for entertainment but have ended up being used for more intuitive reasons. This is because of the educational potential that they afford (for example, *Minecraft and Sid Meier's Civilization series*) some games that have been created for entertainment purposes have provided ways for students to learn and practice various topics. Lastly, there are game-like experiences or "gamified" experiences that apply game design principles to achieve everyday tasks, from becoming more productive at work, eating better and maintaining a healthier lifestyle, to managing finances and developing new skills (for example, *Habitica*).

If you want to learn all about gamification in Unity, I encourage you to have a look at Gamification with Unity 5.x. You can get an eBook or hardcopy version by going to the following link or scanning the QR code: `https://www.packtpub.com/game-development/gamification-unity-5x`.

Now that we have a brief understanding of what games are made of and their use in different contexts, it's time to understand the game design process.

The game design process

As I mentioned before, there are many things that define what *is* game design. For example, it is an opportunity to transport players to realities that we can only imagine to be people that we may only dream of. However, just as important as what it is and isn't, is how it is done. Generally speaking there is a systematic approach that game designers follow to create a game. It begins with the "idea"—the concept of what the game will be. This is usually not static and will change over the course of a game's development. From there, and depending on who is on your team, it will go through many design phases before becoming a prototype. Beyond the prototype phase, the actual game will enter the development process where the actual assets (and not placeholders) will be created and implemented. From this point, the game will go through an iterative cycle, where the game will undergo playtesting, changes, more playtesting, more changes, and then eventually it will be refined to the point where it will enter the last stages. Here, we will briefly explore each of these stages.

Workflow

The workflow process of game design is linear in the sense that there is an order that it takes place: concept development, prototyping, implementation, testing, and hitting release. This concept is illustrated here:

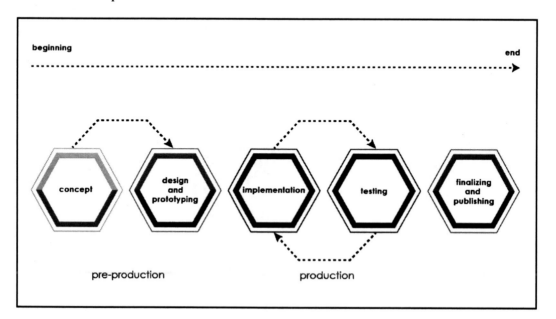

Of course, the diagram only outlines the process in general. As you develop games and work with others, you will find that this process loops in many other parts. Sometimes, through designing and prototyping your concept, you may end up having to change the initial idea. The important thing to remember is that while to some extent game design is a linear process, in terms of developmental stages, these stages do and will often form iterative cycles.

Concept development

We begin the process of game design by first brainstorming and then designing and prototyping a concept. The ideas at this stage can be adventurous, out there, and completely bizarre, because anything goes. It may be useful to get yourself a small notebook to write down your thoughts because they will come to you at any moment. Another thing to think about is who you are designing this game for. Do you know enough about them or do you need to do a bit more research? Defining your demographics early on can help when it comes to refining your idea. For example, if the people you are designing play role-playing games (RPGs) then they are likely to prefer a detailed narrative and character customizations, as opposed to premade characters and a simple story. Therefore, the kind of environment, what kind of narrative that it can afford, and the characters that you will create (and possible options for them) will need to be thought about while you're brainstorming ideas.

Some useful tips when it comes to concept development are listed here:

- Keep all your ideas in a journal or somewhere safe so that you can refer to them later.
- Challenge yourself if you're stuck with ideas on what kind of game to create. Choose the first thing that comes to your mind, flip a dictionary and choose a word at random; there are many ways to really push your creativity.
- Play games that you wouldn't normally play, and if you don't play, then start! By playing more games in different contexts and on different platforms (mobile, PC, PlayStation, and so on), you will begin to learn how experiences change depending on the hardware you're using to interact with. Pay attention to how the player controls differ between a mobile and console game. These little things will help you later when you start to design and prototype your game.
- Deconstruct games, identify the core features, and remake them. At the end of this chapter, there is a nice exercise for doing this but really think outside of the box. The aim is to be inventive, to create something new with the same concept.

- Learn about games! Don't just become the game designer, become a researcher, an explorer of games. Invest a little bit of time to learn what other game designers have done, how they have done it, what worked or didn't. There are many postmortem videos about games that explain the development process. In addition, it also gives you a bit more insight into the overall game design process and the roles and responsibility that each team member has. In this way, if you're thinking about creating a small (or large) team, you can understand what's involved.

- Be critical, be judgmental! If you played a game and didn't like, identify why that was. Was it the controls, perhaps the story was boring? Then take the guise of the designer, and think about how you would fix it: would you change or remove something, how would you make it better?

 Unfortunately, we won't be covering this stage in the book, as everything that we will be using in our projects is pre-made. However, what I do encourage you to do is that after you have learned about the projects that we will be doing in this book, brainstorm your own version of them. Instead of *Angel Cakes* (project 1), develop something that is to do with zombies or even fish! By doing this, you will be able to practice the first stage of game development and develop your brainstorming and conceptualization of game ideas.

Design and prototyping

This is where those crazy ideas become a bit more refined. You begin to weed through all your ideas, deciding which ones are feasible, which ones are not appropriate for your intended audiences, and so on. Start with pen and paper and draw out your game. You don't need to be an artist; prototyping is rough, it's messy, it is completely raw. Don't get caught up in how neat it looks. The point at this stage is to get what's in your head out on paper. Other things that you might find useful during the prototyping stage are post-it notes, colored pens, scissors, dice, counters (for example, beads, buttons, stones, and so on), other game bits and pieces (for example, *Monopoly* money, figurines, and so on). During the prototyping stage, you will want to also see how the interaction flows through the game. For example, does the interaction feel difficult in the sense you can't do or get something that you want to? Perhaps the game feels a bit too easy or hard? At this stage, these are considerations that you will also need to iron out when it comes to properly playtesting your game, so don't worry too much if they still don't feel completely right.

Since we won't be actively designing or prototyping the games in this book, you might want to think about how you would prototype them. One way to do this is to redesign them with your own ideas and then refine them through the design and prototype stage so that you can get a better understanding of this process.

Implementation

This is where you will transfer what you've conceptualized, designed, and prototyped into the actual game. Generally, this is where you begin integrating it into the game engine, working on the actual models that will feature in the game. At this point, you're no longer prototyping, but developing the game. From here on out, you should have a clear idea of what your game is and how it will work from beginning to end. Once you have begun implementing your assets into the actual game, you will go through various iterations. These iterations will often occur after playtesting, albeit informal or formally done (for example, open/closed alpha, beta testing). The projects in this book will start at this stage. This is because we already have assets ready for you to use. But it is important to know at what stage of the game development process that implementation is at.

Testing

This is probably *the* most important part. If you haven't already been doing this, then I would suggest that you stop what you're doing and start. Testing is such an important step in the process because it helps to make sure that your game runs smoothly and efficiently. Not only this, it can raise issues relating to player engagement, glitches/bugs/exploits within your game that can give other players an advantage when it comes to game time (especially in multiplayer games). We will cover playtesting in a later chapter, so we won't go into too much detail now.

Iteration

While you're testing, you will also need to iterate your design. Iterations may be minor, such as the location of objects, others may be large, such as changing the structure of a level or redoing the animation of a character. At this stage, it's about refining what your game is to make it what you want it to become. Each iteration is an improvement that will come with more testing. This is why testing is also very important because, without it, you're not able to refine and improve, or even fix part of your game, so that it gets to the stage that you envisioned it at from the beginning. Of course, you will get to a point where you find a minor change here and another one there, and you may even get caught up in the pursuit of perfection. All game designers have reached that point, so it's a common feeling of wanting "completeness" to the point of perfection, but it rarely comes. So when you get to this stage, you need to let go and move on. Otherwise, you will never complete any game, ever!

Finalizing

This is the polishing stage where you will begin to fine-tune what has already been implemented. This can include a range of different things from tweaking post-processing effects to character speeds. This is the final stage before you release your game on your targeted platform to the public. We will discuss this as we go with each of the three games, and in the final chapter so that your game will be ready to go.

A-Team

Who you have as part of your team can also impact the overall design and development of your game. Having the right resources, skill set, and even personalities can have a large influence on a game's success. Generally, a game development team consists of many different people: artists, designers, animators, programmers, and sound designers. Each of these roles will be sub-divided, for instance between character artists, texture artists, level designers, AI programmers, gameplay programmers, and so on. However, having a range of different skill sets allows for each part of the game's design to be developed in a concentrated environment by someone who has experience in the relevant field. However, not every game is lucky enough to feature an expansive team; you might even be reading this book without knowing anyone from any of these fields, which is why this book is here to guide you through the process and to support and expand your knowledge.

There are many game developers that post information "behind the scenes" of how their games are developed. These sometimes include commentary and interviews with various members of their team. A lot of these videos touch on the challenges that they face during the development of their game and in some cases the heartache of not being able to complete certain features or the game at all. I encourage you to check them out. There is one about the *Making of Assassin's Creed Unity* you can watch by visiting this link or scanning the QR code `https://www.youtube.com/watch?v=30jVQBpQSEU`:

Developing 2D games

There are some major and subtle differences between 2D and 3D game development, as well as some misconceptions. Here, we'll go through the most common ones, and touch on other relevant ones throughout the book. While you don't need a complete understanding of these differences, the ones here are important to keep in mind if you're new to 2D game development.

X, Y, and Z-axis

The first obvious difference between 2D and 3D is that 2D utilizes only two axes: X and Y; whereas 3D has an additional Z-axis. To explain how this works from a games perspective, see the following diagram:

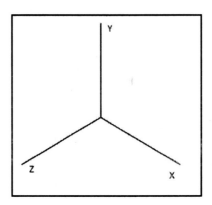

Generally speaking, the z-axis is used for depth and is utilized so that the player can explore an environment like they would in reality whether it is from a third person or first-person perspective camera. The z-axis allows the added third dimension to an environment. 2.5D games utilize the z-axis to provide a sense of depth because the game is still fixed to the x and y-axes.

In saying that, it is important to know the differences between 2D, 2.5D, and 3D games. While there are many different stories, quests, and adventures that games can take us on, these experiences, at least in terms of their appearance and design, will differ depending on what axis they are using—x, y, or z. Before we start creating any game in this book, we'll just briefly go through some examples of 3D and various types of 2D style games. In this way, you will learn about the differences between the two and what types of experiences that they can afford.

Full 3D

These games are everything from *Assassin's Creed* (featured in the following screenshot to *Skyrim* and everything in between. They are completely 3D immersive, explorable, and interactable environments. When you think about the design of a 3D game, you need to think about what the physical environment will look like. What kind of objects will be in it? How does the player navigate around them and through the world? For example, think about where you are right now.

If you had to turn your current environment into one that would be in a video game, what kinds of objects would you need to create? Perhaps a desk or chair, maybe a lamp? Then, how would players interact with these objects? What kind of effects would occur, such as a player turning the lamp on or off?

There are many basic and intricate details that go into making a 3D environment. Of course, they are not exclusive to 3D environments, as we will see in the other types of games, but these are some fundamental considerations.

Screenshot of Assassin's Creed

Orthographic (3D)

Just like the name suggests, orthographic 3D is a 3D game that is played from an orthographic perspective. Sometimes, these are also referred to as *Isometric* games and are given this name because of the perspective that they are played in. Some popular orthographic games include *Diablo, Q*bert, Clash of Clans,* and *Monument Valley* (featured next).

Unlike 3D, and depending on the type of gameplay that is required (for example, can the player rotate the environment?), the player will more than likely not see all sides of the game environment.

Screenshot of Monument Valley

2D with 3D graphics, also known as 2.5D

Think of 2.5D simply as a 3D environment constrained to a 2D plane (for example, x, y-axis). In other words, the player can only move up and down, left or right; they are not able to move on the z-axis. The use of 3D is merely used mostly for an aesthetic purpose, such as to show the depth of an environment. An example is shown next, with a screenshot taken from the game *New'n'Tasty*. In this screenshot, you can see the characters are constricted to a platform, with various levels (depths) of environmental assets visible in the background. When designing for 2.5D games, only a portion of the environmental assets are seen, as if you walked into a room and that is it, you can walk no further.

There are different practices and approaches to modeling assets for games like this, so I encourage you to explore them if 2.5D is something that piques your interest. Some other great examples of 2.5D games are *Little Big Planet, Trine, Bastion,* and *Raymond Origins.*

Screenshot of New'n'Tasty

Full 2D

Games that are restricted to the x and y-axis (and don't show any depth) are what we call 2D games, such as *Pac Man* (featured next). They can be top-down or side-scrolling (up/down/left/right). Unlike 3D games, players only see one side of the game object at any given moment. Sometimes this can be quite linear in the sense that there is no perception of depth (with the exclusion of parallax).

Often though, sprites can be brought to life, as can the environment, with beautiful (frame-by-frame) animations and effects. Other popular examples of 2D games are *Mario, Donkey Kong, Space Invaders, Monaco: What's Yours Is Mine, Mark of the Ninja,* and *Castlevania: Symphony of the Night*.

Screenshot of Pac Man

2D with a perspective camera

Like 2.5D games, 2D games can also utilize "depth" by using a perspective camera or utilizing a concept known as **parallax**, while not having any 3D assets within the environment. To understand the concept of the parallax effect at a more scientific level, let us look at the following diagram:

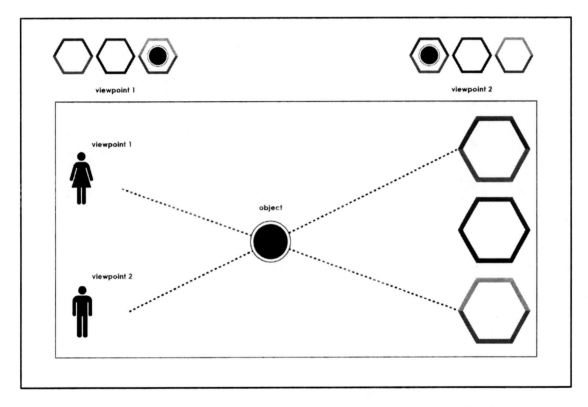

Depending on where you are, certain items are in view instead of others. If a player is at **viewpoint 1**, then they will see the black circle and blue hexagon; if they are at **viewpoint 2** then they will see the black circle and a red hexagon. Moreover, you can also think of it like this as well, when you move within a game space, the "background" that is closest to you moves faster than the "background" that is further away. It is the same when you're driving in an area, such as the country, and you can see the mountains moving slower than the fence. There are many games that use 2D with a perspective camera/parallax effect, such as *Braid* (featured next).

Other great examples of 2D games that feature parallax environments include *Terraria* and *Limbo*.

The Unity Engine

You've made it, you've decided you want to learn Unity, good for you! There are a few things that we need to do before we even open Unity (assuming you haven't downloaded it or used it before). If you have already downloaded Unity and set it up, you can skip the next section: *An overview of built-in features in Unity*; if you haven't please read on.

Downloading Unity

Now, let's start getting everything set up to create our games.

To begin, you can grab your own free copy of Unity by heading to the following URL: `https://unity3d.com/get-unity/download`.

 If you choose to download Unity 2018 Beta, it should not affect anything that you will do in this book. However, it is possible that some things will be slightly different than they are presented here. Please keep this in mind when deciding on which version to download. For this book, we are going to use the latest stable version at the time of writing.

Each plan has its own benefits, some with more added features than others. Depending on your long-term needs, a pro or plus plan might be useful. However, for all the projects in this book, we will be using the personal (free) version of Unity. Once you have chosen the version that suits your needs the most, download and install it.

While this book aims to teach you the basics of 2D game development, I encourage you to check out these four things (all available on the official website):

1. Tutorials `https://unity3d.com/learn/tutorials`
2. Documentation `https://docs.unity3d.com/2017.3/Documentation/Manual/`
3. Community `https://unity3d.com/community`
4. Social (for example, Twitter, Facebook groups, and so on)

Not only will you be able to explore a lot of the added 2D (and 3D) options that Unity offers, which aren't covered here, you can also learn about them through their own tutorials. Lastly, I highly encourage you to become part of the Unity Community and engage with their social media. In this way, you will be able to connect with other Unity game developers while at the same time being up to date with the latest news and be immersed in a great platform for you to share your own projects and questions with other game developers.

Once you have installed Unity, you will be required to log in. If you haven't created an account, don't fret, it's a straightforward process. Simply click on the *create one* link to do it. The process is simple, free, and will take little time to go through. Once you're done, come back and enter your login details, and click **Sign In**.

More detailed information can be found here: `https://unity3d.com/unity/activation/personal` or by scanning the following QR code.

Once you've done this, there will be a short survey about you (basic demographic information) and your intended use of Unity. This is the final step before we will use Unity. When you have submitted the survey response, you will see a screen with three different options: **Projects**, **Learn**, and **Activity**, like this:

Projects simply show all your current projects that are either found on your computer (**On Disk**) or online (**In the Cloud**). However, what I want to draw your attention to is the **Learn** tab, which is shown here:

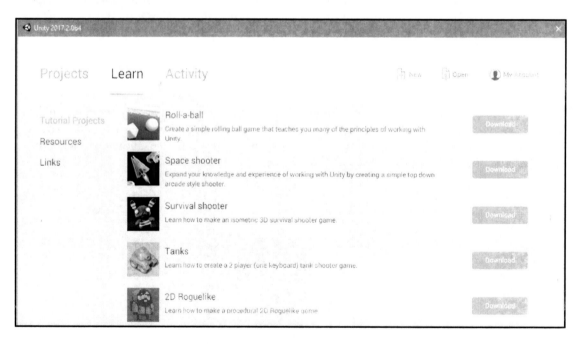

There are several types of tutorials that you can explore at your own pace, like the ones in this book, which will teach you some interesting things about Unity. You will need to download each tutorial to go through it and depending on your connection, it may take a little to no time. Here is an example of the **Survival shooter tutorial**, along with the instructions within the browser (left):

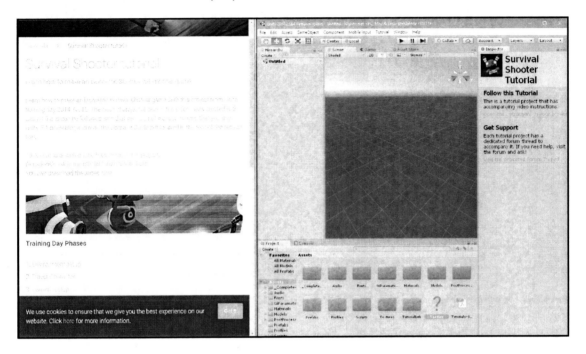

(left) The Survival Shooter tutorial that Unity offers. (right) The tutorial as viewed within Unity itself.

An overview of built-in features in Unity

Unity has some great built-in features. Let's begin by exploring some of the basics. Unity has many fantastic features, and we don't have enough time to cover them all. However, as we venture further into this book we will start to cover the fundamental and important ones. As you progress through the projects, we will begin to cover more advanced features.

Creating a new 2D project in Unity

To begin a new project within Unity, we first need set up the project files. When you open Unity, be sure to click on the **New** icon in the top navigation menu, on the right. Once you have done this, you will see a screen like this:

Do these things first:

- Give your project a unique name, something that isn't too long, but also descriptive enough.
- Next, in this window, we need to specify a location for your project that has enough space available and isn't going to be modified by other people (other than team members). This is more the case when it comes to shared workspaces and networks.
- Once you have done that, click on the radio button for **2D** as shown in the preceding screenshot.
- Now, click **Create Project**. We don't need to add any asset packages at this stage as we will be adding them manually later for each project.

Once you have done this, unity will open the project space, which we will discuss in more detail in the next section.

A brief overview of the Unity User Interface (UI)

Unity will begin setting up the project and once it's completed, you will see a screen like this:

This is an example of the Unity UI once you open Unity. As you can see there are no project files at this stage.

This might be a bit overwhelming if you're new to Unity, but don't worry, you will be up to speed in no time. We'll go through each part of it in more detail later in this chapter and throughout the book, starting in the top left corner with **Hierarchy**, **Scene**, **Game**, **Inspector**, **Console**, and finishing in the bottom left corner, with the **Project** panel.

The main components of the UI in Unity

These are the main "default" components that you will see. By default, this means they are here once you launch Unity for the first time or when you reset the workspace; we'll discuss how to do this later.

Hierarchy Window

The **Hierarchy Window** contains all of the **GameObject** within the current **Scene**. A **GameObject** can be anything from a prop or character to the scenery. In essence, GameObjects are like a *container* that we can place things into what we refer to **Component**. In Unity, **Component** can be for lighting, animation, character control, rendering, physics, colliders, and so on. It is these that give **GameObject** functionality. An example of the default **Hierarchy** window is this:

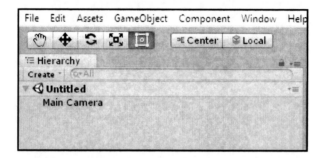

To put it simply, **GameObject** contain **Component**, which provides the functionality for **GameObject** within a **Scene**. As we begin to add and remove **GameObject** from the **Scene**, they will appear and disappear from the **Hierarchy** window as well. In addition, another handy thing to know is that anything within the **Hierarchy** window can be parented. Parenting simply establishes a hierarchy when it comes to the connection between **GameObject.** For example, a 3D asset may contain various parts that need to be moved and scaled together.

Therefore, the main **GameObject** becomes a *Parent* and all the other objects become *Children*. You can easily parent and unparent **GameObject** by simply selecting the main object and dragging it to where you want it to sit within the hierarchical structure. You can see this process illustrated here:

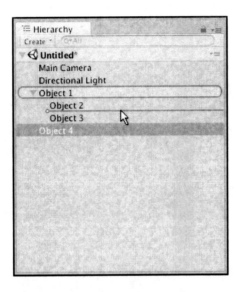

Lastly, it is possible to have more than one **Scene** opened in the **Hierarchy** window, but we won't need to do this in the projects in the book. If you would like to know more about it, head on over to the official Unity documentation by going to this link or scanning the QR code: https://docs.unity3d.com/Manual/MultiSceneEditing.html

Next, we will look at the "big picture" or the **Scene View** within Unity.

Scene View

The **Scene View** is where all the magic happens. In here is where you will create your game. You can see this part of the Unity UI, in the following screenshot. This is an interactive space where you can select, rearrange, and position all the **GameObject** within your project. We will cover **Scene View** navigation and how to move **GameObject** around in the next chapters.

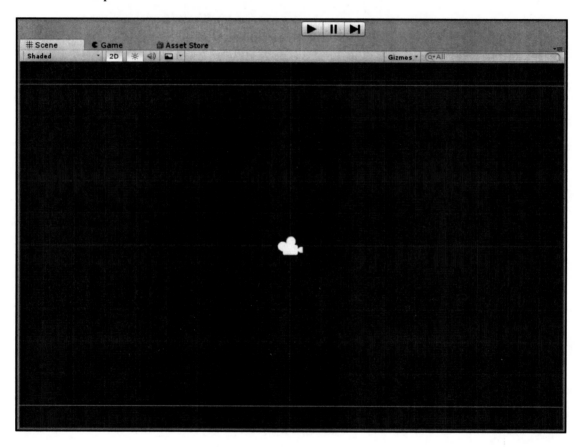

Game View

The **Game View** is very similar to the **Scene View**, giving a window into your game. In particular, the **Game View** shows which is the final result, what the player will see in your game. Also, the **Game View** can simulate different screen ratios. This allows you to control how your game will look on the different screens on which your game will run. Although this is a good preview, before a final release, you should still test on as many as real screens possible to ensure the best quality of your game. This is how it looks in Unity:

Inspector window

The **Inspector** window is where all the information related to the selected **GameObject** is presented. It will become one of the most used windows within the Unity UI. As we have already discussed, Scenes contain **GameObject** and these contain **Component**, and it is in the **Inspector** window (like in the following screenshot) that all the information of this Component is visible. This information relates to the properties and settings of not just **GameObject**, but to pretty much everything else within Unity, such as assets, materials, audio, and so on.

We will go into more details about properties that are listed within the **Inspector** window throughout the book, but for now, this is just an overview of what it does.

To get an idea of how it looks like when an object is selected here is an example of the **Inspector** when the default camera is selected:

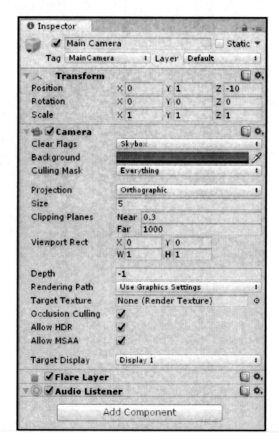

Console window

The **Console** window, which is shown next, shows errors, warnings, and other messages either generated by Unity or your own game code that relate to various parts of the project. These messages can be simple syntax errors within code or more problematic issues relating to performance. We will go into more detail about the different types of errors, how to resolve common ones, and how to run checks known as **Debugging**—to check where errors are occurring, in later chapters.

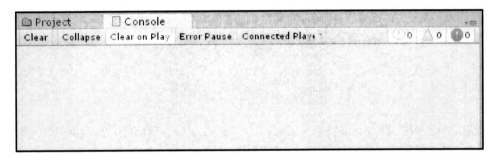

You will notice these errors as you play a Scene or try to run scripts. Each error will present itself with a name and a brief description of what the error is, and where it can be found within the script (for example, line number within a code file). Here is an example of a simple log:

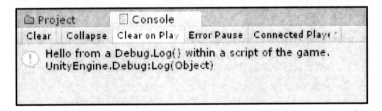

Project Window

The **Project** window will display every file within your project that you have either imported or created within Unity, such as models, scripts, plugins, and so on. Everything within your Unity project is (and should be) contained within a folder structure, with the Assets folder being the root—or parent folder, like in the following screenshot:

When you select a folder within the **Project** window the contents will be shown in the panel to the right, like in this screenshot:

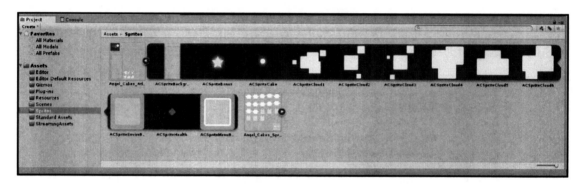

In this image. you can see the various Sprites that have been cut from the Sprite Sheet for Angel Cakes.

Customizing the workspace

It is quite easy to customize the layout of the workspace within Unity. There are many different panels which serve different purposes: the **Window** menu item in the top bar can be navigated to open additional panels or panels that have been closed earlier. To change the layout, move the mouse cursor over the panel's name you want to move and then press and hold the left mouse button. Holding down, drag the tab where you would like it to be. It can be a floating (for example, separate window, see the following screenshot) or anchored to another part of the Unity UI.

You can see the difference between floating (image on the left) and anchored next to the **Hierarchy** tab (image on the right) of the **Project** panel:

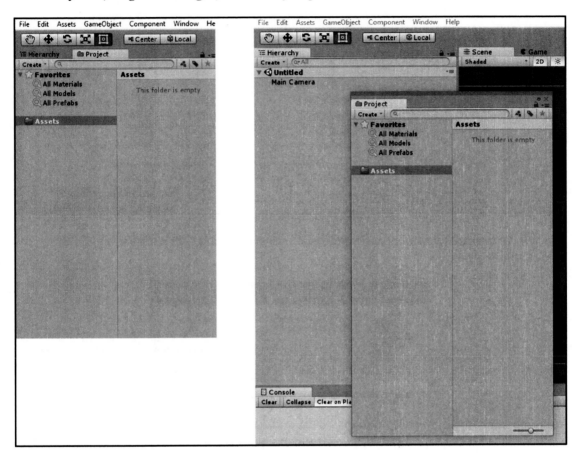

If you have rearranged the workspace and don't like it, you can reset to Unity's default layout. To do this, go to **Window** | **Layouts** | **Revert Factory Settings...**, as here:

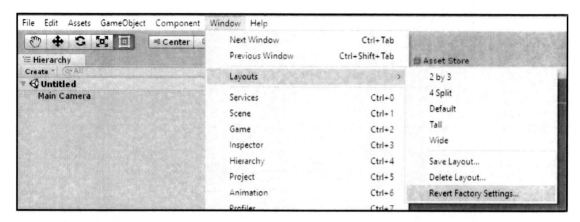

You will be prompted with a confirmation box, as shown here, click **Continue** and the layout will be reset.

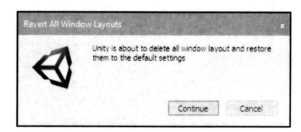

From the same menu, It is also possible to save and load custom layouts. By doing this, you can switch between your favorites layouts when you need to work on different aspects of your game.

Hotkeys to keep in mind

We all like to take shortcuts from time to time, and working with Unity, hotkeys can help make performing simple tasks a whole lot more efficient. Here is a list of useful hotkeys for actions that you'll perform on a regular basis throughout this book. Feel free to make a copy of this page or print it to reference later (the list has been taken from the official documentation of Unity at the following link: `https://docs.unity3d.com/Manual/UnityHotkeys.html`). Here are the most used ones:

Tools	
Keystroke	Command
Q	Pan
W	Move
E	Rotate
R	Scale
T	Rect Tool
Z	Pivot Mode toggle
X	Pivot Rotation Toggle
V	Vertex Snap
Ctrl/command + LMB	Snap

GameObject

Ctrl/command + Shift + N	**New empty game object**
Alt + Shift + N	New empty child to selected game object
Ctrl/command + Alt + F	Move to view
Ctrl/command + Shift + F	Align with view
Shift + F or double-F	Locks the scene view camera to the selected GameObject

Window	
Ctrl/command + 1	**Scene**
Ctrl/command + 2	**Game**
Ctrl/command + 3	**Inspector**
Ctrl/command + 4	**Hierarchy**
Ctrl/command + 5	**Project**
Ctrl/command + 6	**Animation**
Ctrl/command + 7	**Profiler**
Ctrl/command + 9	**Asset store**
Ctrl/command + 0	**Version control**
Ctrl/command + Shift + C	**Console**

Asset Workflow

When it comes to working with assets in Unity, there are some things specific to asset types to keep in mind. Below, we will go through different types of assets that are used within Unity and how they should be handled. We will also discuss some of these assets in more detail as we use them within our projects later in the book.

Primitive and placeholder objects

When you first start to build levels in Unity, primitive and placeholder objects can help you "block out" your level or use as player characters. Blocking out is simply just placing objects within the environment where the final version (even if it's not yet created) is intended to go.

These objects are a cube, sphere, plane, capsule, cylinder, and quad, and they are displayed here:

In the image above, you can see an example of each type of primitive/placeholder objects within Unity, along with their pivot point (arrows located in the center point to each of the 3 axis - x, y, and z).

You can add them by navigating through the top bar **GameObject / 3D Object**. Since these are 3D objects, we won't be discussing them in this book, but you can read more about these objects by visiting the link in the official documentation at `https://docs.unity3d.com/Manual/PrimitiveObjects.html` or by scanning this QR code:

Images

In general, the most common image files types are `BMP`, `TIF`, `TGA`, `PNG`, `JPG`, and `PSD` (photoshop file). Each file format serves a different purpose, with different settings, and varying file sizes. For example, `PNG` file formats allow you to have an alpha channel, which allows part of an image to be transparent, where a `JPG` does not. These are important things to keep in mind when deciding on what image format that you will need to export from your graphics program. We will cover how to import images with alpha channels, as well as sprite sheets and tilemaps later in the book.

If you save your layered Photoshop (.psd) files into your Assets folder, they will be imported as flattened images. This means that you cannot access the layers directly within Unity. If you need to make changes to a layer within your .psd file, you will need to do so within Photoshop.

3D model files

Whether you're a user of Maya, Max, Blender or anything in between, Unity can import a range of different 3D model file types (for example, .fbx, .dae (Collada), .3ds, .dxf, .obj, .blend, and .skp).

Meshes and animations

Some 3D models just remain static—they don't move; others, like characters, do. Importing meshes (3D models) with animations in Unity is a pretty straightforward process. We won't go into much detail about it here since this relates to 3D games, but you can read more about 3D meshes online by visiting this link https://docs.unity3d.com/Manual/HOWTO-importObject.html or by scanning the QR code here:

If you would like to find out more information about importing animations, you can do so by visiting this link to the official documentation https://docs.unity3d.com/460/Documentation/Manual/AnimationsImport.html or by scanning the QR code:

Audio files

Whether it is background music or sound effects, games often feature sounds. In Unity, just about every common audio file format can be imported (for example, `.mp3`, `.ogg`, `.wav`, and so on). We will discuss audio in more detail in `Chapter 3`, *Let's Make Some Prefabs*.

Naming conventions for assets (and in general)

You are free to create and use your own naming conventions, but to get you started, I encourage you to explore whatever kinds of naming conventions exist and find one that suits you and/or your team. We will explain the one that we will use in more detail in `Chapter 2`, *Working with Assets*.

Importing into Unity

Most assets that are used within Unity have been created externally, such as sprites, tilemaps, audio files, models, and so on. There is the possibility to save the source files in the actual Unity file so that whenever updates are made, they are automatically updated within Unity. You can learn more about this in detail by visiting the link the official documentation `https://docs.unity3d.com/Manual/ImportingAssets.html` or by scanning the QR code:

Special folders

Usually, when you create a project you will also need to create various folders to keep everything organized within the **Project** window. However, when naming your folders, there are a few names that Unity will interpret as an instruction for the folder's contents to be treated in a certain way. For example, for Editor scripts to work you must place them in a folder named `Editor`.

The folders `Assets`, `Editor`, `Editor Default Resources`, `Resources`, `Gizmos`, `Plugins`, `Standard Assets`, `StreamingAssets`, and `Hidden Assets`, which are described in more detail later, are not automatically created within Unity. Therefore, each time that you create a new project, you will need to create them manually. Keep in mind the names will trigger Unity to treat them accordingly, so be sure to not use them if they're not going to do what you intend them to. Here is a screenshot of what the Unity **Project** window would look like if you have created all the special folders.

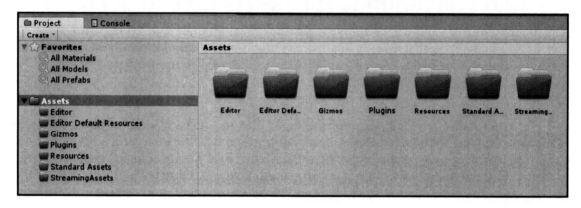

Image of the special folders setup

Assets

To begin, the `Assets` folder is the main folder. Think of it as the root directory, the `parent` folder, folder number one. The `Assets` folder contains the Assets (models, audio files, and so on) used in a Unity project. It will also contain any other folders, including the other special folders listed beneath `Assets` folder. Most API functions assume that everything is in the `Assets` folder, and therefore don't require it to be mentioned explicitly. This can be an oversight for game designers new to Unity, who may name the `Assets` folder differently. As you are likely to learn over time, there are some functions need to have the `Assets` folder, which is part of a file's pathname. For example, certain functions in the `AssetDatabase` class require that the `Assets` folder is included in the pathname. As a result, it is better to include this from the beginning of your path to Unity and your project structure.

Editor

Scripts placed in a folder called **Editor** are treated as Editor scripts rather than runtime scripts. In their essence, Editor scripts add or improve functionality within Unity, which is particularly relevant during development. In their essence Editor scripts extend Unity to suit your needs by implementing additional functionality (for example, new menus). On the other hand, Runtime scripts execute during gameplay and are the essence of your gameplay. We will focus more on runtime scripts during the rest of this book (for curiosity, you can keep reading this section, if you don't understand at first, that is fine; in fact, Editor scripts are an advanced topic in Unity development).

Lastly, like the location, the important thing to know is that Unity does not allow components inside the `Editor` folder to be assigned to a **GameObject** even if they derive from MonoBehaviour. What this means is that all runtime scripts that will be used in your game (for example, movement scripts), should be kept outside of the `Editor` folder.

It is important to keep in mind that where you place your `Editor` folder makes a difference with respect to other scripts that you have in your project. There is an order that Unity compiles and runs scripts, it is as follows:

- **Phase 1**: Runtime scripts are in folders called `Standard Assets`, `Pro Standard Assets`, and `Plugins`
- **Phase 2**: Editor scripts in folders named Editor that are anywhere inside top-level folders called `Standard Assets`, `Pro Standard Assets`, and `Plugins`
- **Phase 3**: All other scripts that are not in a folder/subfolder called `Editor`
- **Phase 4**: All remaining scripts (those that are inside a folder called `Editor`)

Since we won't be needing to create any Editor scripts, this will not be an issue, but if you want to know more about the script compilation order, then check out this link: `https://docs.unity3d.com/Manual/ScriptCompileOrderFolders.html`

Lastly, if this has peaked your curiosity, then there are some (intermediate) tutorials in the official documentation about Editor Scripting (among others), which can be found here: `https://unity3d.com/learn/tutorials/s/scripting`

Editor default resources

Editor Scripts can make use of Asset files loaded on-demand. This is done by using the `EditorGUIUtility.Load` function. This function looks directly at the Asset files in a folder called `Editor Default Resources`.

Place the needed Asset files in the `Editor Default Resources` folder (or an appropriate subfolder within it). Remember, if your Asset files are in subfolders, always include the subfolder path in the path passed to the `EditorGUIUtility.Load` function.

> You can only have one `Editor Default Resources` folder within a Unity Project. This folder must be placed in the root of the **Project** directly in the `Assets` folder.

Plugins

You can add plugins to your project so that you can extend many features in Unity as well as improve your own efficiency and workflow processes. Essentially, Plugins access third-party code libraries, system calls, and other Unity built-in functionality.

> These plugins are usually platform-depend (Win, Linux, Mac, Android, iOS, WP, and so on) and might be written with glue-code to allow calling specific OS level functions (APIs) that Unity doesn't provide access to through its classes. Those plugins are oftentimes also written in different programming languages like C/C++, Obj-C, C#, Java, and so on Moreover, the plugins folder allows differentiating between platforms by adding sub-folders per platform: x86, x86_64, Android, iOS, and so on.

We won't cover much 1of these things within our book, so don't worry. Furthermore, they are often easy to implement and use, especially if the plugin is well-done. The key thing to remember is that when you get a new plugin be sure to place it in a folder called `Plugins`. In this way, Unity will know how to handle them.

> Like many other types of folders, you can only have one `Plugins` folder and it must be placed in the `Assets` folder. You can refer to the screenshot at the beginning of this section to see this in action.

Gizmos

Gizmos allow you to add graphics to the Scene View. By doing so, they help you to visualize design details that are otherwise invisible. There are various Gizmos that can be displayed within the Scene View, which can be selected or deselected via the **Gizmos** menu. You can find the **Gizmos** menu at the top-right of the Scene View toolbar, like here:

Once you have clicked on this, a drop-down menu will be displayed:

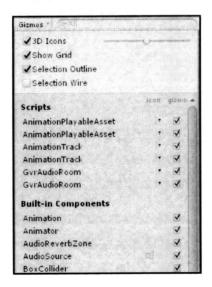

Gizmo menu

The Gizmos.DrawIcon function places an icon in the Scene to act as a marker for a special object or position. You must place the image file, which is used to draw this icon, directly in a folder called Gizmos. Otherwise, it cannot be located by the DrawIcon function.

 Like many of the other special folders, you can only have one Gizmos folder and it must be directly within the Assets folder.

Place the needed Asset files in this Gizmos folder or a subfolder within it. If you are placing an asset within a subfolder, remember to include the path in the Gizmos.DrawIcon function.

An example of Gizmos within Unity can be seen in the following screenshot (and their keyboard shortcuts):

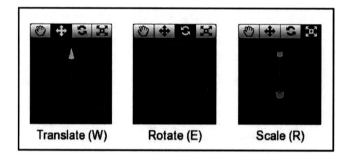

Example of Gizmos within Unity

Standard Assets

When you first import a Standard Asset package into Unity (**Assets | Import Package**) they will be automatically placed into a folder titled Standard Assets. This is also the case when you create a new project in Unity and opt to import Standard Assets, such as a first-person controller, skyboxes, lens flares, Water prefabs, Image Effects, and so on. As we saw earlier, when it comes to script compilation, these folders are also affected by that order.

 It is important to remember that you can only have one Standard Assets folder. In addition, any subfolders that it contains will also need to be placed inside of the Assets folder.

Some other important things to keep in mind about the `Standard Assets` folder is that depending on what version of Unity that you used to create your project, the assets may or may not be the same because Standard Assets that are included when you select them for a new project are only relevant to the build of Unity that you are using. Therefore, if you update/upgrade Unity, the assets won't update along with it, and you will have to do it manually. You can do this easily by following these steps:

1. Open your project
2. In the **Project** window, right-click on **Assets** and then select **Import Package** submenu
3. Select from the list the Assets that you wish to replace, and click **Import**

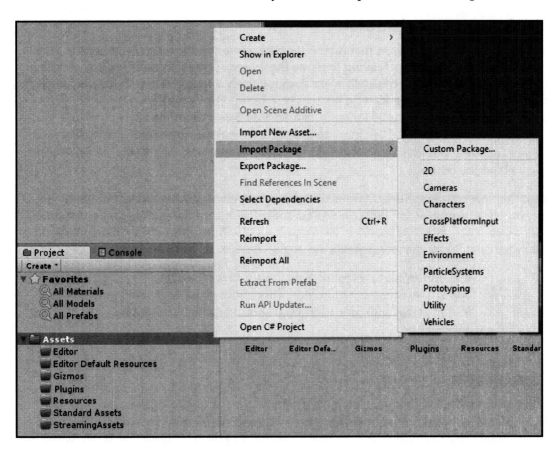

It is important to remember that when you update your assets it will replace files with the newer version. However, it will not remove obsolete files from the earlier version of the Standard Assets. For projects where you are not using all the files, you may want to consider backing up and then removing the old Standard Assets from the project before installing the updated version. This will also help to keep things clean and organized once your project gets larger and you're working with a large number of files. One thing to keep in mind, which we will discuss in a later chapter is that when we will be packaging our games, Unity has a nifty feature that only includes assets that are being used within the project. That way when your project is built it will not have any assets that aren't being used reducing the file size, among other things.

StreamingAssets folder

The first thing that I want you to notice is that the name of this folder is one word. This is because we have used camel casing to name the folder. Camel casing is writing words or phrases (without spaces) with each word begging with a capital letter. Often, the beginning of a camel casing name begins with a lower case letter. For example, `camelCasingIsWrittenLikeThis`. Of course, you can write it like so, `CamelCasingIsWrittenLikeThis`. Just be sure to remain consistent. Lastly, the `StreamingAssets` folder is the only special folder that uses camel casing, so no need to worry about the others.

What this special folder allows you is to stream an asset, such as a video, on the device. Keeping the example of the video, it will be copied as it is in the package game (and not like other assets, such as *MovieTextures*). As a result, you will be able to play (using streaming) that video on your device, for instance on an iOS device.

> It is important to remember that you can have only one `StreamingAssets` folder. This folder must be located in the `Asset` folder, along with any additional subfolders that it contains.

Resources

Unlike the previous folder, you can have as many `Resources` folders as you wish and they can be placed anywhere in your project (keep in mind that if they are sub-folder of an `Editor` folder, that resources will be available only to Editor Scripts). However, when you load assets from this folder, they will all be merged, and they will seem like a single folder.

What this folder allows you to do is to load assets on demand, so they are not in memory (RAM) until you explicitly load them with the `Resources.Load` function.

Hidden Assets

When you begin to import files into Unity, it is important to know that some files and folders are completely ignored by Unity. The reason for this is to avoid importing special and/or temporary files that are created by the operating system (for example, Windows, OSX) and other applications. The types of files and folders that are ignored are those:

- That start with `'.'`
- That end with `'~'`
- Named `.cvs`
- That contains the extension `.tmp`

Preparing for the projects in this book

By the end of this book, you will have three pretty cool projects to add to either your own portfolio or show your friends and family. Each project will build on the skills learned in the previous one. In this way, you will not only be consolidating your own skills but also adapting them to different situations—a versatile skill for anyone who truly wants to grasp game design. All the assets that we will be using are free and links will be provided to you to download all the content for each game. Here, I have included a brief description of each of these projects to give you an idea of what we will be tackling throughout the rest of this book.

Project 1 - Angel Cakes

Our first project is titled *Angel Cakes* and as you can guess there are an *Angel* and *Cake*. In this game, you will control a little angel that will navigate around the environment. Similar to *Pac-Man*, you will also collect little cakes in order to progress to harder and more challenging levels. There will be enemies, power-ups, and health should you need to collect it. Think of this game as an intro to the basics of setting up a 2D Unity game project.

You can download the asset package for Angel Cakes here: `http://player26.com/product/angelcakes/`.

Project 2 - intergalactic shooter: Quark

Our second project will be a simple intergalactic shooter that will have us controlling a small spaceship shooting at nearby planets and enemies to score as high as possible within the time limit. It is quite arcade-like and very basic, but it will draw upon the skills that you learned from *Angel Cakes* while also extending on them to create more complex interaction.

You can download the asset package for *Quark* here: `http://player26.com/product/quark/`.

Project 3 - RETROformer

Our third and final game will be a platformer game titled *RETROformer*. In this final game, the player can collect coins, shoot enemies, and explore the environment. Essentially, this project will combine everything that you have learned previously with *Angel Cakes* and *Quark*, and build upon it. By the end of the project, you will have developed a strong understanding of what is involved in making games in different genres with different game elements and mechanics.

You can download the asset package for *RETROformer* here: `http://player26.com/product/retroformer/`

Summary

Throughout this chapter, we have explored what games are made up of and how they are developed and learned about the processes involved in making a game. From brainstorming to publishing, this chapter has provided you with a brief overview of the process of developing a game either by yourself or within a team. In addition, this chapter has shown you how to download, install, and get Unity ready for a 2D game project, while also covering some general features.

In `Chapter 2`, *Working With Assets*, we will begin using Unity to develop our first project, *Angel Cakes*. You will learn how to import various delectable game assets and get them ready to use and apply scripts to. So what are you waiting for, turn the page!

2
Working with Assets

Welcome to Chapter 2, *Working with Assets*. In a way, you can think of this as leveling up as you begin to progress through the book. Give yourself a pat on the back, you're persisting through the early stages of game development. Good for you! Now, this chapter gets a little bit hands-on; it will prepare you for what is to come in Chapter 3, *Let's Make Some Prefabs*. We will get you familiar with all the different settings and tools in Unity when it comes to handling Sprites. In addition, we will also begin our journey into 2D game development. Our first game will be a 2D top-down arcade-style game, like the famous *Pac-Man*; you can see an example of what our (finished) game will be like in the following figure:

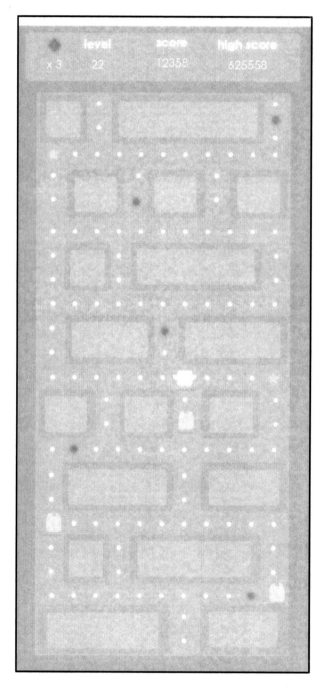

This is what Angel Cakes will look like once we have finished implementing all our assets

Throughout this chapter and by making this game, you will learn a bit about what is involved in creating a game that is focused on collecting objects. We will do this by exploring some famous examples in other games both old and new. You will then begin to import assets into Unity and get all the graphics set up and ready to go. By the end of this chapter, you will have your images sliced up and ready to be implemented.

The following is an overview of what we will be covering throughout this chapter and what you will learn by the end of it:

- What are Textures and Sprites?
- What is the Sprite Renderer?
- Sprite Editor
- Sprite Packer
- Sprite Creator
- How to set up the Angel Cakes project, including how to generate Sprites from an Atlas and Sprite Sheet
- Best practices for getting the project ready for applying scripts and sound effects

By the end of this chapter, you will know the following:

- The core tools for creating, modifying, and editing Sprites and Textures
- How to use the core tools and utilize them for the assets within the project

So, let's get going!

An overview of collecting games

Before we start making our first game, we can begin to learn and understand what games that focus on collecting are about and how they use the act of collecting as part of their core mechanics. There are many examples of these types of games in both 2D and 3D, and to give you some examples and inspiration for your own games, here is a brief overview.

Key features of collecting in games and things to keep in mind

Like we have seen with the preceding examples, it goes without saying that the key feature of a collecting game is, well... collecting something. This could be coins or items; such things may also be used to represent other elements, such as collecting hearts for health. The core mechanic is that the player must collect something to meet a certain condition, such as gaining lives, leveling up, or progressing. There are various other components and parameters that you can implement into a collecting game, such as enemies, the value of items, the frequency of rare items, and so forth. In this way, it is not only about what the player is collecting, but you as a game designer must also define how, when, and how often the player is able to collect the items.

There isn't much that can go wrong when it comes to creating a collecting game per se. Ideally, you want the game to be balanced and challenging. This becomes an issue when it is time to assign points to various of parameters. The right number that you should assign to these will be refined through playtesting, so don't be too worried if they aren't right in the beginning. To get a better understanding of how games focused on collecting are balanced, I encourage you to play any of the preceding games if you can access them or watch some playthroughs on YouTube.

What will you learn in the remainder of this chapter?

By now, you should have a better understanding of games that focus on collecting items. Now we're going to create our own. Of course, you're welcome to use your own graphics and images, but for this tutorial, you are welcome to download the free asset pack online. We'll cover this later in this chapter.

Textures and Sprites

Before you start anything within Unity, it is useful to know that Textures and Sprites within Unity are two separate things, although they are used in similar contexts. To begin, a Sprite is an image that can be used as a 2D object. It has only two coordinates: x-axis and y-axis. Therefore, all the graphical components of 2D game development are called **Sprites**. Sprites can be repositioned, scaled, and rotated like any other game object in Unity. You can move, destroy, or create it during the game. Sprites, by default, are rendered directly against the camera; however, you can easily change this if you are using the **Sprite Renderer** in a 3D scene. They work with the Sprite Renderer, unlike a 3D object, which works with the **Mesh Renderer**. Aside from Sprites, there are other graphical components called **Textures**. These are also images, but they are used to change the appearance of an object in both 2D (for example, Sprites and background) and 3D (for example, an object or character's appearance). But Textures are not objects. This means that you cannot get them to move during gameplay. Saying that, you can create images with Textures that animate, with Sprite Sheets/Atlases. What this means is that each frame of an animation is placed on a Sprite Sheet, which is a Texture, that will eventually be cut up so that each frame of the animation is played sequentially. Throughout this book, we will use the terms Sprite Sheets and Atlases. While they are pretty much the same thing, the subtle difference between the two is that a Sprite Sheet generally has Sprite (frame-by-frame) animations, whereas an Atlas will contain images such as tileable Textures for the walls and other environmental components (for example, objects). Their purpose is to maximize the space by combining multiple images into one Texture, whether for characters (and their animations) or environmental Textures.

More generally speaking, when it comes to handling Sprites and Textures, Unity has various tools that deal with them in different ways and are used for different purposes. A brief overview of each of them follows. We will discuss them in more detail throughout this chapter:

- **Sprite Editor**: This is used to edit Sprites. This is done by selecting them individually from a larger image, known as a Sprite Atlas, or by changing their Pivot point, and so on.
- **Sprite Creator**: This is used to create a Sprite placeholder. This is useful if you do not have any Sprites to use but want to continue implementing the functionality of a game. Sprite placeholders can be replaced later with actual Sprites.
- **Sprite Packer**: This is used to *increase* the *efficiency* of your project's usage of main memory. It achieves this by packing various Sprites into a single place using the **Packing Tag** attribute. This appears in the **Inspector** window when you select a Sprite in the **Project** window.

Sprite Render

The **Sprite Render** displays images that have been imported as the type Sprite. There are a number of different parameters within the Sprite Render that allows you to modify a Sprite. We will discuss them here:

- **Color**: Color allows you to change the color value and the value of the Alpha channel (transparency) of a Sprite
- **Flip**: Flip is what defines the axis that the Sprite needs to be flipped on
- **Material**: Material refers to the material that Unity will use to render the Sprite
- **Sorting Layer**: Sorting Layer defines which layer the Sprite should be rendered on (it basically indicates the order in which the different Sprites are drawn, for example, which one is on top of the others)
- **Order in Layer**: Order in Layer is the order within the Sorting Layer

Sprite Editor

In some cases, you may have a Texture that contains just one graphic element; in other cases, you may have multiple ones. The latter is more effective for many reasons, such as saving computational resources and keeping things organized. A case in which you are likely to combine many Sprites into one Texture may be frame-by-frame animations of a character, where other Sprites may be parts of a character (such as clothing and items), and will need to be customizable, such as different items (and their effects). In Unity, you can easily extract elements from a single Texture by using the Sprite Editor. The Sprite Editor is used to take multiple elements from an Atlas or Sprite Sheet and slice them into individual Sprites.

How to use the Sprite Editor

To open the **Sprite Editor**, perform the following steps:

1. Drag and drop some images (anything you have on your computer, so you can have them as test images) into the **Project** panel.
2. Select the 2D image you want to edit from the **Project** view.
3. In the **Inspector**, change the **Texture Type** into **Sprite (2D and UI)**, so you will be able to use it within the **Sprite Editor**.

4. Click on the **Sprite Editor** button in the **Texture Import Inspector** and the **Sprite Editor** displays.
   When you open the **Sprite Editor** window, you can move it around like any other window within Unity; you can also dock next to others such as the **Hierarchy** or **Project** windows.

5. To select the **Sprites**, simply click and drag on the **Sprite** that you wish to select. As a result, you will have bounding boxes around each **Sprite** element that you have selected, as in the following screenshot:

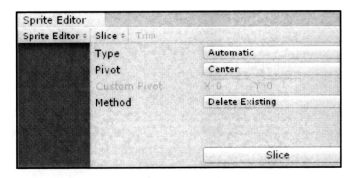

6. If you happen to click and drag too much around a **Sprite**, don't panic! You can easily resize the bounding box by clicking on any of the four corners or edges of the bounding box, like in the upcoming screenshot. Alternatively, you can also reposition the bounding box by clicking and dragging in the middle of the box itself.

7. While you're creating these selections, it is important to make sure that you name them appropriately. To do this, click on the box surrounding the **Sprite** that you wish to name. You will notice that a box appears.

8. Now, next to where it says **Name** is where you enter the name that you wish to call your Sprite.

Another thing that is also to keep in mind here is the **Pivot** of the **Sprite**. Think of this as the Sprite's center. For example, if you rotate a Sprite, it will rotate wherever its **Pivot** is .0.

A few more elements that you will also find useful while you are slicing up your **Sprites** are the options located at the top of the **Sprite Editor** window. We will discuss them now.

You can only see the **Sprite Editor** button if the **TextureType** on the image you have selected is set to **Sprite** (2D and UI). In addition, you cannot edit a Sprite which is in the **Scene** view.

- **Slice Menu**: One great feature of Unity is the opportunity to automatically slice Sprites. What this means is that if you have a large Sprite sheet with various animations, images, and so on, you can automatically cut each image out. You have two options to do this:

    - **Automatic**: Automatic is better for when you have unevenly distributed Sprites, such as the case with an Atlas. When choosing the location of the Pivot, it will, by default set it to the center.

    - **Method:** Method tells you how to deal with existing Sprites within the **Sprite Editor** window. For example, if you select **Delete Existing**, it replaces any **Sprites** that exist (with the same name) with new **Sprites**; Smart will try to create new Sprites while at the same time adjusting existing ones, and Safe will add new Sprites without changing any that currently exist.

- The **Grid** is better for when you have Sprites that are evenly distributed, such as frame-by-frame animations. In these cases, it is not recommended to use Automatic because the size differences between each Sprite may cause unintended effects in terms of how they appear within the game, such as the Pivot being in the wrong location, resulting in an inaccurate animation. An example of the **Grid** menu is shown in the following screenshot. **Pixel Size** sets the size of the **Grid** in the unit of **Pixels.** This number will be determined based on the size of your **Sprite Sheet** and distribution of Sprites:

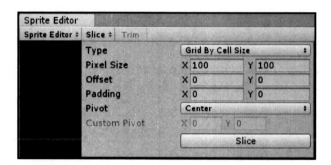

Sprite Packer

Using the **Sprite Packer,** you can combine multiple elements such as large sets of Sprites into a single Texture known as an Atlas. However, before using it, we must first make sure that it is enabled within Unity. To do this, go to **Edit | Project Settings | Editor.**

Once you have done this, look at the **Inspector**; you can change the **Sprite Packer** from **disabled** to **Always Enabled** or vice versa. You can see an example of this in the following screenshot. By selecting **Always Enabled**. The Sprite Packer will always be enabled whenever you start a new project. That way, you will not need to worry about enabling it again:

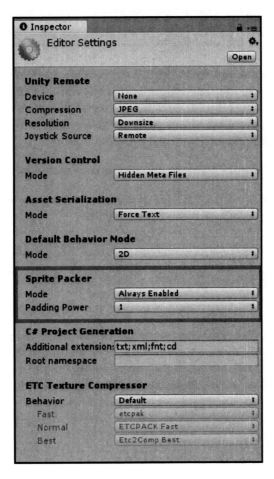

One of the benefits of using this is that it can boost the performance of your game by reducing the number of **Draw Calls** each frame. This is because a significant portion of a Sprite Texture will often be taken up by the empty space between the graphic elements. As a result, it wastes video memory at runtime because it needs to compute this empty space even if there is nothing there. By keeping this in mind, when you are creating your own Sprites, try to pack graphics from several Sprite Textures together and as close as possible to one another within an Atlas. Lastly, keep in mind that depending on the sizes of your Sprites, an Atlas should not be larger than 2048 x 2048 or 2^{11} (or at least, this guarantees compatibility with many devices). Therefore, if you need to resize some elements within your scene, revisit the power of 2 table in Chapter 1, *Press Start*, to see what values you can use to better utilize the dimensions of the Atlas. This is handy only if you want all the Sprites to be in one Atlas. Otherwise, if your Sprites are bigger than the Atlas's maximum dimensions, or you're trying to pack more Sprites than a single Atlas can handle, it will create multiple pages. We will cover this in more detail later in the book.

Unity handles the generation and use of Sprite Atlas Textures behind the scenes so that the user does not need to do any manual assignment. The Atlas can optionally be packed on entering **Play** mode or during a build, and the graphics for a sprite object will be obtained from the Atlas once it is generated. Users are required to specify a Packing Tag in the Texture Importer to enable packing for Sprites of that Texture.

To use the Sprite packer, simply go to the top navigation menu and select **Window | Sprite Packer**.

Once you have done this, it will open the **Sprite Packer**.

Sprite Creator is your friend when you have no assets

While we have Sprites, in this case, you might not always have them. If you don't have Sprites, you can always add placeholders or images in the place of where they are likely to be. This is a useful thing to use when you're prototyping an idea and you need to get functionality working before your images are ready to go. Using the **Sprite Creator** is quite simple.

We can create a placeholder Sprite by doing the following:

1. First, select **Assets** | **Create** | **Sprites**.
2. Next, select the placeholder Sprite you want to make, like in the following screenshot. Unity offers only six different placeholder Sprites: **Square**, **Circle**, **Triangle**, **Diamond**, **Hexagon**, and **Polygon**. Before creating the Sprite, it is important to make sure that you select the folder that you want the Sprite to be created in. This just saves time later from having to move it to the correct folder. This is because, when creating a Sprite with the **Sprite Creator**, it will automatically place it in the Asset folder that you currently have open in the **Project Window**.
3. Lastly, from the list, select the placeholder Sprite that you wish to use:

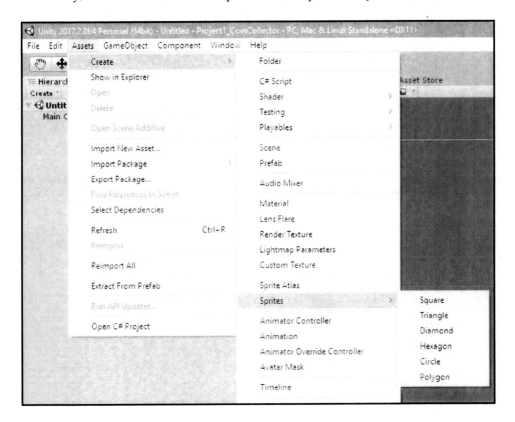

Once you have chosen your Sprite, it will appear as a white shape. The Texture created by Unity will use the .png file format and contain default image data of 4x4 white pixels. At this stage, the new Sprite will have a default name based on its shapes, such as **Square** or **Circle**. You have the option to rename it, but if you don't change it, don't worry, as each additional Sprite that is the same shape will simply have a number following its name. You can, of course, always change the name of the Sprite later by clicking on it in the Asset folder where it is located:

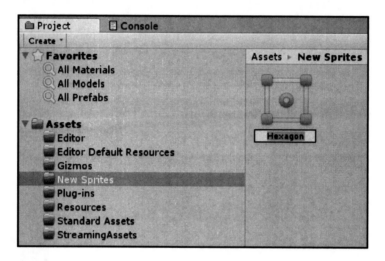

Once your new Sprite has been created, simply drag and drop your placeholder Sprite into the **Scene** view or **Hierarchy** to start using it in your project. An example of this can be seen in the following screenshot:

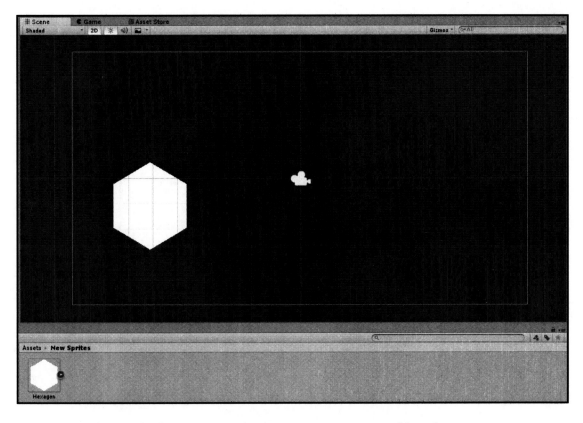

Once you're done, whether it is a mock-up, prototype, or something else, you may want to change the placeholder Sprite to the actual image. Once you have imported the new image(s), simply do the following:

1. Click on the **Sprite** within the **Scene** view so that it is selected.

2. Now, in the **Inspector**, locate **Sprite Renderer Component**. An example of this is shown in the following screenshot:

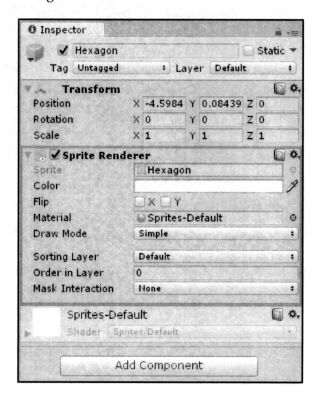

3. Now, where it says **Sprite**, click on the small circle located next to the Sprite name, in this case, **Hexagon**. This is highlighted in the following screenshot:

4. Now, a small window will be displayed, like in the following screenshot:

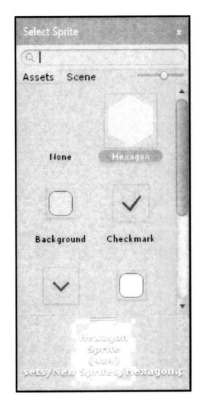

The Sprite Creator makes 4x4 white PNG outline Textures, which is a power of 2-sized Texture that is actually generated by an algorithm.

Setting up the Angel Cakes project

Now we're going to discuss how to set up our first project! For the rest of the chapter, we're going to discuss how to import the assets for the *Angel Cakes* project into Unity and get the project ready to go. We'll cover the interaction part of this game in Chapter 3, *Let's Make Some Prefabs*, so for now, we'll cover the process for importing and setting up while getting you familiar with 2D assets.

To begin, let's get the *Angel Cakes* asset pack, which is featured in the following screenshot:

To download the assets, simply visit `www.player26.com/product/Angelcakes` and download the `.zip` file. Once you have finished downloading it, simply unzip the file with a program such as WinRAR.

Folder setup

Like we discussed in Chapter 1, *Press Start*, you need to make sure that you have some foundational folders created to use with your project. To briefly recap, have a look at the following screenshot. Remember that the Assets folder is always the root or parent folder for the project files:

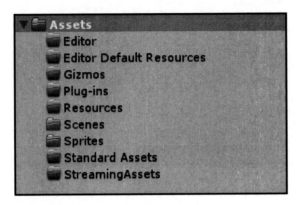

Importing assets into the engine

With your folders set up, we now begin to import some images for our project: the background, the player, an enemy, player collision (wall, objects), and collectables (*Angel Cakes*, health, and bonuses). Importing the assets into Unity is easy. As we discussed in Chapter 1, *Press Start*, Unity accepts most image formats, including the ones within this package:

1. First, click on the folder that you want the Sprites to be imported into, inside the **Project** window; for this project, we will use the folder titled Sprites
2. Next, in the top menu, click **Assets** | **Import New Assets** and navigate to the folder that they are located in
3. Once you have found them, select them and then click **Import**

4. Once they are imported, they will appear in the folder, like in the following screenshot:

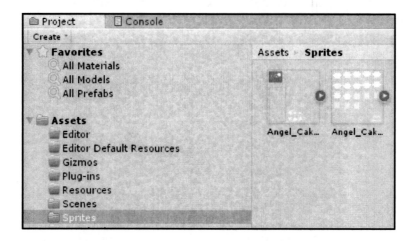

Configuring assets for the game

The assets used in this game do not need much configuring, in comparison to the ones that we will use later.

Once you have imported the two Sprites into Unity, do the following:

1. Select each one within the **Project** window.
2. Now, in the **Inspector**, change the **Sprite Mode** to **Multiple**. This is because we have multiple images of each Texture. One is an Atlas (the environmental objects) and one is a Sprite Sheet (character animations).
3. Once you have done this, click **Apply**:

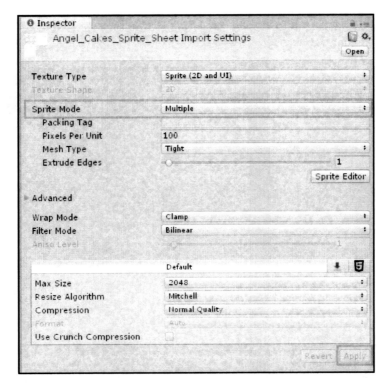

Once you have changed the **Sprite Mode** to **Multiple**, click **Sprite Editor.** Now you should see something like the following screenshot:

1. First, click on **Slice** and select **Grid By Cell Size**
2. Next, in **Pixel Size**, change the values of **X** and **Y** to **50**, like in the following screenshot, then click **Slice**:

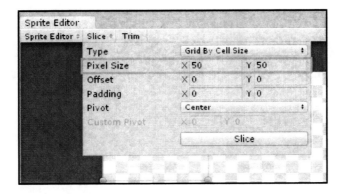

Now, if you hold down *Ctrl* (or *command* on a Mac) you will see all the freshly cut slices, like in the following screenshot:

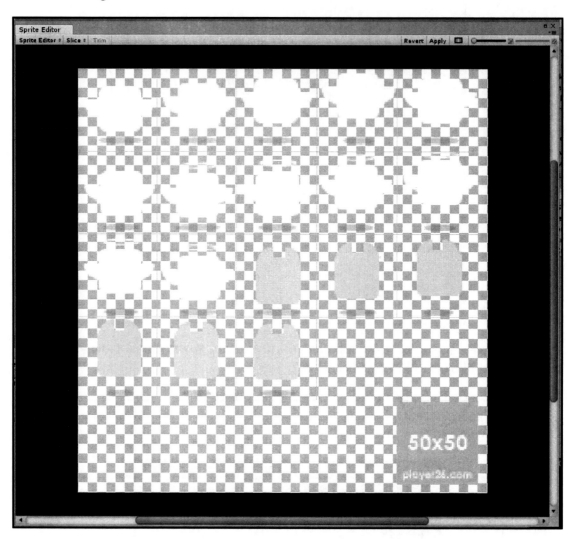

If you click on each slice, you will notice that a **Sprite** information box will appear, like in the following screenshot:

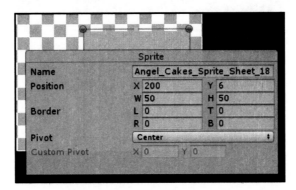

In this information box, you can rename the Sprite to whatever you would like. Each Sprite has been given a number so that you can understand the corresponding name conventions that are described following screenshot:

For this project, we will call each Sprite set the following:

- **Numbers 1-6**: ACSpriteChar1...2...3...4...
- **Numbers 7 - 12**: ACSpriteCharEvo1...2...3...4...
- **Numbers 13 - 18**: ACSpriteCharEnemie1...2...3...4...
- **Number 19**: Delete

Once you have done this, you can now see all your Sprites within the **Project** window. To do this, simply click on the triangle that is highlighted in the following screenshot:

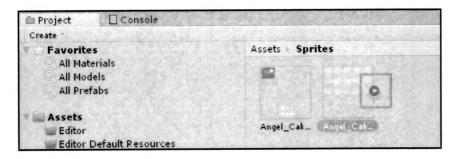

Once you have clicked this, it will expand, revealing all of your Sprites and their names, like in the following screenshot:

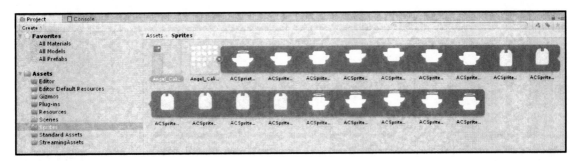

There are many things that we will now be able to do with these images, such as animations, which we will cover later in this book, such as Chapter 9: Look it Moves, as well as place them within the **Scene**.

The next thing that we need to do now is slice up the environment Atlas. Locate the Sprite file within the **Project** window and open it up in the **Sprite Editor**. Remember that you need to change the **Sprite type** to **Multiple** in the **Inspector**, otherwise you will not be able to edit the Sprite.

Once you have it in the **Sprite Editor**, it should look something like the following:

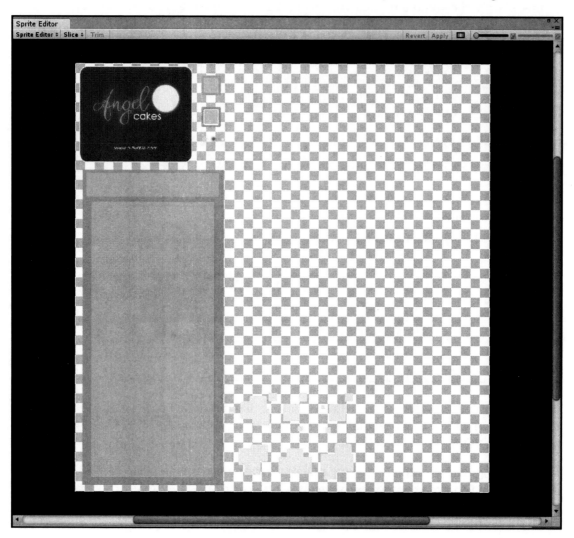

This time, instead of selecting the Slice type **Grid By Cell Size**, we will do it manually. This is because if we choose to do it via the type **Automatic**, we will find that there are other slices, like those on the clouds on the right of the following screenshot. This can be tedious when there are lots of little parts of a single Sprite, such as the Clouds:

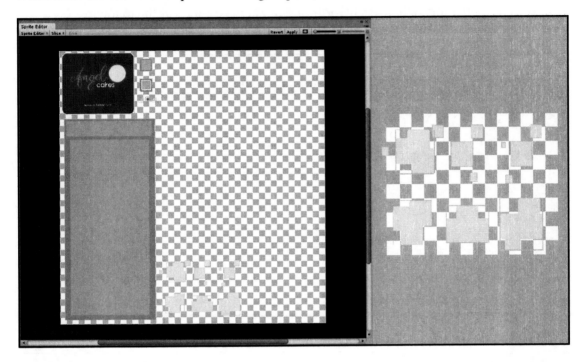

So, for now, manually drag and click around each of the Sprites, making sure that you get as close to the edges as possible. You may find that you will need to zoom in on some parts (by using the mouse scroll wheel), like the *Angel Cakes*. Also, the options in the top-right corner might help you by filtering the image (for example, black and white). As you begin refining the bounding box, you will feel the outline pull or snap toward the edges of the Sprite; this helps you to get as close as possible to the edges, therefore creating more efficient Sprites. Don't forget to name the Sprites either!

For this project, we will call each Sprite set the following:

1. ACSpriteEnviroBlock
2. ACSpriteMenuBlock
3. ACSpriteBonus
4. ACSpriteHealth

5. ACSpriteCake
6. ACSpriteBackground
7. ACSpriteCloud1...2...3...and so on

To give you a better idea where each Sprite is located, have a look at the following screenshot. The Sprites are numbered so that you can easily locate them.

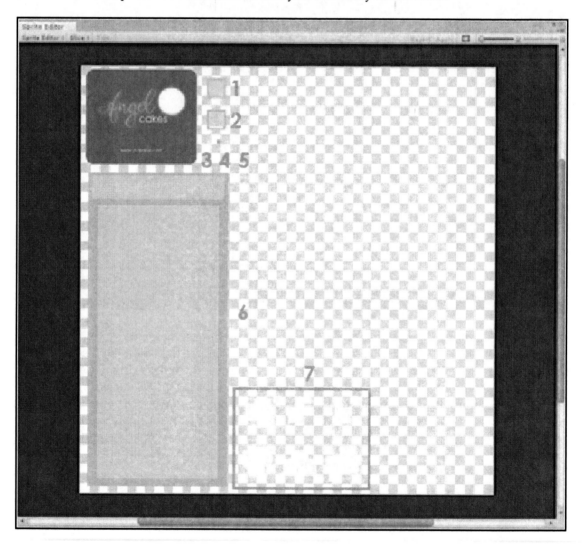

Once you have done this, click on **Apply** in the top-right corner of the **Sprite Editor**. As a result, you should be able to see all the Sprites in the **Project** window by clicking on the triangle. It should look like the following screenshot:

9-slicing Sprites

A nice little feature of Unity that allows you to scale elements such as Sprites without distortion is 9-slicing. Essentially, what 9-slicing does is allow you to reuse an image at various sizes without needing to prepare multiple **Assets**. As the name suggests, it involves splitting the image into nine segments. An example of this splitting is shown in the following screenshot:

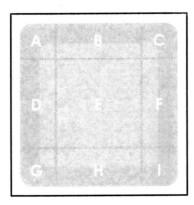

The following four points describe what will happen if you change the dimensions of the preceding image:

- If you change the four corners (**A**, **C**, **G**, and **I**), they will not change in size
- If you move sections **B** and **H**, they will stretch or tile horizontally
- If you move sections **D** and **F**, they will stretch or tile vertically
- If you move section **E**, the image will stretch or tile both horizontally and vertically

You can see these four points illustrated in the following screenshot:

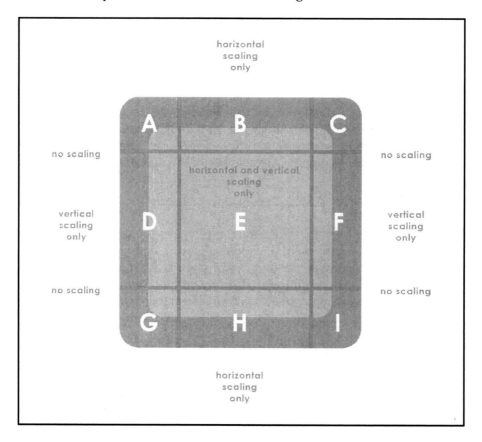

By using 9-slicing, you can re-size the Sprite in different ways and keep the proportions. This is particularly useful for creating the walls within our environment that will create obstacles for our little Angel and enemies to navigate around.

We will need to do this for our **ACSpriteEnviroBlock** so that we can place it within our level for the player to navigate around. To do this, we need to make sure that the Sprite that we have created has been set up properly. First, you need to make sure the **Mesh Type** is set to **Full Rect**. To do this, select the **Angel_Cake_Sprite_Atlas** (contained in **Project** window | **Asset** | **Sprites**), then head to the **Inspector** and change **Mesh Type** from **Tight** to **Full Rect**, like in the following screenshot:

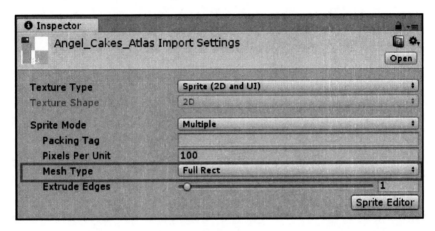

Now we need to define the borders of the Sprite. To do this, perform the following steps:

1. First, select the **Sprite (Angel_Cake_Sprite_Atlas)**.
2. Next, in the **Inspector**, click the **Sprite Editor** button.

3. Now, click on the Sprite that you want to apply the 9-slicing to. In our case, this will be the **ACSpriteEnviroBlock**, like in the following screenshot:

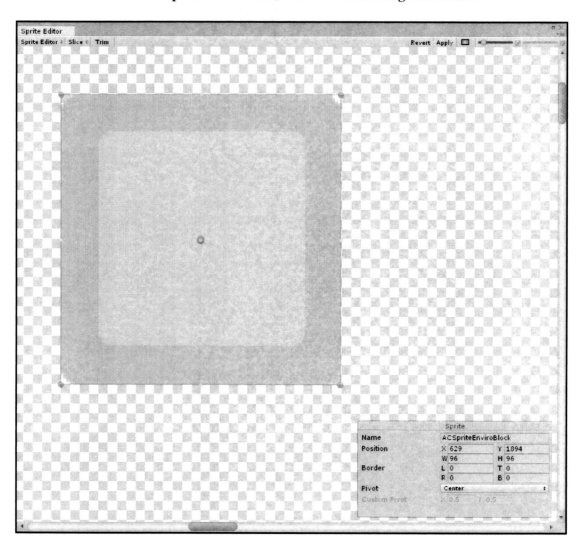

Looking at the **Sprite** information box in the bottom-right corner, we need to adjust the values for the **Borders** of the **Sprite**. For this **Sprite,** we will use the value of 20 for **L, R, T,** and **B** (left, right, top, and bottom, respectively):

Sprite			
Name	ACSpriteEnviroBlock		
Position	X 629	Y 1894	
	W 96	H 96	
Border	L 20	T 20	
	R 20	B 20	
Pivot	Center		‡
Custom Pivot	X 0.5	Y 0.5	

In some cases, you might need to tweak the position of the borders; you can do this by clicking and dragging the green dots located at the intersections of each border (top, bottom, and sides). You can see this in the following screenshot:

To test your 9-sliced Sprite, drag it from the **Project** window into the **Scene**, like in the following screenshot:

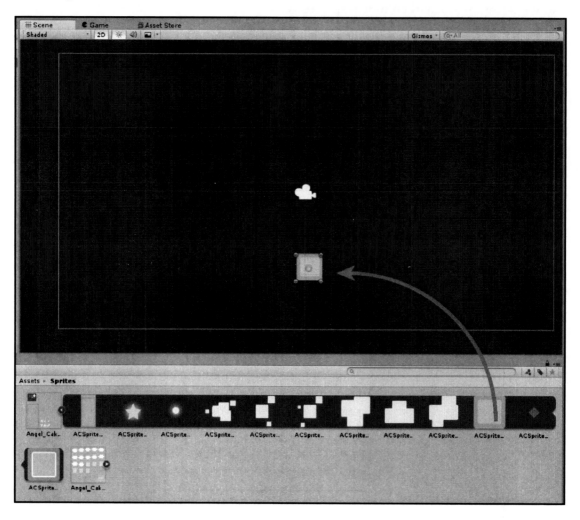

Next, in the **Inspector**, change the **Draw Mode** from **Simple** to **Sliced**, like in the following screenshot:

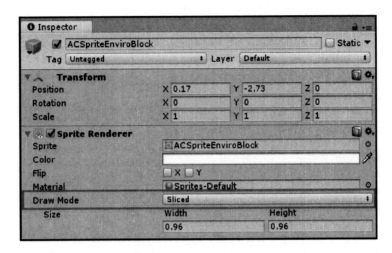

Now you can resize the **ACSpriteEnviroBlock** without it deforming. Give it a go! You should have something like the variations in the following screenshot:

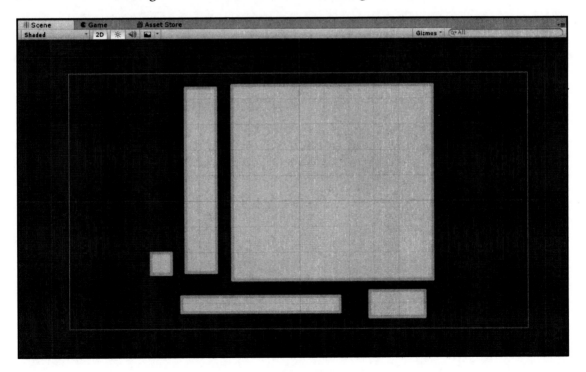

You will notice that it isn't quite like the **Sprite.** This is okay, we can adjust this setting in the **Inspector.** Simply click on the **Atlas** Texture in the **Project** window and, in the **Inspector**, change the value of **Pixels Per Unit** to **250:**

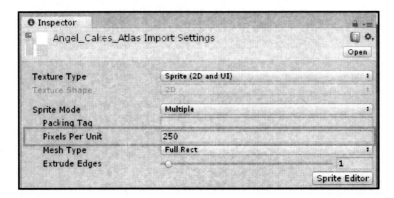

Click **Apply**, then click and drag another **ACSpriteEnviroBlock** onto the **Scene** and try to resize it. You will end up with something like the following screenshot:

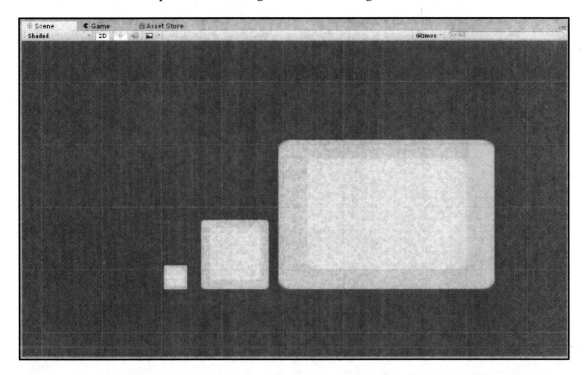

As you can see, there is a little distortion. This just means that you will need to edit the **Borders** inside the **Sprite Editor** until you get the location of them correct. For now, tinker with the locations of the borders. In `Chapter 3`, *Let's Make Some Prefabs*, you will get the correct ones. Lastly, we will also cover other Draw Modes such as Tiled in later chapters with our third project. For now, this is all that you need to know to get you prepared for `Chapter 3`, *Let's Make Some Prefabs*.

Best practices

At some stage when you're creating 2D games, you will probably need to create your own 2D Sprite, and eventually your own Sprite Sheets. For those new to this, there are a few other things to keep in mind (other than the power of 2) when doing this. We'll discuss some of these things in the following section.

Textures

While we have been emphasizing the Power Of Two, it is for a reason. Not only will they be more efficient, they also won't need rescaling at build time. As we have already said, in Unity you can use up to 4096x4096 pixels (make sure that you use these units in your graphics program), but 2048x2048 pixels is the highest available on many graphics cards and platforms. In other words, your game might not run with Textures higher than 2048x2048. So, if you build an absolutely fabulous 4096x4096 pixels Texture, it probably won't be such an absolutely fabulous experience for those on low-end devices. The best way to overcome this issue is to create Textures in a high resolution (4096x4096 pixels) and then downsize to a smaller power of 2 depending on your targeted device, as this is likely to vary. This goes for all repeated elements (for example, windows, doors, environmental assets) that will be within your scene.

Moreover, **Power Of Two (POT)** Textures (which have dimensions with a number of pixels corresponding to a POT) are recommended over **Non-Power Of Two (NPOT)** Textures because they are better for computational reasons (for example, more efficiency at runtime). We will look at the disadvantages and advantages of both, so you can see why:

- **POT advantages**: Always supported by any graphics card.
- **POT disadvantages**: Requires more disk space. Needs to be handled by the engine to only draw the parts that are needed if the image data inside the Texture does not use all pixels (in most cases, this is true and means extra work to be done by the graphics/game engine).

- **NPOT advantages**: Uses Textures as they are; no waste of disk space per Texture file.
- **NPOT disadvantages**: Not supported by all graphics cards. Might cause slower draw calls. Some graphics cards will show empty white or black rectangles, or the whole application will just crash. While saving some disk space to store the image file, it is going to waste VRAM when the Texture is uploaded to the graphics card as it will still be aligned in memory as if it were a POT image. The wasted pixel data might even cause pixel bleeding, which will show up as some fuzzy borders that haven't been drawn anywhere in Textures but are added by graphics card drivers through mipmapping Textures.

 There's also the possibility to mix POT sizes per axis, for example, 128x1024. This can work but it doesn't have to on all graphics cards, so POT with the same size for both axes is the best way to go for maximum co-compatibility.

Maximizing the space that you have

Another important thing to remember when creating your own Textures is to maximize the space within the Texture itself when you're combining multiple images. However, be aware of different materials requiring different parts of the same Texture. You can end up using or loading that Texture multiple times. In addition, some Textures may also have an alpha channel, which makes part of the Texture transparent. Lastly, for parts of a texture that are tiled, you don't need to add the image tiled more than once. In general, you only need the part that is tileable; Unity will take care of the rest. Not only will this help to increase the resolution of a tileable image, it will also save space. Fortunately, there are a few programs out there that help to make this whole process easy, such as **TexturePacker**, which you can find by either visiting https://www.codeandweb.com/texturepacker/unity or by scanning the QR code:

Scaling

This is an issue for 2D as much as it is for 3D. Setting a scale within your graphics program will give you much fewer (if any at all) headaches later when it comes to bringing things into Unity. Different programs use different measurements by default, so you will need to make sure that if you're using graphics programs such as Adobe Illustrator or Photoshop, your measurements are consistent – 3 mm is very different from 3 cm and 3 px.

Naming

As we have already discussed in `Chapter 1`, *Press Start*, naming your Sprites is as important as naming any other file. Whether you're cutting up Sprite Sheets or creating placeholder Sprites, consistent names are important.

 If there is one piece of advice any newcomer to Sprite Sheets should learn early on, it is this: one thing that can be painful, and by painful I mean you might prefer to walk on hot coals, is updating a `Sprite` file. To put it bluntly, you know every name that you have given to every single sprite within an image file? Well, when you update the image file, it must be resliced and every slice must be renamed...again. Even with something as simple as changing the name of the file, unless it is absolutely necessary due to issues relating to project files (e.g. an error with the naming convention); you will still have to go through this process. So, the old saying "*measure twice, cut once*" absolutely applies here.

Summary

In this chapter, we have seen some examples of games that focus on the mechanics of collecting. We have seen some of the key features of collecting games and things to consider when designing them, including considerations for our project. We explored many features within Unity that focus on 2D Sprites that handle them as well as create them. Finally, we have learned how to set up and configure the Sprites for our project and get it ready for applying scripts to and creating prefabs. Lastly, we looked at some best practices for creating Sprites and utilizing the Sprite tools.

Next, in `Chapter 3`, *Let's Make Some Prefabs*, we will learn how to write some basic C# scripts and apply them to our Sprites. We will also learn what Prefabs are in Unity, and how to create and use them within our project. Lastly, we will also explore how to add basic audio and sound effects to our game.

3
Let's Make Some Prefabs

Previously, in Chapter 1, *Press Start*, we looked at what games are made of and how to set up Unity. In Chapter 2, *Working with Assets*, we started to import assets and get them ready for Unity. Now, in Chapter 3, *Let's Make Some Prefabs*, we're going to do something cool: we're going to create our first game.

We will cover the following topics:

- What are Prefabs and how do we create and use them?
- Basics of C# in Unity
- What is a PlayerController?
- How to create a collection system
- Basic overview of Audio in Unity
- Create a PlayerController for our game
- Create Prefabs for player, wall, and collectables
- Adding basic audio and sound effects (sound FX or SFX)

By the end of this chapter you will be able to achieve the following:

- Create a basic Prefab
- Script and implement basic C# scripts
- Create a PlayerController for the Angel character
- Create collectable *Angel Cakes* for the PlayerController to pick up
- Import audio and apply it to various aspects of the game environment

Now with that said, let's make our first game.

Basics of audio and sound FX in Unity

Adding sound in Unity is simple enough, but you can implement it better if you understand how sound travels. While this is extremely important in 3D games because of the added third dimension, it is quite important in 2D games, just in a slightly different way. Before we discuss the differences, let's first learn about what and how sound works from a quick physics lesson.

Listening to the physics behind sound

What we hear is not just music, sound effects (FX) and ambient background noise. The sound is a longitudinal, mechanical (vibrating) wave. These "waves" can pass through different mediums (for example, air, water, your desk) but not through a vacuum. Therefore, no one will hear your screams in space. The sound is a variation in pressure. A region of increased pressure on a sound wave is called a compression (or condensation). A region of decreased pressure on a sound wave is called a rarefaction (or dilation). You can see this concept illustrated in the following image:

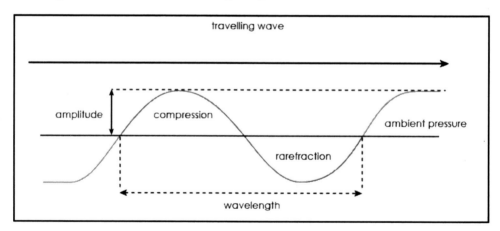

The density of certain materials, such as glass and plastic, allows a certain amount of light to pass through them. This will influence how the light will behave when it passes through them, such as bending/refracting (that is, the index of refraction), various materials (for example, liquids, solids, gases) have the same effect when it comes to allowing sound waves to pass. Some materials allow the sound to pass easily, while others dampen it. Therefore, sound studios/booths are made of certain materials to remove things such as echoes. It has a similar effect to when you scream underwater that there is a shark. It won't be as loud as if you scream from your kitchen to tell everyone dinner is ready.

Another thing to consider is what is known as the **Doppler Effect**. The Doppler Effect results from an increase (or decrease) in the frequency of sound (and other things such as light, ripples in water) as the source of the sound and person/player move toward (or away from) each other. A simple example of this is when an emergency vehicle passes by you. You will notice that the sound of the siren is different before it reaches you when it is near you, and once it passes you. Considering this example, it is because there is a sudden change in pitch in the passing siren. This is visualized in the following image:

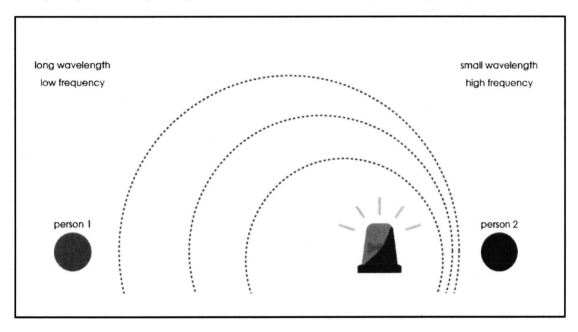

So, what is the point of knowing this when it comes to developing games? Well, this is particularly important when creating games, more so in 3D, in relation to *how* sounds are heard by players in many ways. For example, imagine that you're nearing a creek, but there are dense bushes, large pine trees, and a rugged terrain. The sound that creek makes from where a player is in the game world is going to sound very different if it was a completely flat plane free from any vegetation. When it comes to 2D games, this is not necessarily as important because we are working without depth (z-axis) but similar principles apply when players may be navigating around a top-down environment and they are near a point of interest. You don't want that sound to be as loud when the player is far away as it would be if they were up close.

Within the context of 2D and 3D sounds, Unity has a parameter for this exact thing called **Spatial Blend**. We will discuss this more in the *Audio Source* section.

A

There are several ways that you can create audio within Unity, from importing your own/downloaded sounds to recording it live. Like images, Unity can import most standard audio file formats: AIFF, WAV, MP3, and Ogg, and tracker modules (for example, short instrument samples): .xm, .mod, .it, and .s3m.

Importing audio

Importing audio into Unity follows the same processes as importing any other type of asset. We will cover the basics of what you need to know in the following sections.

Audio Listener

Have you heard the saying, *If a tree falls in a forest and no one is there to hear it, does it still make a sound?* Well, in Unity, if there is nothing to hear your audio, then the answer is no. This is because Unity has a component called an **Audio Listener,** which works like a microphone. To locate the Audio Listener, click the **Main Camera**, and then look over at the **Inspector**; it should be located near the bottom, like in the following image:

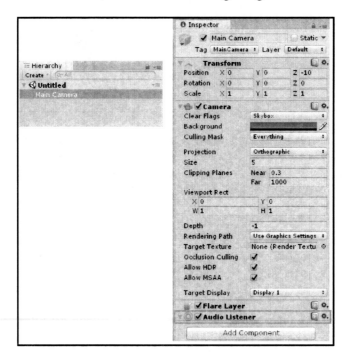

If for some reason, it isn't there, you can always add it by clicking the following button titled **Add Component**, type **Audio Listener**, and select it (click it) from the list, like in the following image:

The important thing to remember is that an **Audio Listener** is the location of the sound, so it makes sense as to why it is typically placed on the **Main Camera**, but it can also be placed on a Player. A single scene can only have one **Audio Listener**; therefore, it's best to experiment with the one that works best for your game.

 It is important to remember that an **Audio Listener** works with an Audio Source, and must have one to work.

Audio Source

The Audio Source is where the sound comes from. This can be from many different objects within a Scene as well as background and sound FX. The Audio Source has several parameters; later we will briefly discuss the main ones.

To see more information about all the parameters, you can check out the official Unity documentation by visiting the link or scanning the QR code:

https://docs.unity3d.com/2017.2/Documentation/Manual/class-AudioSource.html

You may be wondering why we should have a slider for **Spatial Blend**, instead of a checkbox. This is because we need to fade between 2D and 3D, and there is a good reason for this. Imagine that you're in a game and you're looking at a screen on a computer. In this case, your camera is going to be fixated on whatever is on the screen. This could be checking an inventory or even entering nuclear codes. In any case, you will want the sound that is being emitted from the screen to be the focal audio. Therefore, the slider in the Spatial Blend parameter is going to be closer to 2D. This is because you may still want ambient noises that are in the background incorporated into the experience. So, if you are closer to 2D, the sound will be the same in both speakers (or headphones). The closer you slide toward 3D, the more the volume will depend on the proximity of the Sound Listener to the Sound Source. It will also allow for things, such as the Doppler Effect, to be more noticeable, as it takes in 3D space. There are also specific settings for these things.

Choosing sounds for background and FX

When it comes to picking the right kind of music for your game, just like the aesthetics, you need to think about what kind of "mood" you're trying to create. Is it a sombre or uplifting kind of mood, are you ironically contrasting the graphics (for example, happy) with gloomy music? There is really no right or wrong when it comes to your musical selection if you can communicate to the player what they are supposed to feel, at least in general.

For this game, I have provided you with some example "moods" that you can apply to this game. Of course, you're welcome to choose sounds other than this that are more to your liking! All the sounds that we will use will be from the Free Sound website: `https://freesound.org`. You will need to create an account to download them, but it's free and there are many great sounds that you can use when creating games. In saying this, if you're intending to create your games for commercial purposes, please make sure that you check the Terms and Conditions on Free Sound to make sure that you're not violating any of them. Each track will have its own attribution licenses, including those for commercial use, so always check! For this project, we're going to stick with the "Happy" version. But I encourage you to experiment!

Happy

- **Collecting Angel Cakes**: Chime sound (`https://freesound.org/people/jgreer/sounds/333629/`)
- **Being attacked by the enemy**: `Cat Purr/Twit4.wav` (`https://freesound.org/people/steffcaffrey/sounds/262309/`)
- **Collecting health:** correct (`https://freesound.org/people/ertfelda/sounds/243701/`)
- **Collecting bonuses:** Signal-Ring 1 (`https://freesound.org/people/Vendarro/sounds/399315/`)
- **Background:** `Kirmes_Orgel_004_2_Rosamunde.mp3` (`https://freesound.org/people/bilwiss/sounds/24720/`)

Sad

- **Collecting Angel Cakes:** Glass Tap (`https://freesound.org/people/Unicornaphobist/sounds/262958/`)
- **Being attacked by the enemy:** `musicbox1.wav` (`https://freesound.org/people/sandocho/sounds/17700/`)
- **Collecting health:** `chime.wav` (`https://freesound.org/people/Psykoosiossi/sounds/398661/`)
- **Collecting bonuses:** short metallic hit (`https://freesound.org/people/waveplay/sounds/366400/`)
- **Background:** improvised chill 8 (`https://freesound.org/people/waveplay/sounds/238529/`)

Retro

- **Collecting Angel Cakes:** `TF_Buzz.flac` (`https://freesound.org/people/copyc4t/sounds/235652/`)
- **Being attacked by the enemy:** Game Die (`https://freesound.org/people/josepharaoh99/sounds/364929/`)
- **Collecting health:** `galanghee.wav` (`https://freesound.org/people/metamorphmuses/sounds/91387/`)

- **Collecting bonuses:** SW05.WAV (https://freesound.org/people/mad-monkey/sounds/66684/)
- **Background:** Angel-techno pop music loop (https://freesound.org/people/frankum/sounds/387410/)

Not everyone can hear well or at all, so it pays to keep this in mind when you're developing games that may rely on audio to provide feedback to players. While subtitles can enable dialogue to be more accessible, sound FX can be a little trickier. Therefore, when it comes to implementing audio, think about how you could complement it, even if the same effect that you're trying to achieve with sound is subtle. For example, if you play a "bleep" for every item collected, perhaps you could associate it with a slight glow or flash of color. The choice is up to you, but it's something to keep in mind. On the other end of the spectrum, those who can hear might also want to turn the sounds off. We've all played that game (or several) that really begins to become irritating, so make sure that you also check this while you're playtesting. You don't want an awesome game to suck because your audio is intolerable and there is not an option to TURN THE SOUND OFF! You've been warned.

Integrating background music in our game

Once you choose which music better suits the kind of feel you want to create for your game, import both the sound and the music inside the project. If you want, you can create two folders for them, SoundFX and Music, respectively.

Now, in our scene, we need to do the following:

1. Create an empty game object (by clicking **GameObject | Create empty**), rename it Background Music.
2. Attach an **Audio Source** component (in the **Inspector**, click **Add Component | Audio | Audio Source**).
3. Next, we need to drag and drop the music we decided on/downloaded into the **AudioClip** variable and check the **Loop** option, so the background music will never stop. Also, check that **Play on Awake** is checked as well, even if it should be by default, so the music will start playing as soon as the game starts.
4. Hit Play to start the game.
5. Lastly, adjust the volume, depending on the music you chose. This may require a bit of playtesting (remember to set the value after the play mode, because the settings you adjust during play mode are not kept).

In the end, this is how the component should look (in the image, I chose the happy theme music, and set a **Volume** of 0.1):

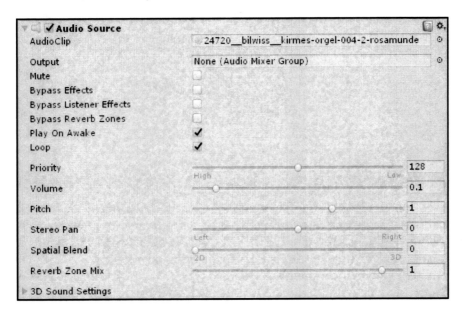

Creating the Angel and the PlayerController

In this section, we will focus on how to create our main character, the Angel. BUT! Before we move on, it's important to note that we will use the built-in physics engine in Unity. Since this book teaches by example, we will only cover it briefly and by creating our game. If you want to have a nice in-depth explanation of the Physics engine in Unity, you can refer to Chapter 5, *Freeze! Creating an Intergalactic Shooter*, of Getting Started with Unity 5.x 2D Game Development (https://www.packtpub.com/game-development/getting-started-unity-5x-2d-game-development). Despite the title, the book is perfectly suitable even if you use more recent versions, such as 2017. Here is the QR code:

Alternatively, you can also check out the official tutorial by visiting `https://unity3d.com/learn/tutorials/topics/physics` or scanning the following QR code:

A brief overview of Unity's physics system

There are two different physics engines in Unity, one for 3D and one for 2D. While both use the same concepts, such as gravity, force, and velocity, they are implemented in slightly different ways, especially since there isn't a third dimension in 2D games. There are several components and properties when it comes to 2D physics in Unity. However, the two main important components to understand this book will be `Colliders` and `Rigidbody`, since we are going to use them both to implement our **PlayerController**.

Rigidbody

A `Rigidbody` is the main component that allows game objects to engage in physical behavior (that is, movement). When a `Rigidbody` is attached to a `GameObject`, the object will immediately respond to gravity. Since a `Rigidbody` takes over the movement of the `GameObject` it is attached to, you shouldn't try to move it from a script by changing the Transform properties such as position, rotation, or scale. Instead, you should apply forces to push (for example, other characters, objects, projectiles) the `GameObject` and let the physics engine calculate the results. There are some cases where you might want a `GameObject` to have a `Rigidbody` without having its motion controlled by the physics engine. For example, you may want to control your character directly from script code but still, allow it to be detected by triggers. This kind of non-physical motion produced from a script is known as **kinematic motion**. The `Rigidbody` component has a property called **Is Kinematic** that removes it from the control of the physics engine and allows it to be moved kinematically from a script. It is possible to change the value of **Is Kinematic** from a script to allow physics to be switched on and off for an object, but this comes with a performance overhead and should be used sparingly.

If one or more `Collider` components are also added, the `GameObject` is moved by incoming collisions. We discuss `Collider` components in the next section.

Colliders

`Collider` components define the shape of an object for the purpose of physical collisions. You can think of this as an invisible box that is an object that permits it from passing through it but without coming into contact. They don't have to be the same shape as the visual representation (Mesh, Sprite) of the object; in some cases they can be a simple primitive type (for example, Box `Collider`, Sphere `Collider` (only in 3D), and Capsule `Collider`), but the closer to the actual shape, the better. If you're using many different primitive types of colliders within Unity, you can combine them to create what is called a Compound `Collider`.

In 2D, you can also use what is called a Polygon Collider 2D or Edge Collider 2D. A Polygon Collider 2D is a collider that is shaped by freeform edges that you can adjust so that it better suits your Sprite. It must also enclose the edges of the area that it is trying to provide a collider around. An Edge Collider 2D is defined by a freeform edge made of line segments, so you can adjust it to fit the shape of a Sprite with great precision. In general, Edge colliders are best for surfaces (for example, game platforms) because you are only generating geometry where you need it.

Another important thing to consider when using colliders is the type of Material that they are made of. For example, a player jumping on a springboard is going to result in a very different behavior than landing on spikes. Applying Physics Materials to objects can be done to 2D objects by using Physics Material 2D. It is important not to forget the "s" as Physic Material (without the "s" in Physics) is reserved for 3D Physics Materials. Lastly, Physics Materials in Unity 2D have two properties: Friction and Bounciness, as in the following image. We will touch on these later for *Project 3 - RETROformer*:

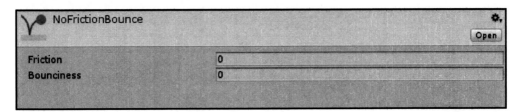

Assembling the Angel

First, we need to create a new Sprite, and assign as Graphics "ACSpriteEvo1." We can rename the new Game Object as `Player`.

Then, we need to attach a collider to our Player character. This is a component, which allows the character to have a physical shape. Since we want our character to have a circular shape, we need to attach a `CircleCollider2D`. In the scene view, you should see a green circle around our character, and the default one should be good to go. In case you would like to tweak the dimensions of the green circle to encapsulate your character in a different way, you are free to change the **Radius** setting, along with the **Offset** one, if you need to translate the circle from the pivot point.

Another component we need is `Rigidbody`, which is a component that tells Unity that this object is subject to the Physics engine. Since we are building a 2D game, we need to use `RigidBody2D`. Once placed on the character, we need to make two important changes, which are as follows:

1. We need to disable gravity, since our game is top-down, and therefore there is no gravity. To do so, you need to set the **Gravity Scale** to zero.
2. We don't want our character to rotate due to collisions, so we need to freeze rotation in the z-axis. There is a checkbox under the constraints drop-down. Here is a screenshot of how the component should look in the end:

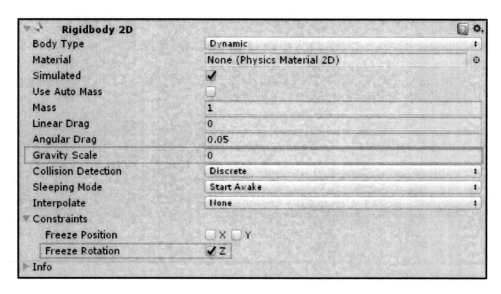

Tagging the player

Later, we will start implementing the collecting system, but first we need to distinguish the **Player** from other objects. One way to do it is to assign a **Tag**. When you install Unity, it comes preloaded with a set of default tags. However, if you want to add your own (custom) tags, you can do it by navigating to **Edit | Project Settings | Tags and Layers**, like in the following menu:

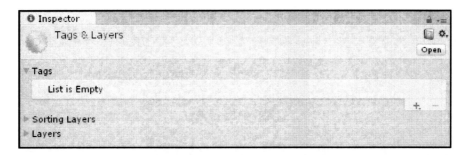

In our specific case, we can select the **Player**, and just beneath the name we can set **Player** as a tag, which is a default tag, as shown in the following screenshot:

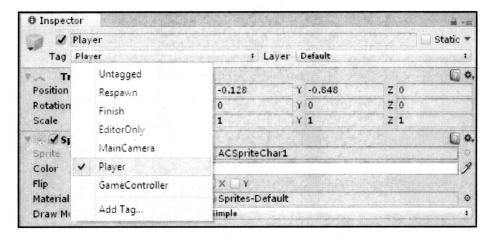

Creating the Script

Now, we are good to go to start writing some scripts. This is the first script of this book, and since it's a book with examples, we will jump straight into one, and learn how to code by deconstructing what we are doing. Don't be scared if it is not clear to you at the beginning, because it might be hard if it's the first time you see the code. Don't give up; being able to code is worth the effort.

To create a Script, we need to create a new folder, called `Scripts`, as shown in the following screenshot:

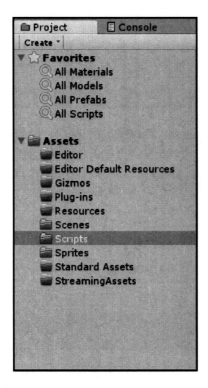

1. Inside the folder, right-click and then **Create I C# Script (Alternatively using the top-menu Assets I Create I C# Script)**
2. Rename the script to `PlayerController` so we will always know later what the script is supposed to do
3. The script can be used as a component, meaning that it can be attached to a GameObject

As we have seen in the previous chapter, not all the scripts are components. For instance, Editor scripts are not components, and in general, every script that does not derive from **MonoBehavior** is not a component.

So, let's drag it onto our character GameObject, and it will appear in the **Inspector**, like the following screenshot:

If you double-click the **Script** component, an editor will open depending on your preferences in the settings. The default is MonoDevelop, but also Visual Studio (www.visualstudio.com) is excellent.

Once opened, this is how the script looks:

```
using System.Collections;
using System.Collections.Generic;
using UnityEngine;

public class PlayerController : MonoBehaviour {

    // Use this for initialization
    void Start () {
    }
    // Update is called once per frame
    void Update () {
    }
}
```

At the beginning, there are three lines that allow us to use libraries. At this stage, we won't touch them.

Then, there is the class definition, in this case, named `PlayerController`. Inside it, there are two functions: `Start()` and `Update()`. The first is called every time this script starts, whereas the second is called at every frame. You can explore the whole execution order of the different functions and scripts by following this link: https://docs.unity3d.com/ Manual/ExecutionOrder.html.

Enforcing components

Since we need to use this script along with the collider and the `RigidBody` we have attached before on our player, we need to enforce this by saying that every time we use this script, the object on which this script is attached must have a collider and a `RigidBody`. As a result, we won't wrongly use this script without those components.

We can achieve this by adding two lines of code above the class definition, as highlighted here:

```
using System.Collections;
using System.Collections.Generic;
using UnityEngine;

[RequireComponent(typeof(Rigidbody2D))]
[RequireComponent(typeof(CircleCollider2D))]
public class PlayerController : MonoBehaviour {
  //[...]
}
```

If you want to do a more general script, you can have Collider2D instead of CircleCollider2D. As a result, you will be able to use any collider, but then you need to remember which one is the right collider for the character you want to use.

Exposing variables in the inspector

When in Unity, we attach components to our GameObject, there are some parameters (or variables) that designers can adjust. We would like to adjust the speed of our character from the **Inspector**. In this case, we will use a float, so decimal values can also be used.
The easiest way to expose a variable in the **Inspector** (there are other ways, but for now we won't see them) is to declare a variable public. Optionally, you can assign a value, which will be the default one in the Inspector. So just inside the class, we can add the following highlighted line:

```
//[...]
public class PlayerController : MonoBehaviour {

    public float speed = 10.0f;

    //[...]
}
```

As a result, if we go back in Unity, and see our character, we will see that now the speed is exposed in the **Inspector**, as shown here:

We get a reference to the `Rigidbody`, so we can use it to move the character. Sometimes during the execution of the script, we need to reference some other components that are attached to the object. The `Start()` function is a perfect place for this purpose. In fact, now, we need to retrieve the Rigidbody component. To do so, let's declare a variable, this time private since we don't need to expose it to the **Inspector**, as shown here:

```
//[...]
public class PlayerController : MonoBehaviour {

    public float speed = 10.0f;

    private Rigidbody2D rigidBody;

    //[...]
}
```

Next, we need to assign the `rigidbody` of the character within the variable. So, inside the `Start()` function we can use the `GetComponent()` function to retrieve the `RigidBody2D` instance that is attached to the same game object this script is attached to, in the following way:

```
void Start() {
        rigidBody = GetComponent<Rigidbody2D>();
    }
```

Please note that we don't do any check of the validity of `Rigidbody` (if it exists), because at the beginning of the script we have enforced that `Rigidbody` must exist to use this script. As a result, we can avoid checking the validity of the variable (null-check), since we know `Rigidbody` will always exist.

From the player input to a new position in the world

Every time the player presses a key on the keyboard, or use the thumbstick on a controller, we need to retrieve this input. Then, we need to elaborate it so that we can calculate the next position of our character after a frame.

Since it's a calculation we need to do for every frame, it's reasonable to do it in the `Update()` function. However, since we are going to use physics, we need to use a similar function, called `FixedUpdate()`. So, let's rename Update to `FixedUpdate()`, as the following:

```
void FixedUpdate () {

    }
```

To retrieve the player input, we can use the default key mapping in Unity.

 In case you would like to change this mapping, you can do it by clicking the top bar and then **Edit | Project Settings | Input**.

In particular, we can use the `Input.GetAxis()` function, and using as a parameter a string with the name of the axis. In our case, we have the *Horizontal* and the *Vertical* axis. These are values that range from -1 to 1 depending on how tilted the thumbstick is (or, in the case of a keyboard, they can just be -1, 0, and 1). Thus, we need to multiply these values by the speed variable, and then multiply it by the `Time.deltaTime`, which is the time since the last frame. Finally, we need to add the current position of the character with transform.position and the corresponding axis. It sounds complicated, but it's not once the code is written down. For those of you who are familiar with equations, this is what we will be using:

$$pos_t = pos_{t-1} + velocity * \Delta Time$$

So, finally here is the code, in which we do the same operation once for the x-axis and again for the y-axis, and store values within variables:

```
void FixedUpdate () {
        //Get the new position of our character
        var x = transform.position.x + Input.GetAxis("Horizontal") *
Time.deltaTime * speed;
        var y = transform.position.y + Input.GetAxis("Vertical") *
Time.deltaTime * speed;
    }
```

Moving the character to the new position

The last step for our PlayerController is to move the character to the new position that we calculated in the last section.
We could do this by changing the transform of the character, but since we are using the physics engine of Unity, and we don't want to force the character to go against a wall ignoring the collisions, we need to find another way.
Thankfully, the Rigidbody that we created a couple of sections ago, has a built-in function to move the Rigidbody into a new position and respect the collisions. Exactly what we need! The function is called MovePosition() and we can use it as shown here:

```
void FixedUpdate () {
        //Get the new position of our character
        var x = transform.position.x + Input.GetAxis("Horizontal") *
Time.deltaTime * speed;
        var y = transform.position.y + Input.GetAxis("Vertical") *
Time.deltaTime * speed;

        //Set the position of our character throught the RigidBody2D
component (since we are using
        physics)
        rigidBody.MovePosition(new Vector2(x, y));
    }
```

And with this, you can save the PlayerController script, and we have finished with it.

Testing the PlayerController

Before we move on, it's best practice to test what we have achieved so far.

If we Hit play, we can move the character in the world by using the arrows key if you are on a keyboard. If you want to test whether the angel is colliding properly, you can just place a wall, add a `BoxCollider2D`, and test it out.

Collectable system

In this section, we start our collectible system. This includes the ability of the Player to collect the cakes, keep track of how many cakes the player has collected and in how much time, and trigger the end of the game once all the cakes have been collected.

We will finish the collectible system in `Chapter 4`, *It's about U and I*, when we will integrate the UI. Now, for the moment, we will start at step one, by creating it by allowing the player to collect *Angel's Cakes*.

Setting up the Angel Cakes

Let's create a new Sprite in our scene and name it *Angel's Cake*. Then, in the Sprite Renderer assign the Graphics **ACSpriteCake**.

Then, we need to add a collider component. Yes, a collider! Why? Because even if the cake won't collide because we don't need actual physics response, we still use the Physics engine to check when the player collects a cake by colliding with it. This is called a **Trigger**, and we need to specify that we are willing to use this collider as a Trigger. Triggers won't stop other rigid bodies to enter their space, they just pass through and trigger events instead.

Add to *Angel Cakes* a `BoxCollider2D`, likewise, we did with the character, but this time we check the checkbox **Is Trigger,** as shown here:

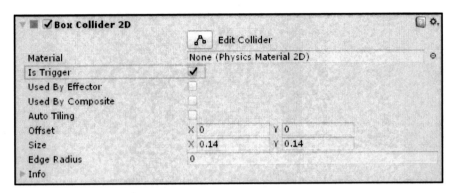

In this case, we don't need a `Rigidbody`, since we won't move this object in the physics world. However, since we would like to play a sound when the player collects the cake, we need to add an `AudioSource` component. As shown here:

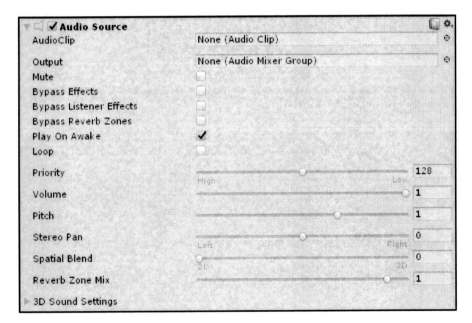

And with this, we are good to go to create the script. To change from how we create a script for the player character, we can go to the **Inspector** panel and click **Add Component** | **New Script** and type the name of it, as shown here:

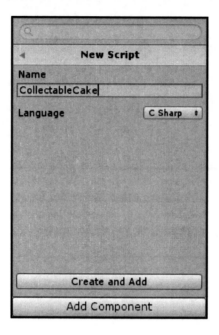

Then, double-click the script to open it.

By doing in this other way, it's faster, but the script is created in the Assets folder, and you need to move it in the Script one manually.

Enforcing components, again!

As we did for the PlayerController, we need to enforce some components, again. This time, the required component to make this script work is the BoxCollider2D and the AudioSource. Here is how:

```
using System.Collections;
using System.Collections.Generic;
using UnityEngine;

[RequireComponent(typeof(BoxCollider2D))]
```

```
[RequireComponent(typeof(AudioSource))]
public class CollectableCake : MonoBehaviour {

    //[...]

}
```

Triggering cake

We can remove both the `Start()` and the `Update()` functions, since we won't need them, and add a new variable:

```
public AudioClip collectableSound;
```

This variable is public, so it will be exposed in the **Inspector**, and as you can imagine it stores the `AudioClip` we want to play when the player collects the cake.

Then, we need to add a new function:

```
void OnTriggerEnter2D(Collider2D other) {
}
```

This is a special function, which is called every time an object enters within the trigger collider of our cake, and this other object is stored in the other variable.

The first thing we need to check is whether the other object is actually the player, we can do this by using the tag we set before. As a result, we can easily check whether the player has collected the cake:

```
void OnTriggerEnter2D(Collider2D other) {
    //Check if the player collides with the angel's cake
    if (other.tag == "Player") {

    }
}
```

Inside the If-statement we need to increase the number of cakes that the player collects, but we will postpone this task to the Chapter 4, *It's about U and I*, when we will integrate the UI. In the meantime, we can leave a reminder:

```
void OnTriggerEnter2D(Collider2D other) {
//Check if the player collides with the angel's cake
if (other.tag == "Player") {
//If so, increase the number of cakes the player has collected (see in the
next chapter)
//TODO: to implement
}
}
```

The next step is to play the audio. To do so, we need to retrieve the AudioSource component, which we can do with the same function we used for the PlayerController (GetComponent()), and use it to play the sound we stored in the collectableSound variable:

```
void OnTriggerEnter2D(Collider2D other) {
        //Check if the player collides with the angel's cake
        if (other.tag == "Player") {
            //If so, increase the number of cakes the player has collected
(see in the next chapter)
            //TODO: to implement

            //Play the collectable sound
            GetComponent<AudioSource>().PlayOneShot(collectableSound);
        }
    }
```

Then, we need to hide the cake from the player, and we can do this by disabling the Renderer component. In fact, we cannot destroy the cake yet, since it needs to finish to play the sound. So, after having disabled the renderer, we destroy the cake after a delay that is long as the **AudioClip** in the collectableSound variable. Finally, we remove the script, so the player cannot collect the same cake twice (even if it is hidden):

```
void OnTriggerEnter2D(Collider2D other) {
        //Check if the player collides with the angel's cake
        if (other.tag == "Player") {
            //If so, increase the number of cakes the player has collected
(see in the next chapter)
            //TODO: to implement

            //Play the collectable sound
            GetComponent<AudioSource>().PlayOneShot(collectableSound);
```

```
            //Hide the cake by disabling the renderer
            GetComponent<Renderer>().enabled = false;

            //Then, destroy the cake after a delay (so the sound can finish
    to play)
            GameObject.Destroy(gameObject, collectableSound.length);

            //Destory this script, in case the player hits again the cake
    before that is destroyed
            Destroy(this);
        }
    }
```

Save the script, and come back to Unity, since it's time to test it.

Testing the cake collectable system so far

First of all, you need to drag and drop the sound FX you decided on when the player collects the cake, and place it within the script we have just created for the cake. You should end up with something similar to this:

If we duplicate (*Ctrl* + *D* or command + *D*) many cakes, then we can hit play, and test that our angel can collect these cakes, and we know since they will disappear, and the audio will be played. However, there is no counter to keep track of how many cakes the player collects, and this will be done in the next chapter.

Prefabs for our Game Objects

A Prefab is a type of asset, just like Sprites, and Audio. It is a reusable `GameObject` stored in the **Project Window**. Prefabs can be inserted (multiple times) into any number of Scenes within your Unity game project. When you add a Prefab to a Scene, you create an instance of it. What this means is that all Prefab instances are linked to the original Prefab and are essentially a clone of it. This is particularly useful when you want to have multiple instances of an object, such as a health pickup. Instead of having to adjust each one individually, you just update the original Prefab (for example, color, graphics, properties) and it will automatically update all the other instances of the health pick-up within the game. You may find that at some stage, you're editing an instance and want these changes to be reflected in the original Prefab. Unity allows you to do this easily by way of the **Inspector**. When you click a Prefab instance within your Scene, you will see buttons: **Select**, **Revert** and **Apply**. The **Select** button selects the original Prefab. This allows you to edit the main Prefab and so change all its instances. However, you can also save overridden values (excluding transform settings) from an instance, back to the original Prefab by clicking the **Apply** button. If you have modified an instance of the Prefab but decided that you don't like the changes, you can simply go back to the default values by clicking **Revert** before clicking the **Apply** button.

Creating the Prefab for the player and the cake

To create the Prefabs for our game, we need first to create a `Prefab` folder in our **Project**. You can do this by following these steps:

1. Right-click (in our `Prefab` folder) and select **Create | Prefab**. We need to do this twice and rename them respectively `Cake` and `Player`.

2. From the **Hierarchy** panel, we need to drag the **Player** into the **Player** prefab and **Angel's Cake** into **Angel's Cake** prefab(as it was obvious). As you can see, they become blue in the **Hierarchy** panel. This is fine because now they are linked to the Prefab, as we were saying in the previous section.

As a result, we can easily drag and drop the components we need ready to go, whenever we need them. We can remove all of the instances of the cakes and the player from the Scene since we can drag and drop the Prefabs from the **Project** panel now. Before we leave the chapter, there is one more thing to do… Build our map!

Building the Map

Now that we have all the pieces, building the map becomes a piece of cake. It is an essential part of the 2D game environment because this is what defines your gamespace - or the area that the player interacts within.

Start by placing an ACSpriteMenuBlock (9-slice it if you didn't in Chapter 2, *Working with Assets*), and remember to change the **Draw Mode** into **Sliced**. Then, stretch it until you have something like this:

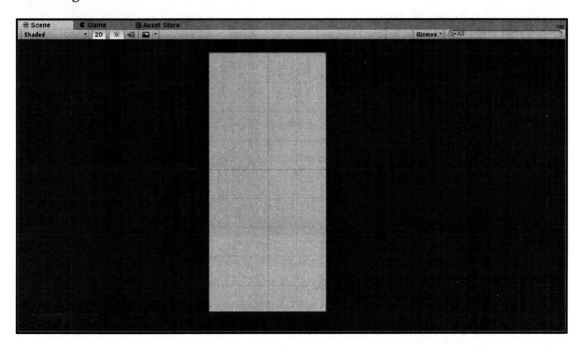

Next, drag the walls into the map, and stretch them as required. (Remember to keep the sliced mode! As a result, you won't stretch the scale). Duplicate the pieces as required, until you will reach something like the following:

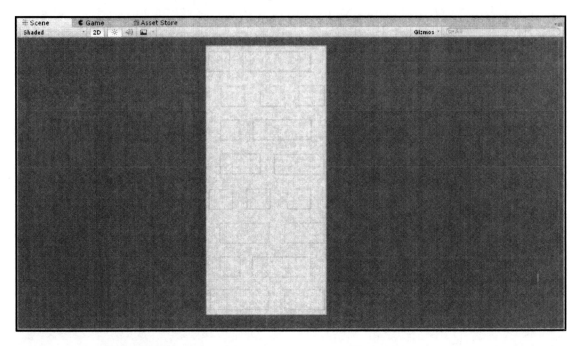

Once you finished working on the walls, I suggest you place them inside an empty game object to keep your scene tidy.

Also, you will need to create four walls to enclose the map. However, you need to remove the `Sprite Renderer` component, so that the map looks exactly like before, but the player cannot run away from the map.

Before we move on, we need to select them all and attach a `BoxCollider2D` to all of them. At the moment of writing, there is a bug, since the `BoxCollider2D` won't stretch to fit the dimensions of the wall (since it is a sliced sprite). Until this bug is fixed, I suggest you use this free script that you find at the following URL: `http://player26.com/?p=1363`.

The script is super easy to use: just select all the walls, and attach the script to them. The script will fix the collider, and it will delete itself. Simple, isn't it?

The next step is to place all the cakes on the map. If the Audio icon is bothering you, you can scale all the gizmos icons to zero from the **Gizmos** tab in the Scene View. Once you have placed all the cakes around the map, you should have something like this:

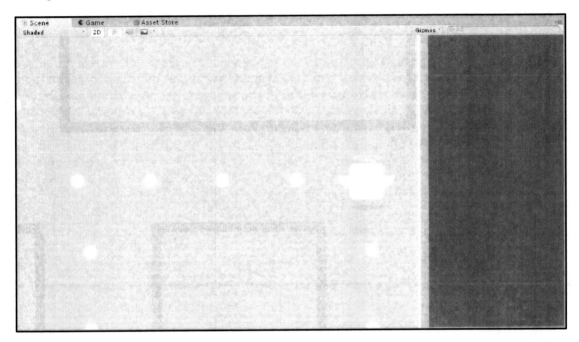

Once again, you can create an empty game object in which to parent all the cakes, so to keep the scene tidy.

The final touch is to add the player and playtest your game so far. The character might be too big to fit the corridors we have created, so scale it as needed.

Summary

In this chapter, we have explored what Prefabs are in Unity, how they are used, and more importantly, how to create one. We have also learned the basics of C# and scripts within Unity.

In addition, this chapter has also shown us how to create **PlayerControllers** and how to implement a collection system so that our Angel can eat cakes. Overall for the player movement, we have created a script, the PlayerController, which is responsible for taking the input and moving the character. Then, for the collecting system, we have created another script, this time attached to the cakes, which is responsible for detecting when the player collects that specific cake. This system is incomplete since we don't count how many cakes the player collects, and therefore the game never ends even if the player collects all the cake in the map. We will fix this in the next chapter, where we will talk about UI, giving feedback to the player, and ultimately establishing game over conditions. Then, we created the player character, an Angel able to collect cakes. To do so, we used the Physics Engine, by using the Colliders and **Rigidibodies**. Lastly, we added some background music and sound FX to our game to give it a little more magic. In Chapter 4, *It's about U and I*, we're going to explore the concept of **User Interfaces (UIs)**, what they are, how to design them, and how to create them in Unity! So, things are about to get a bit more serious between U and I...and Unity.

4
It's about U and I

Welcome to the final chapter of our first game. If you have been following this book chapter-by-chapter, you will have developed a strong foundation for using Unity. This chapter is an important one because it will explain one of the most crucial and difficult elements to get right when it comes to a game's experience. That is the user's interface, or simply, the UI. Don't let the title fool you; while it may be tempting to think of a UI as something trivial, simply on-screen graphics to convey information, there are many aspects of a UI that can cause problems (for example, navigation). We will discuss all of this through this chapter and then how to implement a basic UI in our game.

In this chapter, we will cover:

- The basics of the UI
- Four types of the UI
- Building the UI
- Scripting the UI and integrating with the collection systems
- Building a basic map
- Testing
- Other things that the reader could consider adding to the game later

By the end of this chapter, you will:

- Know how to implement a basic UI into Unity
- Build a basic game map
- Learn about best practices for testing games

If you're interested in reading more about UI, Unity has some official documentation that explains many aspects in more detail. You can find it by visiting `https://docs.unity3d.com/2017.2/Documentation/Manual/UISystem.html` or scanning the following QR code:

Overview of the UI

Imagine a watch without a watch face to indicate the time. An interface provides important information to us, such as time, so that we can make informed decisions (for example, whether we have enough time to get ice cream before the movie starts). When it comes to games, the **User Interface** (**UI**) plays a vital role in how information is conveyed to a player during gameplay. UIs provide important and sometimes vital information (for example, statistics, health, ammunition count) to a player during gameplay. The implementation of a UI is one of the main ways to exchange information with the player about moment-to-moment interactions and their consequences (for example, taking damage). However, UIs are not just about the exchange of information, they are also about how information is provided to a player and when. This can range from the subtle glow of a health bar as it depletes, to dirt covering the screen as you drive a high-speed vehicle through the desert. There are four main ways that UIs are provided to players within a game, which we will discuss shortly.

The purpose of this chapter is to prime you with the fundamentals of UIs so that you not only know how to implement them within Unity but also how they relate to a player's experience. Toward the end of the chapter, we will see how Unity handles UIs, and we will implement a UI for our first game. In fact, we will insert a scoring system as well as a **Game Over Screen**. There will be some additional considerations that you can experiment with in terms of adding additional UI elements that you can try implementing on your own.

While it is not essential for what you will learn in this book, if you want to further develop your skills when it comes to UIs within Unity, I recommend the following book: *Unity UI Cookbook*, Packt Publishing. It has a perfect set of recipes that are ready-to-use. There you will find all the concepts mentioned here and much more, such as different tips and tricks.

You can find it at `https://www.packtpub.com/game-development/unity-ui-cookbook` or by scanning the following QR code:

Designing the user interface

Think about reading a book, is the text or images in the center of the page, where is the page number located, and are the pages numbered consecutively? Typically, such things are pretty straightforward and follow conventions. Therefore, to some extent, we begin to expect things to be the same, especially if they are located in the same place, such as page numbers or even the next button. In the context of games, players also expect the same kinds of interactions, not only with gameplay but also with other on-screen elements, such as the UI. For example, if most games show health in a rectangular bar or with hearts, then that's something that players will be looking for when they want to know whether or not they are in danger.

The design of a UI needs to consider a number of things. For example, the limitations of the platform that you are designing for, such as screen size, and the types of interaction that it can afford (does it use touch input or a mouse pointer?). But physiological reactions that the interface might give to the player need to be considered since they will be the final consumer. In fact, another thing to keep in mind is that some people read from right to left in their native languages, and the UI should reflect this as well.

Just like our book example, players or users of applications are used to certain conventions and formats. For example, a house icon usually indicates home or the main screen, an email icon usually indicates contact, and an arrow pointing to the right usually indicates that it will continue to the next item in the list or the next question, and so on. Therefore, to improve ease of use and navigation, it is ideal to stick to these or to at least to keep these in mind during the design process. In addition to this, how the user navigates through the application is important. If there is only one way to get from the home screen to an option, and it's via a lot of screens, the whole experience is going to be tiresome. Therefore, make sure that you create navigation maps early on to determine the route for each part of the experience. If a user has to navigate through six screens before they can reach a certain page, then they won't be doing it for very long!

In saying all of this, don't let the design overtake the practicality of the user's experience. For example, you may have a beautiful UI but if it makes it really hard to play the game or it causes too much confusion, then it is pretty much useless. Particularly during fast-paced gameplay, you don't want the player to have to sift through 20 different on-screen elements to find what they are looking for. You want the level mastery to be focused on the gameplay rather than understanding the UI. Another way to limit the number of UI elements presented to the player (at any one time) is to have sliding windows or pop-up windows that have other UI elements present. For example, if your player has the option to unlock many different types of ability but can only use one or two of them at any single moment during gameplay, there is no point in displaying them all. Therefore, having a UI element for them to click that then displays all of the other abilities, which they can swap for the existing ones, is one way to minimize the UI design. Of course, you don't want to have multiple pop-up windows, otherwise, it becomes a quest in itself to change in-game settings.

Programming the user interface

As we have seen in the previous section, designing the UI can be tough and requires experience to get into, especially if you take into consideration all the elements you should, such as the psychology of your audience. However, this is just halfway through. In fact, designing is one thing; making it work is another. Usually, in large teams, there are artists who design the UI and programmers who implement it, based on the artists' graphics.

Is UI programming that different? Well, the answer is no, programming is still programming; however, it's quite an interesting branch of the field of programming. If you are building your game engine from scratch, implementing an entire system that handles input is not something you can create with just a couple of hours of work. Catching all the events that the player performs in the game and in the UI is not easy to implement, and requires a lot of practice. Luckily, in the context of Unity, most of this backend for UIs is already done. Furthermore, as we will see at the end of the chapter, Unity also provides a solid framework on the frontend for UIs. This framework includes different components that can be easily used without knowing anything about programming. But if we are really interested in unlocking the potential of the Unity framework for UIs, we need to both understand and program within it.

Even with a solid framework, such as the one in Unity, UI programming still needs to take into consideration many factors, enough to have a specific role for this in large teams. Achieving exactly what designers have in mind, and is possible without impacting the performance of the game too much, is most of the job of a UI programmer (at least using Unity).

Four types of UI

Before, moving on, I just want to point out a technical term about UIs, since it also appears in the official documentation of Unity. Some UIs are not fixed on the screen, but actually, have a physical space within the game environment. In saying this, there are four types of interfaces are diegetic, non-diegetic, meta, and spatial. Each of these has its own specific use and effect when it comes to the player's experience and some are implicit (for example, static graphics) while others are explicit (blood and dirt on the screen). However, these types can be intermixed to create some interesting interfaces and player experiences. For *Angel Cakes*, we will implement a simple non-diegetic UI, which will show all of the information the player needs to play the game.

Diegetic

Diegetic UIs differ from to non-diegetic UIs because they exist in the game world instead of being on top of it and/or completely removed from the game's fiction. Diegetic UIs within the game world can be seen and heard by other players. Some examples of diegetic UI include the screens on computers, ticking clocks, remaining ammunition, and countdowns. To illustrate this, if you have a look at the following image from the *Tribes Ascend* game, you can see the amount of ammunition remaining:

Non-diegetic

Non-diegetic interfaces are ones that are rendered outside of the game world and are only visible to the player. They are your typical game UIs that overlay on top of the game. They are completely removed from the game's fiction. Some common uses of non-diegetic UIs can represent health and mana via a colored bar. Non-diegetic UIs are normally represented in 2D, like in the following screenshot of *Star Trek Online*:

Spatial

Spatial UI elements are physically presented in the game's space. These types of UIs may or not may be visible to the other players within the game space. This is something that is particularly featured in **Virtual Reality (VR)** experiences. Spatial UIs are effective when you want to guide players through a level or to indicate points of interest. The following example is from *Army of Two*. On the ground, you can see arrows directing the player where to go next. You can find out more about implementing Spatial UIs, like the one in the following screenshot, in Unity by visiting the link to the official documentation at `https://unity3d.com/learn/tutorials/topics/virtual-reality/user-interfaces-vr`:

Meta

Lastly, Meta UIs can exist in the game world but aren't necessarily visualized like they would be as Spatial UIs. This means that they may not be represented within the 3D Space. In most cases, Meta UIs represent an effect of various actions such as getting shot or requiring more oxygen. As you can see in the following image of *Metro 2033*, when the player is in an area that is not suitable for them, the view through the mask begins to get hazy. When they get shot or engage in combat, their mask also receives damage. You can see this through the cracks that appear on the edges of the mask:

 So that you become more familiar with the different types of UIs and their uses, try to identify them in the games that you play and see how they aid or complicate a player's navigation.

Usability and function

When you're designing a UI for a multi-device experience, it's important to remember how players are going to be interacting with it, especially since interactions will be different on a computer than on a mobile device. Generally, you can't pinch and grab on a computer (unless it has touchscreen capabilities), just like you can't hover over a certain element on a mobile device.

UI is not UX

In some cases, the **User Experience** (**UX**) is influenced by a UI, in that a badly designed and implemented UI is going to lead to a poor UX. Think of this like going to a supermarket looking for pickles and not having any signs to indicate where they are, so you spend valuable time going down every aisle. If you're lucky, you won't overlook them.

In the context of games, user experience, or simply UX, is the process used to determine what the experience will be like when a user interacts with your game. UX includes user testing, generating personas (a fictional identity that reflects one of the user groups that you're designing for), scenarios, and storyboards. A good UX should consider the beginning of a player's journey from the acquisition of the game, how problems are handled, the playing of the game, and anything post-game. It's the journey that a player will be taken on from the first impressions to the end, whether it's the game's conclusion or any additional bonus material, such as DLC. UX can only be designed to a certain extent, because what is designed and what happens when players actually play your game are two different things, and, in some cases, completely different things. We will cover testing in a later chapter within this book. Now, with that said, let's look at how to create UIs for games.

Designing UIs for games

When it comes to designing UIs for games, there are a few things that you need to keep in mind. Not only will chosing the right UI for your game greatly add value to its ability to convey information it will also help to improve the user's experience. We'll go through the different types of UIs, along with some examples, in the following sections.

Feedback

One thing that a UI can offer is feedback to a player based on their interaction. Feedback can take on many forms and can be something as simple as a meter increasing/decreasing (for example, the health bar) to a player's avatar changing over time as the player upgrades and customizes them. In other instances, entire menus may change to reflect a player's progression through the game, like in *Spec Ops: The Line* in the following image:

You want feedback to be instantaneous, but not in the player's face. You want to alert them that a change has occurred based on an interaction but without annoying them. Could you imagine if every time you got a pellet in *Pac-Man* you got some large sparkly text saying "Well done" or "Good Job" plastered on your screen? Most likely not, and this is why, when you want to highlight a significant form of interaction, such as destroying a level 99 boss, you would adorn the player's screen with these kinds of things. It's a monumental event, let them know that their 1382nd attempt at the level was appreciated. Therefore, how you are going to alert the player to changes in the UI is as important as when.

When it comes to discrete changes to a UI, you may want to consider a subtle animation of a UI element. This can be as simple as a glow around the UI element. Another option is to use sound. Coming back to *Pac-Man*, the use of sound was implemented each time a player picked up a pellet. It is important to remember that audio can be just as effective as an animation, though it may not always be heard. For example, sometimes, players opt to disable the sound if they are in public or do not have headphones, others may have hearing impairments, like we discussed in Chapter 3, *Let's Make Some Prefabs*. Therefore, keep this in mind if you are using sound as the only way to indicate a change in the UI to the player. Lastly, you can implement subtle feedback from the starting point of an interaction, such as the main menu. In this way, you have the ability to communicate things such as progress, like that in the (previous)image of *Spec Ops: The Line*. As you progress through the game and complete each chapter, the main menu screen changes from something that is relatively neutral (top-left corner) to a devastating war-torn country (bottom-right corner), which reflects what has occurred in the game. While it is subtle, it in some ways sets the mood for the game and provides a sense of progression to the player before they continue their journey.

Be bold, not ambiguous

Be loud but don't shout in the user's face, you want the impact of your UI to be exciting and meaningful and not aesthetic noise.

Loud noises can immediately get people's attention, and so can UI elements. Therefore, you want to make your more important elements the focal point. The key here is to have fewer elements so that the player doesn't feel overwhelmed. For example, in a game, you may want the health bar to be the main item of focus. Therefore, place it somewhere where it will be noticed and not in the corner in the player's peripheral view. One way to achieve this is to have the UI elements contrast the environment, ideally within the same color palette so that they stand out, but not draw so much attention that they are distracting. A great website to create great color schemes is Adobe Color CC (https://color.adobe.com/). An example of it can be seen in the following screenshot:

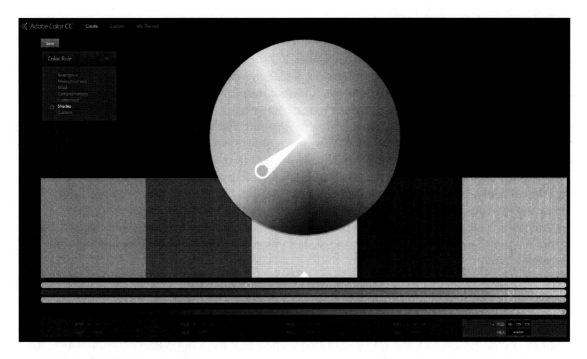

Color is a great way to convey information to players for various reasons. Just like a red traffic light means stop and green means go, the same approach can convey something immediately to a player with little effort. A common example of this in games is with a health bar. In general, when it is full, it is green. As the player engages in combat and takes damage, it begins to deplete and turn red, therefore instantly telling the player they're at risk of dying.

Just like we have seen with audio, similar considerations need to be made with color. UI design and feedback shouldn't rely on color alone. This is because some players may have some degree of colorblindness.

Keep it simple, consistent, and focused

When it comes to the components of a UI, they should be presented or highlighted in the order that you want your player to focus on. In other words, keep the important stuff on top and visible, with non-important elements not demanding visual real estate. Think of this as a visual hierarchy, from most important to least important. A simple example of this is to make a UI component bigger to make it the focal point. In this way, it cannot be ignored by a player: something that is useful for indicating a player's depleting life.

In saying that, the use of consistent color is important to maintain. For example, if you use one color to represent coins, try to avoid using it for other similar items (for example, gems or other resources). If the colors of items are too similar, then the player is going to have a hard time distinguishing between them, especially during moments that require fast interactions. You don't want players going crazy to collect coins thinking that they are super valuable gems, only to be bitterly disappointed when they check their inventory. It does happen.

Ergonomics: devices, hardware, and gestures

Phones and tablets don't have mice, so clicking options vary. This is an important thing to keep in mind because not all devices are created equally. When it comes to touchscreens, there is two kinds—capacitive and resistive touch. Capacitive is what you will experience with most modern devices, and you interact with the screen simply by touching it. Resistive, on the other hand, requires that a certain level of pressure is applied, such as with a stylus.

Multi-device design

Another thing to keep in mind is that if you are designing for multiple devices, try to keep the experience the same. With many applications being multi-platform, you don't want the user getting used to an experience on a cellphone that is presented in one way, and then to log on to the computer version, and it's completely different. Therefore, while you are designing the UI, determine how it will look on each device. Is the home icon too small on a cell phone to understand what it is? Is the navigation menu too large for a desktop version? Making sure that the UI is optimized will ensure that users who use your application across multiple devices will have a seamless transition and won't have to try to figure out how to access the features all over again.

Meaning and integrity

When it comes to creating a meaningful UI, you don't want to have unnecessary or deceptive interactions. What I mean by this is that you don't want players clicking a trophy button and then it takes them to a purchase page for coins, gems, or other virtual currency. Buttons aren't and shouldn't be used as click bait, even if things such as microtransactions are part of your business model.

Goals

You want to make sure that your goals are met with the UI that is presented to the player. If you want the player to follow a certain navigational path to encourage communication and the sharing of resources among players, you want the way that it is meant to be done presented in a clear and concise way.

Enjoyment

No one likes navigating through five menus to do one thing, nor do they want to keep track of necessary components (for example, health or remaining ammunition) by having to look at different locations on the screen. You want the UI to be as natural as possible so that it doesn't interfere but also so that it can be enjoyed and utilized by players.

Test

It goes without saying, and if I haven't said it enough, I will say it again, test, and test on multiple devices. The UI may look incredible on a PC, but if it's all shrunk up on a smaller-than-average smartphone, that isn't going to be fun. Even though you should be thinking about this from the beginning, in terms of screen resolution, devices sometimes give us unexpected surprises.

Introduction to the UI system in Unity

Welcome, you've made it to base camp for UIs in Unity. By now you will have read through what a UI is (and isn't) and things to keep in mind while you're creating it. If this was Mount Everest, you should be acclimatized now so that we can keep on with our journey.

Building UIs in Angel Cakes

Everything that we have read until now has brought us down to this moment. Now, we're ready to start building our first game. So let's get started!

Scripting a UI and integrating with the collection systems

It's finally time to add some UIs to our game. We will keep it simple because we talked a lot about design in the previous sections. Here, we will focus on the functionalities. After that you will have learned how to design, and how the UI system works in Unity, then you will be free to go on your own and improve the UI created in this section.

Importing a new font

Since we are going to display the score to the player, it's important to plan which font we will be using for it. For *Angel Cakes*, to keep the style consistent, the font I chose is **Century Gothic Regular**. You can grab a free copy of it from `http://www.911fonts.com/font/ download_CenturyGothicRegular_4365.html`.

Once we have the file, it's likely to have a strange name, so my suggestion is to rename it simply `Century Gothic Regular` (of course, keeping the same file extension). Then, inside Unity, we can create a specific folder, named `Fonts`, and drag and drop our new font. From now on, we can use the font within our project.

Setting up the UI

First of all, we need to create a canvas by right-clicking in the **Hierarchy** panel, then **UI** |
Canvas, and naming it HUD. Unity should automatically create an **EventSystem**. In case it
doesn't, you can manually add it by again right-clicking and then clicking **UI** |
EventSystem. Then, we need to create a **Panel** within the **Canvas**, and we can do it
similarly to how we created the **Canvas**. Among the different anchor presets, we can select
the one on top, as shown in the following screenshot:

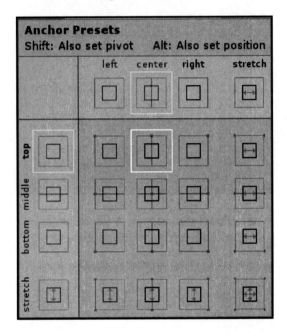

Next, resize the panel so that it occupies the upper part of the screen. In the end, you should end up with something similar to the following:

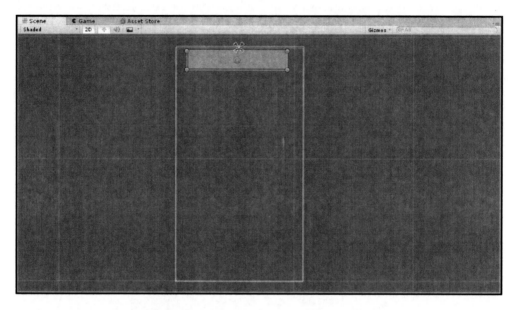

If you want to be sure how the panel will appear in-game, you can switch to the game mode view. This is how the panel should appear according to our design:

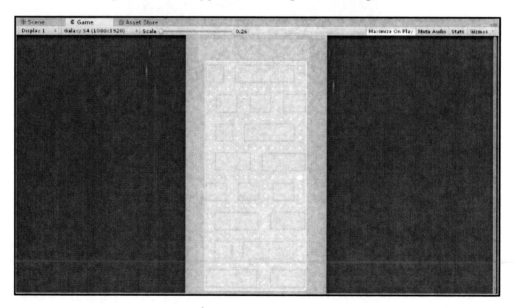

We need to create one more thing: a label where we'll display the score to the player. So let's create a **Text**, and rename it ScoreLabel. Now, in the **Inspector**, we need to tweak some values of the Text Component. In particular, we want to change the font, to the one we imported before, and the font size to better fit the panel. It's important to adjust the dimensions of the box containing the text, and the anchors (in my case, I used that they stretch), and the alignment. Also, as a text we can insert the string Score: 0, so we can have a better idea of how it will look once the score starts to increase; don't worry much about it though because this text will be replaced by our script. Of course, feel free to change any other settings you'd like to fit your personal style and mood. These are the settings I used:

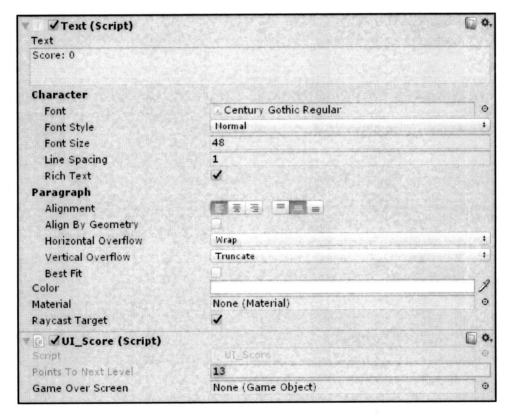

Programming the scoring system

Finally, we get to get our hands dirty with a bit of code. Don't worry, it will be simple. As usual, let's start by creating a new C# script, name it UI_Score, and open it up in your editor of choice.

First of all, if we want to use the UI system within a script, we need to import it in the context of our script. We can achieve that with a using statement at the beginning of our script, as highlighted here:

```
using System.Collections;
using System.Collections.Generic;
using UnityEngine;
using UnityEngine.UI;
public class UI_Score : MonoBehaviour {
    //[...]
}
```

Once we have done this, we are ready to use all the Unity UI components in our script. In fact, the first variable we need is a reference to the Text Component we created in the previous section:

```
//Reference to the Text component, set in the Start() function
private Text uiText;
```

Then, we need a variable to store the actual value of the score, and another one that stores the number of points required to pass to the next level. Please note that in this case, we used the [SerializeField] attribute before the private variable to still make it editable from the **Inspector**:

```
//Current score of the player
private int score;
//Points required to the next level (set in the Inspector)
[SerializeField]
private int pointsToNextLevel;
```

In a similar fashion, we need to get the reference to the **Game Over Screen**, which we will create later. Thus, we can write:

```
//Reference to the game over screen GameObject (set in the Inspector)
[SerializeField]
private GameObject gameOverScreen;
```

Then, we need to get the reference to the Text Component in the `Start()` functions, therefore it becomes:

```
// Use this for initialization
void Start () {
    //Get a reference to the Text component
    uiText = GetComponent<Text>();
}
```

Finally, we need to create a function that takes, in an input, the number of points to add to the player's score and visualize it in the UI. The function should also check whether the new score is equal to or greater than the points needed for the next level, and if so, it shows our **Game Over Screen** and disables the player input. As a result, this is the function we need:

```
public void IncreaseScore(int points) {
    //Increase the points
    score += points;
    //Check if the player has collected all the points to the next level
    if(score >= pointsToNextLevel) {
        //If so, show the game over screen
        gameOverScreen.SetActive(true);
        //Disable the player controller, so the player cannot move while
the Gameover screen is on
        FindObjectOfType<PlayerController>().enabled = false;
    }
    //Update the Score count
    uiText.text = "Score: " + score.ToString();
}
```

And with this, we can save the script, since we have finished with this script. However, we still need to call this last function every time the player collects a cake. But before we do that, don't forget to attach this script to the **ScoreLabel**!

Increasing the score when the player collects a cake

Now that our UI system is set up, we need to actually call the function of the last section when the player collects a cake. To achieve this, we need to open the `CollectableCake` script from `Chapter 3`, *Let's Make Some Prefabs*. If you recall, we left a To-Do which was to link the moment the player collects a cake with the UI.

In fact, we start by creating another variable (settable in the Inspector), and this time public, to store the value of the single cake. As a result, you will be able to change the value of every single cake. This is useful in case we want to add other collectable cakes, maybe that are more rare, which scores more for the player. Here is the variable declaration:

```
//Stores the value of the cake in terms of Player's score
public int cakeValue = 1;
```

Then, we need to substitute the TODO line of code with the following, so we actually call the UI script we wrote before:

```
if (other.tag == "Player") {
    //If so, increase the number of cakes the player has collected
    FindObjectOfType<UI_Score>().IncreaseScore(cakeValue);
    //[...]
}
```

And that's it. Now, let's create a **Game Over Screen** before we tweak the last settings in the **Inspector** and finally get our first game finished!

Creating a Game Over Screen

To create a **Game Over Screen**, we start by creating another panel. This time, we can rename it Game Over Screen.

Next, create a new **Image** and call it Panel. In fact, we can use it as background for our Game Over menu by using the ACSriteMenuBlock graphics. In a similar fashion to the text for the score, we can add a title to the menu, such as **GAME OVER**.

Then, at the bottom, we can add a **Play Again?** button, and change the graphics again into ACSriteMenuBlock. Don't forget to set the proper font, the anchors, the alignment, the font size, the font color, and so on. In the end, you should have something like this:

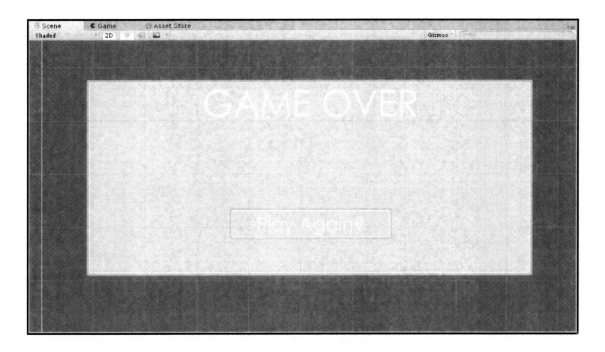

Scripting the Game Over Screen

Now we would like to restart the level when the player clicks **Play Again?** To do so, let's create another script and name it `UI_GameOver`. This time the script is going to be much simpler. In fact, we want to create a function to reload the current level, that's it.

First of all, we need a using-statement to import the library to manage the scenes, so here it is:

```
using System.Collections;
using System.Collections.Generic;
using UnityEngine;
using UnityEngine.SceneManagement;
public class UI_GameOver : MonoBehaviour {
    //[...]
}
```

Then, just create the function to reload the current scene (the `buildIndex` is the identifier that Unity assigns to this specific scene in the built version, thus retrieving the line for the current scene, we can reload the level):

```
<pre>public void PlayAgain() {
//Reload the current scene
SceneManager.LoadScene(SceneManager.GetActiveScene().buildIndex);
}
```

Save the script, because we are close to the end. Just a few settings away to complete our game!

Last tweaks

To make our game fully functioning, we need to tweak a couple of things.

First of all, we need to link the previous function to reload the scene when the player presses the **Play Again?** button. To do so, add the `UI_GameOver` script to the button, then in the `On Click()` tab of the **Button** component, press the + button to add an event. Drag and drop the script just added, and select the `PlayAgain()` function. Here is how the final setup should look:

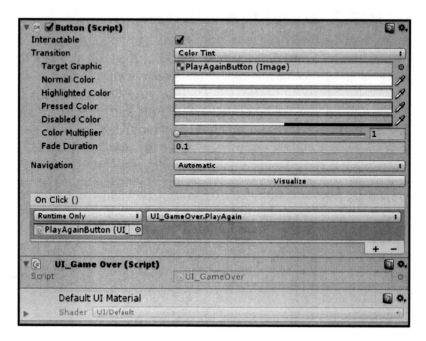

Next, we don't want the **Game Over Screen** to always be visible when we start the game, so we need to disable it. To achieve that, select the **Game Over Screen** in the **Hierarchy** panel, and in the **Inspector** uncheck the checkbox next to its name. Here is a screenshot of that:

Lastly, we need to select our **Score Label**, because we need to set both the number of points to the end of the game, and the **Game Over Screen** reference. For the former, just insert the number of cakes in the game (unless you inserted special cakes with different values; in that case, you need to insert the sum of all the values, but see the last section for more info). For the **Game Over Screen** reference, just drag and drop it from the **Hierarchy** panel. Here is the final result:

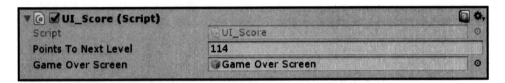

Finally, we are ready to test our game!

Testing

One of the things that you want to make sure you do along the way is to test your game, and not just on one device, on but many.

More kinds of cakes

Of course, the first challenge is to add different kinds of cakes, or at least, different collectables. In the first place, you can still use the CollectableCake script and change their values. But remember to create a prefab, and add all the proper colliders. For instance, in the package you can find a purple diamond, that is a good start to make objects with more values.

However, when you've got different cakes and/or objects with different values, you don't want to calculate the sum of their values by hand. In this case, we can set the `pointsToNextLevel` variable in the `Start()` function of the `UI_Score` script.

Here is a possible example:

```
// Use this for initialization
void Start () {
    //Get a reference to the Text component
    uiText = GetComponent<Text>();
    //Get the sum of all the cake values around the level
    foreach(CollectableCake cake in FindObjectsOfType<CollectableCake>()) {
        pointsToNextLevel += cake.cakeValue;
    }
}
```

Other suggestions include creating a second score system similar to the first one for another kind of collectible or adding some power-ups. So when the player collects this specific object, the script increases the speed in the `PlayerController`. But these are just a few examples.

Adding more levels

Another good challenge for your level is to include other levels in your game. Every time the player reaches the number of points to the next level, instead of displaying the **Game Over Screen**, the player can jump to a second or third level. In order to do so, you might want to visit the official documentation of Unity regarding the **Scene Manager** here: `https://docs.unity3d.com/ScriptReference/SceneManagement.SceneManager.html` You can also add the number of levels in the interface.

Adding animations

In the next projects, we will learn more about how to animate our characters. However, this package already comes with animations, and if you are up to the challenge, you can try to explore the animation system by yourself. Here a little hint is to select all the sprites that compose an animation and drag them in the scene. Unity will ask you to save the animation file, and I'd suggest you create another folder for those. Then, the characters should already be good to go. From there, you can see the effects of animating a character.

In any case, you can keep reading this book, and come back here later.

Devils

The greatest challenge for you would be to add some devils (enemies). They don't need to be complex and chase the player; in fact, they can just move from one spot to another on the map, and the player needs to avoid them.
Here are some suggestions on how to implement them.

Remember to attach the proper colliders and set them as a trigger. Every time the player hits the devil, you can show the **Game Over** menu. You can just use the same line of code for the UI_GameOver script:

```
SceneManager.LoadScene(SceneManager.GetActiveScene().buildIndex);
```

To make the enemy move from one spot to another, you need to create some empty game objects in the game called waypoints. Then, you need to give a set (or even just two of them) in the script that controls the devil and makes it move toward one. When the devil reaches that waypoint, it comes back to the first one (or continues on the list, if you want to implement a list of waypoints). To check whether a devil reached a waypoint, you can calculate the distance between the devil and the waypoint. If this is below a certain threshold, then you can consider that the devil has reached the waypoint.

Of course, this is quite a challenge, but I'm sure you will do fine if you persist. Also, you can first finish reading the book, and then improve all the games you have created once you have more confidence in Unity.

Summary

We have learned the fundamentals of UI design and explored many different aspects of what it entails. We have also seen some examples of different kinds of UIs and how the four types of UI—diegetic, non-diegetic, spatial, and Meta all differ from each other and how they can be used within a game.

Then, we explored some concepts of how Unity handles UIs before diving into implementing the UI for our *Angel Cakes* game. In particular, we have created a script for the **Score**, which integrates with the CollectableCake script of Chapter 3, *Let's Make Some Prefabs*. We have also included a **Game Over Screen** to show when the Angel collects all the cakes.

Lastly, we have explored some suggestions about how to go on developing our game to make it even more awesome than it currently is. Of course, this chapter only provided a brief overview of some of the many important components of UIs, so I highly recommend that you also explore the design and practicality of UIs with other online/offline resources. One resource is the Interaction Design Foundation, ;www.interaction-design.org. While it focuses more on UX, there are many great resources on UIs to check out.

Now, with this chapter, we have concluded our first game. It is, therefore, time to start another one. For our next game, we will go into deep space to meet new friends in Chapter 5, *Freeze! Creating an Intergalactic Shooter*. So set your phasers to stun, because things are about to get a whole lot more interesting.

5

Freeze! Creating an Intergalactic Shooter

Welcome to Chapter 5, *Freeze! Creating an Intergalactic Shooter*. If you have been following this book up until now, you should have one pretty cool game under your belt; if not, we're about to step it up with game number two. In this chapter, we're going to learn about the second game, a top-down arcade-style intergalactic shooter, so brace yourself. We'll also cover some other import settings, which will build upon what we covered in *Angel Cakes* (our first game). Later in this chapter, we will add a bang, by learning about Unity's animation system, to create an explosion.

Throughout this chapter, we will cover the following:

- An overview of game #2 and the shooter genre
- How to set up the Unity project for game #2
- How to import assets (intermediate import settings)
- Introduction to the animation system within Unity
- Creating a basic "explosion" animation for our game
- Setting up the player controller

By the end of this chapter, you will:

- Be able to import and set up assets for a shooting game
- Have a basic understanding of Unity's animation system
- Know how to create basic animations from Sprites

Excited? Well, me too, let us dive into creating an intergalactic experience!

An overview of game #2

Ever wanted to be beamed out to space on an intergalactic mission, perhaps like our beloved *Cassini*? For our second project, we will be making a top-down arcade-style shooter that will transport you into the world of galactic fantasies. In this game, you will control a small spacecraft that must navigate around planets and asteroids to collect power stars and health (if you get hit):

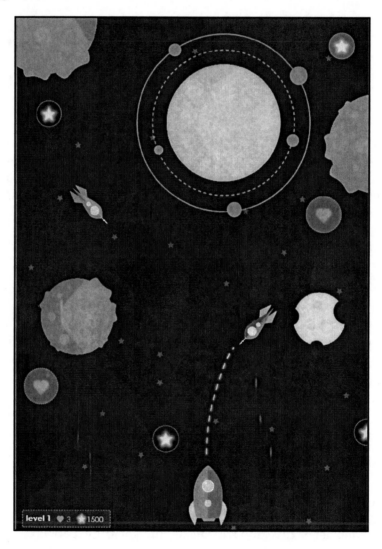

Overview of shooting games

There are many different types of shooting games, each designed differently from the next. To offer you a better understanding of their differences, and to provide you with a bunch of different examples that may inspire your own games, we'll discuss these different types.

First-Person

Our first example is perhaps the most common type that people think of when they hear about the "shooter" genre. From a 3D perspective of the player, a **First-Person Shooter (FPS)** is all about putting you in the virtual shoes of the game's avatar and seeing the game's world through their eyes. FPSs can be traced back to the 1970s, and since then, they have developed into spectacular and immersive worlds that take us far from our own reality, such as in *Metro 2033*, pictured here:

Third-Person

In a literal step back from an FPS, **Third-Person Shooters (TPS)** have you controlling the player from behind or over the shoulder. Like FPSs, TPSs also has a long history that can be traced back to the late 1970s. An excellent example is *Spec Ops: The Line,* pictured here:

Top-down

If FPSs are *in* the player's shoes and TPSs are from behind, let us talk about shooters where the perspective is from above, or top-down. Think of these types of shooters as played from a birds-eye perspective. Many arcade games feature top-down shooters, such as *Asteroids* and *Space Invaders* (pictured here):

As you can see, the style of shooter all depends on the perspective of the camera, at least as far as our examples go. There are many sub-genres of shooters (for example survival, rail, light gun, tactical, and so on). All of these would require a whole chapter or even book to discuss, so I encourage you to explore them to deepen your own knowledge.

Designing game #2

Now that you have a general understanding of shooting games, it's time to design our game. First of all, we like the idea of setting it in space, and, of course, it will be a 2D game. Riding the coattails of the success of *Space Invaders*, we can try to do something similar. So, the player will control a spaceship, which is at the bottom of the screen and can move only to the left or right. We could allow the player to go also up and down, but that would complicate the AI a little too much. Then, we don't like the idea of having shields protecting the player, since we want the game to be more challenging. However, we like that the player has a limited number of lives and that they are shown in the bottom-left corner of the screen.

This is a screenshot of how the game should look at the end of these three chapters:

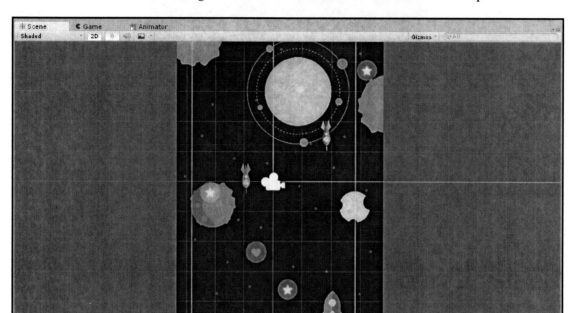

Setting up the project for game #2

This project will follow pretty much the same process as the last one. We will go through the steps briefly, but if you need a more detailed process, if you have, for instance, chosen to start with this project, then I encourage you to review the previous chapters. Now, with that said, let's get started.

You can find the assets to this project at `http://player26.com/product/quark/`.

Once you have downloaded the files, unzip them into the location of your project.

Importing assets for the space shooter

As we have already discussed with the first project, there are few differences when it comes to importing the assets for our second game. Like the last project, the assets for this one also come with a series of Sprite Sheets; these look like the following images:

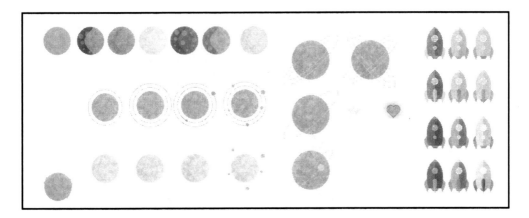

As you can see from the image above, we have spaceships, explosions, and planets. Basically, everything we need to create our space-themed shooting game.

Once you have imported them into Unity, we will need to slice them up and label the Sprites accordingly. You can either follow our naming convention or choose your own. Just remember that if you choose to use your own naming convention when referencing the Sprites, you must also use it within your code, instead of the names we use. The naming convention we will use should be clear, but I invite you to find a naming convention that works for you.

Remember that the Sprite Sheets should be sliced. In the next section, we are going to slice the Sprite Sheet to make the explosion.

Organizing the project

In organizing the project, as we did for the previous game, we need to create a folder to keep everything tidy. In this game, we are going to use the following folders:

- `Animations`
- `Audio and Music` (you need to fill this one with your own music and sound effects)
- `Fonts` (you need to fill this one with your own fonts)
- `Graphics` (where you need to place all the Sprite Sheets of the graphics package)
- `Prefabs`
- `Scripts`

Here is how your **Project** panel should look:

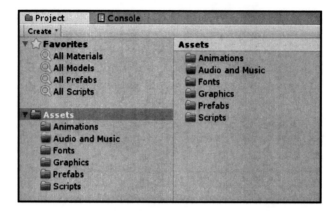

After this has been set up, let us get our hands dirty, starting with creating a big explosion.

Introduction to the animation system

Unity has a brilliant and effective animation system named **Mecanim**. It works wonderfully with 3D animation, as well as for 2D animations. However, we will use some basic features, since we are going to use just a couple of Sprite animations to begin with.

Of course, feel free to explore the official documentation by visiting `https://docs.unity3d.com/Manual/AnimationSection.html` or following the official video tutorial: `https://unity3d.com/learn/tutorials/s/animation`.

When it comes to the animation system in Unity, we can talk about State Machines. Each animation is a node and the character can change animation according to certain variables of the State Machine. You can see an example of an animation State Machine in the following image. Keep in mind that, usually, animation state machines are much bigger and more complex in a real project than the ones used to explain how they work:

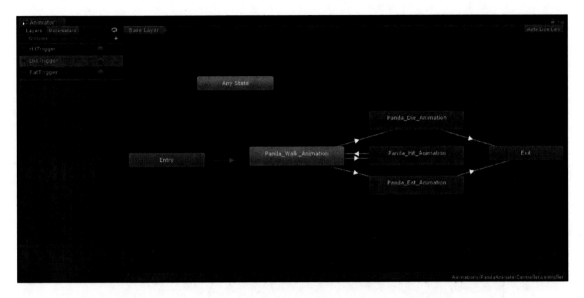

For our game, we will be implementing an explosion animation each time something is destroyed. It is a simple animation, but by showing you how to create it, you will be able to implement other types of animations for other elements of not only the games within this book but also your own projects. However, for our project, the animations will come into effect when the player's spaceship runs out of life, and when enemies' spaceships, planets, and comets are destroyed.

Concepts of Sprite animations

Although the animation system in Unity is very powerful, and it is able to animate to a certain degree, often external programs are used. In the case of 3D animations, programs such as **3DStudioMax**, **Maya**, or **Blender** are used. When it comes to 2D animations, the most-used technique is an animation Sprite Sheet. In short, it is a sprite sheet containing all the frames of the animation. They can be created with any program that manipulates 2D graphics. Some of these programs include Photoshop, GIMP, or Illustrator (in case you want vector graphics).

For instance, in our case, we've got two animation Sprite Sheets, one for each kind of explosion. Let us take one of them, for instance, `explosion02`. Here is what it looks like:

As you can see, there are 12 frames, and each one of them is properly spaced within the sheet. Having things properly spaced is essential to simplify the workflow in Unity. If you select the sheet in the **Project** window, we can see its **Import Settings** in the **Inspector**. We need to select **Multiple** for the **Sprite Mode**, as shown in the following screenshot:

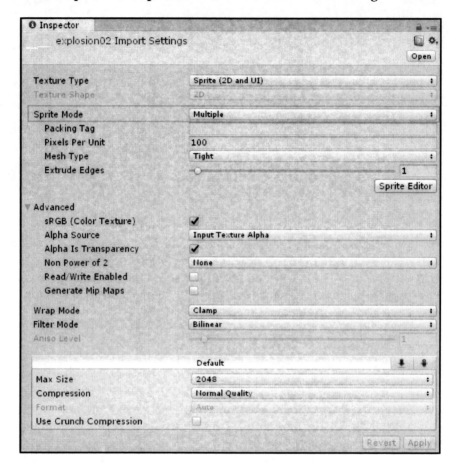

After you have clicked **Apply**, we need to open the **Sprite Editor** by clicking the **Sprite Editor** button, so we can properly **Slice** the animation Sprite Sheet:

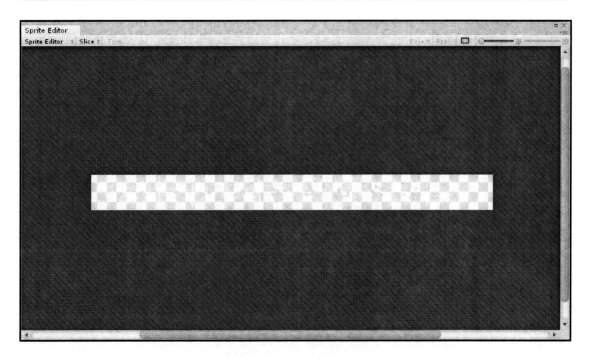

On the top bar of the **Sprite Editor**, click **Slice**. Select **Grid By Cell Count** as the type, and insert 12 columns and 1 row. In case you have a different sprite sheet with a different number of frames, use the number of columns or rows of your animation. Here is what it should look like:

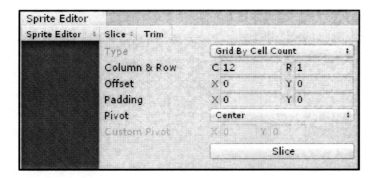

Then, press the **Slice** button at the bottom of the window. As a result, each frame of our animation is a different Sprite, and they are also numbered from zero in order (something that might be very useful in large projects). Click **Apply** in the top-right corner and close the **Sprite Editor**.

Generating the animations from the sprites

The last step to generate the animation is to expand the **explosion** sheet with all the frames as single Sprites in the **Project** panel, as shown here:

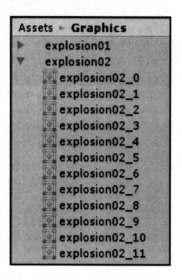

Select all the frames, and drag and drop them on the **Scene** view. Unity will ask you where you want to save the animation and under which name. Select the animation folder (if you do not have one, create it), and type explosionAnimation for the name. Finally, save it.

A few considerations now. If you hit play, you can see the animation playing continuously on the screen, but let us see how it works under the hood. First, navigate to the animation folder, and you will notice that two files have been created. One is the animation that we have just saved, and the other one is the animation State Machine we were discussing just before and it is named as the first frame of the animation Sprite Sheet, in this case, explosion02_0, but you can rename it explosion02_animator. If you double-click the State Machine, the **Animator** window comes up showing you the State Machine, and here is how it looks:

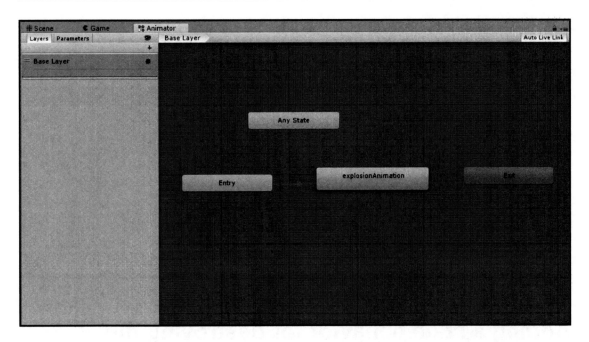

The important thing to pick up here is that, from the **Entry** node, there is a link to our animation represented by another node. This means that as soon as the object running this machine plays, our animation is running, which is exactly what we want. We won't dig any further into animation during the development of this second project, but we will discuss the animation system more in the last project of this book.

Now, coming back to the **Project** panel, if we select the animation, we can see its properties in the **Inspector**. Since the explosion is not a continuous animation, but rather a one-shot animation, we need to uncheck **Loop Time**, as shown in the following image:

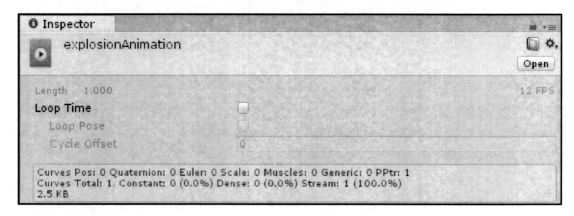

Adding a state behavior for destroying the explosion

If you hit play, the animation will play only once. However, the object won't be destroyed as we would expect. This can be done with a very simple script, which is a StateMachineBehavior. We take this script from the book *Getting Started with Unity 5.x 2D Game Development* (https://www.packtpub.com/game-development/getting-started-unity-5x-2d-game-development), which, once again, I suggest you read to get more insight into 2D game development. Thus, for the detailed explanation of this script, check out *Chapter 4, No Longer Alone - Sweet Toothed Pandas Strike*, of that book. Here, we will just see how to create and use that script, without explaining in detail how the StateMachineBehavior script works.

Create a new script, and name it `StateMachineBehaviour_DestroyOnExit`. Open it, erase all the code in it, and instead paste the following:

```
using UnityEngine;
public class StateMachineBehaviour_DestroyOnExit : StateMachineBehaviour {
    override public void OnStateExit(Animator Animator, AnimatorStateInfo
stateInfo, int layerIndex) {
        //Destroy the gameobject where the Animator is attached to
        Destroy(Animator.gameObject);
    }
}
```

Save the script, and open the state machine of our explosion. Right-click the **animation** node, click **Make Transition**, then click the **Exit** node. As a result, you will see an arrow going toward the **Exit** state, as shown in the following screenshot:

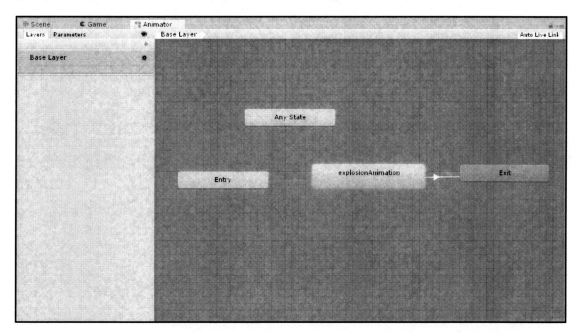

Now, click the **animation** node, and in the **Inspector**, you should see an **Add Behaviour** button click it and add the script we have just created. Then, select the only **Transition** under the **Transitions** tab, and some settings will appear. Set **Exit Time** to 1 and **Transition Duration** to 0. Here is how it looks:

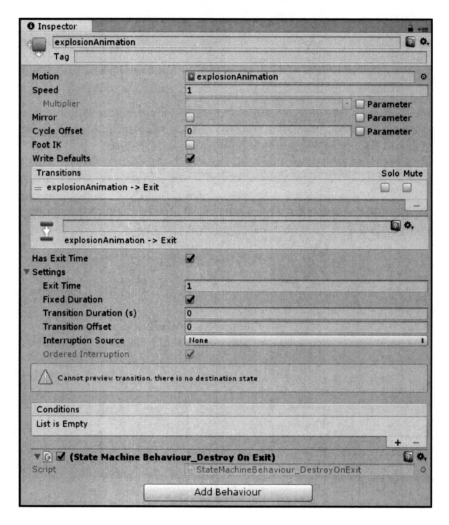

If we play the game now, the explosion should work. For more explanations of this process, you can read the book suggested before, but in any case, we will explore the animation system in the last project of this book.

Saving the explosion as a prefab

We already talked about prefabs in the last project, so you should have a good understanding of their usefulness. The last step for creating this explosion is to save it within a prefab, so we can use it every time we need an explosion, and not only a random explosion every time the game starts.

In the `Prefab` folder, create a new prefab, and name it `ExplosionPrefab`. Then, simply drag and drop it on the **Explosion** object in the **Hierarchy** window. It should become blue after this process, so you will know that it has become a prefab, and you can remove it from the scene. As a result, we can use the explosion prefab any time we need one.

Summary

In this chapter, we covered the basics of the shooter genre; we also described what our second project is and how to set it up. We covered the basics of animation in Unity and how to create a basic explosion animation. In the next chapter, you will learn how to add a bit more substance to our shooter game. You will learn how to create a shooting system so that the player can fire at enemies. You will also learn how to create a prefab for an enemy, as well as an enemy AI to add a bit more action to the game.

6

No One Is Alone Forever

Now, we've laid down the foundations for our second game. In this chapter, it is all about adding a bit more substance to our shooter. In this chapter, we will learn how to create an explosion and use it within our shooting system. In particular, we will learn how to:

- Create the player controller, so that the player can move the spaceship and shoot with it
- Code a simple AI enemy, which results in challenging the players and adding a bit more *action* to the game
- Implement bullets in our game, since without them it wouldn't be a shooter

At the end of the chapter, you will find an exercise section in which you can practice what you have learned in this chapter. However, if you really want to dig deeper into AI, you should consider buying a specific book about it.

By the end of this chapter, you will be able to:

- Create a shooting system for any 2D game
- Implement a basic AI enemy, but that is smart enough to be an obstacle for the player
- Have a better understanding of how to call functions between scripts
- Instantiate game objects, such as bullets or explosions
- Expose many variables in the Inspector for each controller, so that designers can customize and balance the experience
- Make game objects auto-destruct after a certain period of time

Ready to learn all this awesome stuff? Very well, let's dive in!

Creating a shooting system

As we saw in `Chapter 5`, *Freeze! Creating an Intergalactic Shooter,* there are many different ways a player can "shoot" something. As we also learned, in our game, the player will shoot at a range of different objects. Therefore, there are a few things that you may want to consider when it comes to implementing the elements of shooting. One such thing is the "consequence" for shooting or, alternatively, getting shot. For example, when a player shoots at the enemy, how many hits can the *enemy* take before it is destroyed, and vice versa for the player? Are some enemies harder than others, perhaps more powerful? Now, the answers to these kinds of questions become refined through playtesting. It is what we game designers refer to as "balancing", and ideally you want a game to be not too easy or too hard at the beginning, but something that grows in difficulty as the player becomes more skilled at it.

For now, we will work on setting the shooting system up, then we will look at how to balance it later. In particular, the shooting system is not just one script, but in our case, it is made of the interactions between the `PlayerController`, the `EnemyController`, and the `BulletController`. This chapter wants also to show you how it is possible to create challenging enemies without using complex AI algorithms not suitable for beginners since sometimes less is more. So, let's explore these controllers one by one.

Player controller

The `PlayerController` in this instance is slightly different from that in *Angel Cakes*. However, we can use what we learned in the previous project to create this new player controller.

Requirements of the player controller

Let's start by defining the requirements for this player controller.

First of all, we would like to lock the movement to only left and right; we don't want the player going up and down. Of course, this is the choice we made when we designed the game earlier in the chapter. Another consideration is that the left and right movements are limited; the player cannot go off screen. In *Angel Cakes* we have solved this problem by placing walls, so we delegated to the physics system the fact that the player cannot go beyond certain boundaries. In space, there are no walls, and even if we could place invisible ones, for the sake of learning something new, we will see how to limit the movement through the script.

Differently from *Angel Cakes*, the player here can shoot. In particular, the player can shoot straight from the player's location. In our implementation, this means that the player controller has to instantiate a bullet. However, we also need to limit this process, since we don't want the player to shoot billions of projectiles per second, but rather have a reload time before shooting the next bullet. As such, the player controller is also responsible for making this check.

Lastly, the spaceship can take damage, so we need to show the animation of the explosion where the enemy's bullet has hit the player. Again, the player controller has to deal with it. Actually, not only should it show the explosion, but it should also play a sound and decrease the number of lives by one. However, for these two things, we need to wait until Chapter 7, *Getting Serious About Gameplay*, in which we will implement the UI, but it was worth mentioning it here since we are designing our player controller.

Now that we understand the requirements for our player controller, let's implement it. If you remember in Chapter 3, *Let's Make Some Prefabs*, we saw the script piece by piece. Here, to change the approach, we will see all its functionalities one by one.

Creating the script

As we did in Chapter 3, *Let's Make Some Prefabs*, we need to create a **Player Controller (Script)**. Inside the Script folder, right-click and then **Create | C# Script**. We name it PlayerController. Now the script can be used as a component, meaning that it can be attached to a game object:

We can then open the **Script** by double-clicking on it. For those who didn't follow the previous project, here is a short recap. This is the code you should see:

```
using System.Collections;
using System.Collections.Generic;
using UnityEngine;

public class PlayerController : MonoBehaviour {

    // Use this for initialization
    void Start () {
    }
    // Update is called once per frame
    void Update () {
```

```
        }
    }
```

At the beginning, there are three lines that allow us to use libraries. Then, there is the class definition, in this case, named `PlayerController`. Inside it, there are two functions: `Start()` and `Update()`. The first is called every time this script starts, whereas the second is called at every frame.

Moving the player

The first feature to implement is the most vital one: moving the player.

Let's start by copying and pasting the code from Chapter 3, *Let's Make Some Prefabs*. In fact, we need to enforce both **collider** and **rigidbody** components, since we will use them to move the character (and also to detect collisions with bullets or enemies). Then, we actually need to move the character. You can refer to Chapter 3, *Let's Make Some Prefabs*, for a detailed explanation, but we are going to use, once again, the following equation:

$$pos_t = pos_{t-1} + velocity * \Delta Time$$

The only difference is that we don't need to move the player along the y-axis, so the code within the `FixedUpdate()` function becomes shorter than one line. Also, we need to substitute the y variable in the last line of the function with `transform.position.y`.

The final code should look like the following:

```
using System.Collections;
using System.Collections.Generic;
using UnityEngine;

[RequireComponent(typeof(Rigidbody2D))]
[RequireComponent(typeof(Collider2D))]
public class PlayerController : MonoBehaviour {

    public float speed = 10.0f;
    private Rigidbody2D rigidBody;

    // Use this for initialization
    void Start() {
        rigidBody = GetComponent<Rigidbody2D>();
    }

    void FixedUpdate() {
        //Get the new position of our character
```

```
        var x = transform.position.x + Input.GetAxis("Horizontal") *
Time.deltaTime * speed;

        //Set the position of our character through the RigidBody2D
component (since we are using physics)
        rigidBody.MovePosition(new Vector2(x, transform.position.y));
    }
}
```

So far so good, the player is able to move left and right. However, the spaceships movement is unlimited along the x-axis. Therefore, we will need to use a wall to contain the player's movement. To begin we will need to add a variable. We assume that the main camera is centered (as in any 2D default scene). Thus, if the player is on x=0, then the spaceship is in the middle of the left and right sides of the screen. As a result, we are able to use just one variable to limit the motion both left and right symmetrically. We can add to our code the boundX variable, make it public (so designers can tweak it), and assign an initial value:

```
        public float boundX = 10.0f;
```

Now, within the FixedUpdate() function, we need to use a math function to clamp the x value in case it becomes bigger than boundX or smaller than negative boundX.

 A clamp function is a function that takes as input three parameters: a value, a min, and a max. If the value is in between the min and the max, the function returns (gives back) the value itself. Otherwise, the function returns max if the value is bigger than max; similarly, the function returns min if the value is less than min.

In the Unity Math Library, such a function is already implemented, so let's use it between getting the new x value and assign the new position to the **rigidbody**, like the following:

```
    void FixedUpdate() {
        //Get the new position of our character
        var x = transform.position.x + Input.GetAxis("Horizontal") *
Time.deltaTime * speed;
        //Clamp along x-value according to boundX variable
        x = Mathf.Clamp(x, -boundX, boundX);
        //Set the position of our character throught the RigidBody2D
component (since we are using physics)
        rigidBody.MovePosition(new Vector2(x, transform.position.y));
    }
```

Save the script and test it to see if it works before moving on.

It's time to shoot

The next step is to give the player the ability to shoot. In doing so, the player controller creates a `bulletPrefab`. We don't have a `bulletprefab` yet, but we will create it later in the chapter. However, we can create a variable to hold the prefab, so it can be changed later on in the **Inspector**, as the following:

```
public GameObject bulletPrefab;
```

Now, in the `FixedUpdate()` function, after all the lines we already have, we need to instantiate the bullet every time the player shoots. In this case, we are going to check whether the player presses the **Fire1** button or the *E* key. If so, we just instantiate the bullet prefab at the same position as the spaceship and without any rotation applied, which is expressed through the admittedly fancy `Quaternion.Identity` argument (you can find out more about quaternions in Unity at the following links: https://unity3d.com/learn/tutorials/topics/scripting/quaternions and https://docs.unity3d.com/ScriptReference/Quaternion.html:

```
void FixedUpdate() {
    // [...]
    //Check if the player has fired
    if (Input.GetKeyDown(KeyCode.E) || Input.GetButtonDown("Fire")) {
            //Create the bullet
            Instantiate(bulletPrefab, transform.position,
Quaternion.identity);
    }
}
```

This works just fine, but it can be improved. As we anticipated, right now the player can repeatedly press the *E* key and can shoot many bullets. We want in some way to limit this process. In order to achieve this, we need to write a bit more code.

First, we need two variables to store the reload time, which is how often the player can shoot, and the last time the player has shot, which is a private variable to check if the reload time has expired:

```
public float reloadTime = 1.0f;
private float lastTimeShot = 0f;
```

We have to change the code in the `FixedUpdate()` to reflect this change. So, inside the `if statement`, it checks if the player has shot, and we can nest another `if` to check whether the player can shoot or if it is too early (the reload time hasn't expired yet). We can do this by calculating with a subtraction how much time has passed since the last time the player shot and compare it with the reload time. If this results as greater than the reload time, then we need to update the last time the player shot and actually created the bullet. In the end, the code looks like the following:

```
void FixedUpdate() {
    // [...]
    //Check if the player has fired
    if(Input.GetKeyDown(KeyCode.E) || Input.GetButtonDown("Fire")) {
        //Check if the player can shoot since last time the spaceship
has fired
        if(Time.time - lastTimeShot > reloadTime) {
            //Set the current time as the last time the spaceship has
fired
            lastTimeShot = Time.time;

            //Create the bullet
            Instantiate(bulletPrefab, transform.position,
Quaternion.identity);
        }
    }
}
```

That explosion was bad

In Chapter 5, *Freeze! Creating an Intergalactic Shooter*, we created an explosion prefab. This will come in handy now, when we need to make our spaceship explode every time it takes damage.

If you remember from the *Angel Cakes* collecting system, when the player comes into contact with a cake, it is collected. This was done using a special Unity function named `OnTriggerEnter2D`, which detects when the player enters the collider of the cake. Here, we are going to do something similar, but to learn something new, we will implement the explosion in this way: when the enemy bullet hits the player, it's the script of the bullet that makes this check (while in *Angel Cakes* the cake was detecting this), but then it will communicate this to the player controller, which will create an explosion (and eventually decrease the number of lives).

Thus, in order to make the player controller communicate with the future bullet script, we need to create a public function named `Hit()`, which will be called by the future bullet script. What do we need from this function? At the current stage, we just need to instantiate the explosion. This can be done very easily with just a few lines of code.

First of all, add a variable that holds the explosion prefab, so we are able to instantiate it in the `Hit()` function:

```
public GameObject explosionPrefab;
```

Then, let's write the `Hit()` function with a line of code that creates an explosion based on the `explosionPrefab` variable at the same coordinates of where the spaceship of the player has been hit. This means that the coordinates are passed from the bullet script as a parameter of the function:

```
public void Hit(Vector3 hitCoordinates) {
    //Create an explosion on the coordinates of the hit.
    Instantiate(explosionPrefab, hitCoordinates, Quaternion.identity);
}
```

Save the script, and as a result, the spaceship is able to take damage, or at least show that it has been hit. We will deal with proper damage in Chapter 7, *Getting Serious About Gameplay*.

Testing the explosion

If you don't want to wait to implement the bullet script to test this function, you can add in the `FixedUpdate()` so that every time the player presses the key *T*, the `Hit()` function is called. Thus, by following a similar process to shooting bullets, we can add the following lines to the function:

```
//DEBUG CODE: simulates the Hit() function when the player presses
the T key
if (Input.GetKeyDown(KeyCode.T)) {
    Hit(transform.position);
}
```

And this is how it looks in the game:

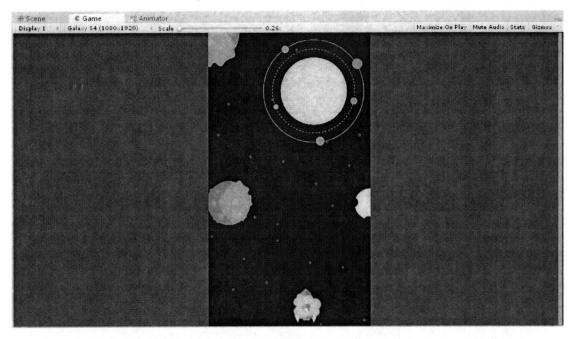

The background you see in the image is a demo image of the package. As a pro tip, you can use the demo image as an example image of the level you are going to build. If you place it underneath, you can have a good sense of whether the explosion is working in the future environment or not and adjust it without waiting for the environment to be built. In our case, we might want to scale down the explosion a bit, and maybe save this scaled down into the prefab. Of course, if you like big explosions, you can leave it as it was before. Also, feel free to change the color if you want.

However, remember to remove these lines (the debug code) once you have finished testing it. Alternatively, you can also comment out the code or surround the debug code with a debugEnabled if statement. However, if the testing code is temporary, erasing it will lead to fewer troubles later on.

Enemy controller

In this section, we will explore how to create the enemy controller.

Requirements of the enemy controller

First of all, we need to move the enemy independently of the player input. As per our design, we want the enemy to continuously move left and right, but also slowly move down. Therefore, we can split the different movements between the two axes. For the x-axis, we can use a sine function to fluctuate (oscillate) between left and right continuously. For the y-axis, instead, we can have the usual movement, just much slower. For instance, the enemy spaceship can do two or three times left-right before it has moved down along the y-axis, a length similar to its dimension.

Another consideration is concerning when the enemy should shoot. In big games, there are complicated AI algorithms to perform a decision-making process. However, here we want to show how it's possible to create a challenging AI with just a few lines of code. So, in this case, we let the enemy shoot randomly, for instance, every one to three seconds. Later in the chapter, we will see a variation, where the enemy shoots when it is above the player.

Besides all of this, we have pretty much all the functionalities of the player controller, so the enemy spaceship moves, moving the **rigidbody** and implementing a `Hit()` function to take damage.

Creating the enemy controller

Create a new C# script and call it `EnemyController`. Since this controller shares many functionalities in common with the player controller, it's better to copy the player controller and modify it. So, copy the whole body of the player controller onto the enemy controller. Don't forget that the name of the class should remain `EnemyController`, and this is very important; otherwise, we will have compilation errors.

New variables for the enemy controller

Since the enemy is now controlled by the computer, we need to script a behavior, like the one we described in the requirements section. Therefore, we need new variables and we need to change some of the old ones.

First of all, we need two different speeds. In fact, the enemies not only move left and right, but they are also coming down slowly. So, let's substitute the speed variable with the following two:

```
public float speedX = 10.0f;
public float speedY = -1.0f;
```

It's not a mistake that the speed along y is negative. The enemy is moving down, so with a negative speed, the enemy will move downwards.

Now, we need to add a couple of other variables. As we have seen in the requirements, the enemy shoots randomly *between* an interval of time, for instance between 1 and 3. To define this interval, we need a variable to specify the minimum, and another one to specify the maximum. We can already initialize them to their default values of respectively 1 and 3:

```
public float minShootingTime = 1f;
public float maxShootingTime = 3f;
```

Modifying the movement

Whereas the player controls the movement of the spaceship, the enemy controller has to do this autonomously.

Since the enemy moves in the two directions in two different ways, we need to implement both the movements. Along y is easy, since we are going to implement once more the usual equation of the motion, which is:

$$pos_t = pos_{t-1} + velocity * \Delta Time$$

Moreover, we don't need to take care of the input of the player, so along y the code within the `FixedUpdate()` function becomes:

```
var y = transform.position.y + Time.deltaTime * speedY;
```

However, when it comes to the x-axis, we have to implement something different. The enemy will keep moving left and right. In order to achieve such behavior, we can use the mathematical sine function. As a result, the equation we are going to implement is the following:

$$pos_t = pos_{t-1} + velocity * \Delta Time$$

Where *A* is the amplitude of the movement. In our case, we can delegate the amplitude to the boundX variable that we have from the player controller. Later, by setting the same value of this variable for enemies and player, we can ensure that both have the same limits along the x-axis. In terms of code, the equation is translated with the following line:

```
var x = boundX * Mathf.Sin(Time.deltaTime * speedX);
```

Lastly, we need to remove to clamp, since the sinus (by varying only between -1 to 1) will ensure we won't have any value greater than boundX or smaller than negative boundX.

The full code for the movement in the `FixedUpdate()` function is the following:

```
void FixedUpdate() {
    //Get the new position of our Enemy. On X, move left and right; on
Y slowly get down.
    var x = boundX * Mathf.Sin(Time.deltaTime * speedX);
    var y = transform.position.y + Time.deltaTime * speedY;

    //Set the position of our character through the RigidBody2D
component (since we are using physics)
    rigidBody.MovePosition(new Vector2(x, y));

    // [...]
}
```

Now, it's time to jump onto making our enemy deadly, by making it shoot bullets.

Shooting deadly bullets

Just as, for the player controller, we don't have the bullet prefab yet, but we do have a variable where the bullet prefab will be stored. This is great, but so far our code makes the enemy shoot at the same time as the player; instead, we would like the enemy to be autonomous. In order to achieve this, we need to change the code. The simplest implementation is that the enemy shoots a bullet after a random amount of time, for instance varying from one to three seconds. These two values are stored in the `minShootingTime` and `maxShootingTime` variables.

Thus, let's remove the check of the input of the player, but keep the check on the reload time. Then, inside the if statements, we need to also reset the reload time to a random value between `minShootingTime` and `maxShootingTime`. We can do this with a built-in class of Unity called `Random`, which does exactly this with the `Range()` function. As a result, the enemy will shoot every time the reload time has expired, and the reload time changes every time it shoots. The code now looks like the following:

```
void FixedUpdate() {
    // [...]
    // Fire as soon as the reload time is expired
    if(Time.time - lastTimeShot > reloadTime) {
        //Set the current time as the last time the spaceship has fired
        lastTimeShot = Time.time;

        //Set a random reload time
        reloadTime = Random.Range(minShootingTime, maxShootingTime);

        //Create the bullet
        Instantiate(bulletPrefab, transform.position,
Quaternion.identity);
    }
}
```

And with this said, congratulations. You have now finished implementing the enemy controller, at least for this chapter; in the next one, we will change it slightly.

Alternative enemy controller

In order to give variety to our game, this section explores an alternative to the previous enemy controller. Once again, this shows how to create challenging enemies with just a few lines of code, without complex AI algorithms that can be confusing for beginners.

Creating the second enemy controller

To create the second enemy controller, we can start by duplicating the enemy controller; just select it and press *Ctrl + D* (if you are a Mac user, you need to press *Command + D*). The new script should be renamed `EnemyControllerSmartAttacker`.

Double-click to open it, and change the class name to `EnemyControllerSmartAttacker`, like the following:

```
// [...]
public class EnemyControllerSmartAttacker : MonoBehaviour {
    // [...]
}
```

Changing the aiming system

The previous enemy was shooting every time it had a chance after a random number of seconds. This other one, instead, shoots when it is above the player.

To implement this behavior, let's remove the `minShootingTime` and `maxShootingTime` variables. However, we need two new variables; the first to store the shooting sensitivity, meaning how close the enemy is to the straight line above the player before shooting, and the other variable stores the player transform, so it's easier to retrieve the player's position:

```
private Transform playerTransform;
public float shootSensitivity;
```

As we did for the rigidbody, we need to retrieve the `playerTransform` at the `Start()` function. To do so, we can find the player controller, since we assume there is only one in the scene, and from there retrieve the player's transform:

```
void Start() {
    rigidBody = GetComponent<Rigidbody2D>();
    playerTransform = FindObjectOfType<PlayerController>().transform;
}
```

Now, inside the if statement in which we check if the reload time has expired, we need to place another nested check. In fact, we need to check if the enemy is close enough to shoot. By taking the absolute value of the difference between the x-axis of the enemy and the x-axis of the player, we get the distance between them along x. We can compare this value with shootSensitivity, and if it is smaller, we can proceed with the rest of the code to shoot the bullet. This time we also need to remove that the reload time is random.

In the end, the code will look like the following:

```
void FixedUpdate() {
    // [...]
    // Fire as soon as the reload time is expired
    if(Time.time - lastTimeShot > reloadTime) {
        //Check if the enemy is "close" on the x-axis to the player
        if (Mathf.Abs(playerTransform.position.x -
transform.position.x) < shootSensitivity) {
            //Set the current time as the last time the spaceship has
fired
            lastTimeShot = Time.time;

            //Create the bullet
            Instantiate(bulletPrefab, transform.position,
Quaternion.identity);
        }
    }
}
```

Now, we get not one, but two different enemies we can use. However, we talked a lot about shooting bullets, but we still don't have bullets! Let's create them in the next section.

Shooting with passion

In order to finish implementing our shooting system, the last thing we need to do is to create our bullets. At this stage, it shouldn't be a too complicated.

Creating a bullet prefab

First, we need to drag and drop our projectile sprite that we sliced in the previous chapter into the scene. Then, we need to add a **Box Collider 2D**, and the default settings should be good to go. We also need to enable **Is Trigger**, like we did for the cakes in the previous project:

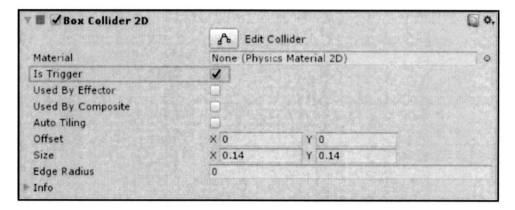

Then, since our bullet will move, we also need to add a **Rigidbody 2D**, and we just need to change the **Gravity Scale** to 0 and freeze the rotation around **Z**; exactly as we did for the player:

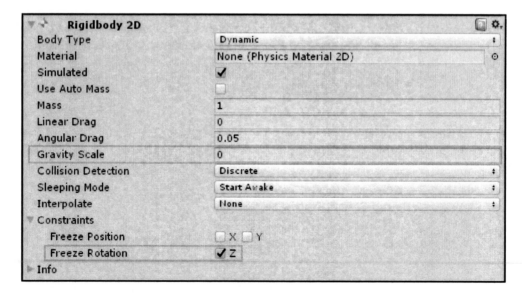

Finally, by using the **Add Component** button, we can create a new C# script and name it
`BulletController`. We are going to implement its functionalities in the next section, but
first, we need to create two new prefabs. Why two prefabs? One is for the bullets of the
player and the other one is for the bullets of the enemies (in case you have different
graphics you can have many more, but in this project, we will just keep two of them). In
fact, even if they don't differ in the graphics, we will make a slight change in a public
variable in the script, but we will see this once we have finished with our script. For now,
you can call the two prefabs respectively `BulletPrefab_Player` and
`BulletPrefab_Enemy`. You can drag and drop from the **Hierarchy** panel the same
BulletSprite on both of them before removing the object from the scene.

Creating a bullet controller

Open the `BulletController` script and remove the `Update()` function, since we don't
need it. It's time to break through the creation of this controller.

Enforcing components

As we did with the other scripts in this book, once again we need to enforce the
components, so we can write:

```
using System.Collections;
using System.Collections.Generic;
using UnityEngine;

[RequireComponent(typeof(Rigidbody2D))]
[RequireComponent(typeof(Collider2D))]
public class BulletController : MonoBehaviour {
//[...]
}
```

Exposing variables in the Inspector

In order to let designers customize the bullet according to the gameplay of the game, we
need to expose some variables by declaring them public. This concept should be clear by
now. In particular, we want to expose the speed at which the bullet moves, and the time
before it is destroyed in case it didn't hit anything. This last one is just an optimization since
we don't want bullets going around in our game world in regions that are not visible.

So, here are the two public variables we need:

```
// [...]
public class BulletController : MonoBehaviour {

    public float speed = 10.0f;

    public float timeBeforeDestruction = 10.0f;

    // [...]
}
```

Getting the reference to the rigidbody

As we already know, we need to get a reference to the **rigidbody** component so we can use it in the `FixedUpdate()` function to move the bullet. As such, let's declare another variable:

```
// [...]
public class BulletController : MonoBehaviour {

    public float speed = 10.0f;

    public float timeBeforeDestruction = 10.0f;

    private Rigidbody2D rigidBody;

    // [...]
}
```

The `Start()` function is always a perfect place to initialize references to other components, so we can just write:

```
void Start() {
    rigidBody = GetComponent<Rigidbody2D>();
}
```

As a result, we are now able to use the **rigidbody** of the bullet.

Auto-destroying the bullet

As we have mentioned, we would like to destroy the bullet after a certain time specified by the `timeBeforeDestruction` variable. Unity comes with a built-in function to destroy a game object after a delay, and once again the `Start()` function is the perfect place for such a thing. In fact, we just need to specify the game object to destroy (in this case the bullet itself), and the time. So, the `Start()` function at the end should be like the following:

```
void Start() {
    rigidBody = GetComponent<Rigidbody2D>();

    //Destroy the bullet if it didn't hit anything after 10 seconds
    Destroy(gameObject, timeBeforeDestruction);
}
```

If you were to place a bullet in the scene now and hit play, it would be destroyed after ten seconds, which is the default value for the `timeBeforeDestruction` variable.

Moving the bullet

In a similar way to the player controller, we need to move the bullet. We use the same equation for the motion and the same lines of code. However, we need to make the movement happen only on the y-axis; there is no clamp, and the bullet moves regardless of the input of the player. Here is the final code, which shouldn't be hard for you to understand:

```
void FixedUpdate() {
    //Get the new position of our bullet
    var y = transform.position.y + Time.deltaTime * speed;

    //Set the position of our bullet through the RigidBody2D component
(since we are using physics)
    rigidBody.MovePosition(new Vector2(transform.position.x, y));
}
```

It's worth mentioning here that if we have the speed as a negative value, the bullet will move down rather than up. We will use this to make the enemies' bullets; their speed will be negative.

Hit spaceships

Here, we face something different from the player controller; we need to check what happens once the bullet hits the player or the enemy. Of course, this is something we are going to do within the `OnTriggerEnter2D()` function. In order to distinguish between whether we hit the player or the enemy, we are going to use a tag. Moreover, we also need to check whether the bullet was shot by the player or by the enemy. In fact, we don't want the player shooting a bullet and immediately exploding. Since in this simple implementation we don't pass any information to the bullet, how can we distinguish between the two? The enemy's bullets will go downwards, and thus they will have a negative speed. So, by checking if the speed is positive or negative, we can determine if the bullet belongs to the player or to the enemy. Once we have checked if the bullet hit the player or an enemy, we need to call the `Hit()` function on the respective controller and destroy the bullet.

Wrapping up, here is the final code for the `OnTriggerEnter2D()` function:

```
void OnTriggerEnter2D(Collider2D other) {
    //Check if the player collides with the bullet (and it has been
shot by an enemy)
    if (other.tag == "Player" && speed < 0) {
        //Send the message to the player that the spaceship has been
hit
        other.GetComponent<PlayerController>().Hit(transform.position);

        //Destroy the bullet
        Destroy(gameObject);
    } else if (other.tag == "Enemy" && speed > 0) {
        //Send the message to the enemy that the spaceship has been hit
        other.GetComponent<EnemyController>().Hit(transform.position);

        //Destroy the bullet
        Destroy(gameObject);
    }
}
```

You can now save the script, and as a result, you have all the basic gameplay scripts working for our space shooter game. In the next chapter, we will finish it up and make it operative by exploring some interesting UI features and building a world.

Exercises

We are halfway through the project, but it's time to improve our skills. Now, you will have learned the basics of creating a simple AI in Unity. I encourage you to experiment with the AI. Here, there is a series of exercises you can do before moving on to the next chapter. I invite you to try to do at least the first two:

- We have seen how to create just one enemy and one kind of bullet. You are free to experiment with the values (such as `speed`, `minShootingTime`, `maxShootingTime` or `shootingSensitivity`) and create a different prefab for each one of them. In the next chapter, we will see how to create the single prefabs of the controllers of this chapter. However, you can get a head start and try to do them now. The package offers different spaceships with different colors, so just have fun experimenting.

- The two enemies we have created are great, and by customizing variables we are able to create quite a variety of enemies. However, you are free to experiment in creating a more complex enemy, maybe a boss. Write down on paper how your boss should behave, where it moves (maybe it can go up and down), how and when it shoots (maybe she/he shoots from two different parts of the big spaceship, making it more challenging for the player). Don't forget to give a nice graphic to your boss and share your results with us.

- The bullet detects the `PlayerController` and the `EnemyController`. However, it doesn't take into consideration that there might be other kinds of objects and/or controllers. In fact, we have `EnemyController2`, and in the next chapter you might implement code for asteroids, planets, and so on, that can explode when hit. Try to fix this problem on your own by figuring out a solution that could work. It doesn't have to be complicated, you can try to do the different casting to the different classes to call the `Hit()` function.

- If you are in the mood for a challenge and know a bit about interfaces in C#, then we can implement the previous exercise in a much smarter way. Create an interface called `CanExplode`, in which we have the definition of just one function: `Hit()`. Then, for each controller we have created in this chapter (such as `PlayerController`, `EnemyController`, and `EnemyController2`) and any other class that needs to explode on impact, we will need to implement such an interface. This allows you to have just a few lines of code in the `BulletScript` at the price of just implementing an interface.

- If your thirst for a challenge isn't quenched after the previous exercise, you can notice that all the controllers share a good portion of the code in common. If you know about inheritance in C#, you can create a master `Controller` class, from which all the other controllers derive. There, implement all the code that they share in common, and leave in the specific class just the code required to distinguish that class from the others.

Summary

In this chapter, we wrote a lot of code. But, it gave us the possibility of bringing our game to life. In fact, we first programmed the `PlayerController`, which is responsible for moving the player's spaceship as well as shooting according to the player's input. Then, we saw how it's possible to automate the process of moving and shooting with just a few lines of code by writing the `EnemyController`. Also, we explored a variant in case you would like to use the second, or maybe both at the same time, to create variety among enemies' behaviors. Finally, we implemented our `BulletController`, which is responsible for moving the bullet on the map, but also for hitting an enemy or the player, creating an explosion.

In `Chapter 7`, *Getting Serious About Gameplay*, we will explore how to incorporate power-up, score, and health into our game, as well as building the environment for our game, and we will finish up by polishing the game. So, without losing any more time, let's jump to the next chapter.

7

Getting Serious About Gameplay

In this chapter, we are going to finish our second project. Here, you will learn about the final tools and scripts you need to finish this awesome space-shooter on your own. In fact, at the end of the chapter, you will find a series of exercises to completely finish the game, and also some ideas on how you can iterate on the design and development of the game. I warmly suggest you try to experiment since it's the best way to learn. After that, you can jump into the last but also most challenging game of this book.

Here are the topics we are going to cover in this chapter:

- Building the UI for our game, with a particular focus on creating a lives counter.
- How to create an infinite scrolling map. This includes a scrolling background as well as falling objects and orbiting satellites.
- Including power-ups by modifying the collection system in *Angel Cakes*.
- Creating a spawning a system to generate both enemies and decorations.
- Testing the game.
- Exercises to improve your skills and further ideas on how to develop your game.

Once you are ready, let's start by including a lives counter for our player.

Building the UI

This time around, our UI is going to be counting a few more things than in our last game. If you remember, we used to increment a score every time a cake was collected. Here, we are going to implement the score, and we will use basically the same thing learned in the previous project. However, we are going to represent the lives of the player with a discrete number of heart icons. Although it's not a super complex UI, it still poses some challenges that we are going to face.

Setting up the UI

The first thing to do is to prepare the UI elements so that they can be easily scripted. Thus, we need to decide where our UI will be shown. As per the design, we want to show both the score and the number of lives in the bottom-left part of the screen.

Let's start to create a panel by right-clicking on the **Hierarchy** panel, and then **UI | Panel**. Drag it to the bottom-left of the screen, as shown in the following screenshot:

Of course, you are free to scale it, as well as change the image and the color to suit your game style. In our case, we are going to use the pre-made rectangle but change the color to suit your needs. As a result, our panel will look like the following:

The next step is to add the three UI elements—the number of the level, the lives represented as hearts, and the score represented with a star icon. In order to achieve this, we are going to use **Century Gothic** font for all the text. Before we move on, just create a text and write `Level 1`. As a result, we have already created one of the three functions of our UI (showing the level), like in the following screenshot:

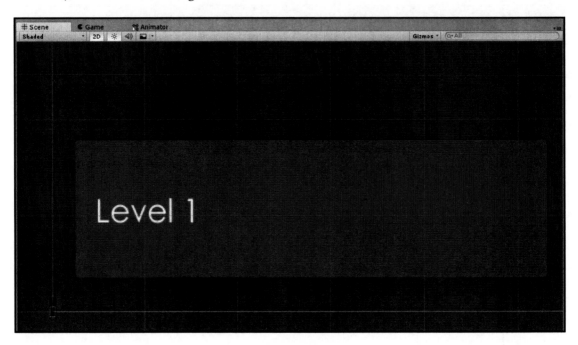

Creating the lives counter

Now it's time to implement the lives counter of the player. As per the design, the player has up to a maximum of three lives, all represented by a heart sprite per life on the screen.

Let's start by creating a new UI image, and use the heart in our package as our icon. Then, duplicate it twice so we have three hearts, and name them `heart_0`, `heart_1`, and `heart_2`. Then, place them on our panel, just after the **Level 1** label, as shown in the following screenshot:

Create an empty game object in your UI, just under the main panel, and place it in such a way that it covers up all the three hearts. Then, parent the hearts to this empty game object (by preserving the order), which we can rename `UIHearts`. Create a new C# script named `LivesCounter` and attach it to the `UIHearts` game object.

Inside the script, we need a variable to keep track of how many lives the player has left, which can be just an integer value. Also, another variable is important to keep track of the maximum number of lives the player can have. So, let's write:

```
public int lives;
public int maxNumberOfLives = 3;
```

Depending on the number of lives that we want to show (or not) we will display a heart. To do this, we need to have an array to store all of them. The array can be private because we can get the references from the `Start()` functions, because the hearts are children of `UIHearts`, where this script is running:

```
private GameObject[] hearts;
```

In the `Start()` function, we need to do two important things. Firstly, initialize the number of lives to the maximum, and secondly, get the references to the three hearts. Since this script can be adapted to as many hearts as we wish, we need to get the references to a heart for each life. We can do it by using a "for loop." Here is the `Start()` function:

```
void Start () {
    //Set the initial number of lives to its maximum
    lives = maxNumberOfLives;

    //Initialise the array of hearts
    hearts = new GameObject[maxNumberOfLives];

    //Cycle among children and get the hearts we need
    for(int i = 0; i<maxNumberOfLives; i++) {
        hearts[i] = transform.GetChild(i).gameObject;
    }
}
```

 Keep in mind that here there are no checks for whether `UIHearts` has enough children for each life. This is something that designers should take care in. In fact, the order of the `UIHeart` game objects in the hierarchy is important. The sorting in the hierarchy is top to bottom, while the location of the visual representation (sprites) is left to right. The index of the array corresponds to the order in the hierarchy.
Alternatively, as an exercise, you can place this check.

Now, we need a function that can be called to increase the number of lives, and we will call it `AddLife()`. This function has to increment the number of lives, clamp the value to the maximum allowed, and finally call a function to update the graphics, which we will implement soon:

```
public void AddLife() {
    //Increment the number of lives
    lives++;

    //Clamp the number of lives to the maximum
    if(lives > maxNumberOfLives) {
        lives = maxNumberOfLives;
    }
    //Update the Graphics
    UpdateGraphics();

}
```

Similarly, we need a function called `RemoveLife()`, which removes one of the player's lives, checks whether the player has no lives, and in this case triggers the game over conditions (in our case, we reload **Level 1**, assuming you have called your level this and put it in the **Scene Build**, which we will cover in Chapter 6, *No One Is Alone Forever*, of this book for the third project). Finally, it updates the graphics (hearts), like before:

```
public void RemoveLife() {
    //Decrement the number of lives
    lives--;

    //Check if the number of lives is zero (or less) and trigger Game
Over, such as reload the level
    if(lives <= 0) {
        //Trigger Game Over, in this case reload current level
        UnityEngine.SceneManagement.SceneManager.LoadScene("level1");
    }

    //Update the Graphics
    UpdateGraphics();
}
```

Lastly, we need to implement the function that actually updates the graphics. Here, we cycle the hearts array and, depending on whether the number of lives is greater (or less) than the current index of the heart, we enable (or disable) that heart:

```
public void UpdateGraphics () {
    //For each heart, check if it should be shown or not, based on the
number of lives
    for(int i= 0; i<maxNumberOfLives; i++) {
        if(i >= lives) {
            hearts[i].SetActive(false);
        } else {
            hearts[i].SetActive(true);
        }
    }
}
```

Save the script, but we haven't finished yet. Right now, the lives system works, but no lives are removed when the spaceship is hit. Therefore, let's open `PlayerController` and modify the `Hit()` function. Here, we need to place a call to `LivesCounter` (assuming that there is just one instance in the game) to remove the player's life:

```
public void Hit(Vector3 hitCoordinates) {
    //Create an explosion on the coordinates of the hit.
    Instantiate(explosionPrefab, hitCoordinates, Quaternion.identity);

    //Remove a life
    FindObjectOfType<LivesCounter>().RemoveLife();
}
```

Save this script, and now you can pat yourself on the back because the lives system is working properly.

Creating the star score counter

The creation of a scoring system should be well known to you by now. If not, you can always go back to the previous project and revise how the scoring system is done. Then, try to implement it by yourself for this project. You should end up with something similar to the following screenshot in the **Game** view:

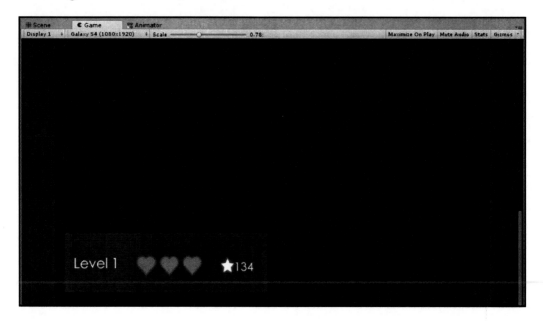

Building an infinite scrolling map

So far, we have the main functionalities of the game running. This section will explore how to create the map in which our shoot takes place. Here, we will implement the main parts, such as making the map perform infinite scrolling or making a satellite rotating around a planet. However, implementing other elements and polishing the game are left as exercises in the next section.

Repeating the background

In an infinite scrolling game, we need a background that repeats continuously. Of course, adding variation to the background (or many layers of background, called parallax) improves the visual appeal greatly. However, usually, there is a basic tileable background that repeats at the very end.

 Parallax scrolling means having two or more layers that move at different speeds to achieve a sense of depth. Usually, layers farther away from the game camera move slower than layers near it.

The concept is that the image scrolls downward followed by another identical image. Since destroying and creating game objects aren't cheap functions from a computational point of view, it's good practice to use just a couple of image game object instances (instead of many that are created at the top and destroyed at the bottom). Both images scroll, then as soon as one goes off-screen, both are repositioned to their initial position. As a result, you create the illusion that the background repeats indefinitely.

From an operative point of view, we have two images: one that occupies the whole screen, and the other one just above. They will scroll down, and as soon as the second image fills the whole screen, both images are repositioned. We will create a single script that we will attach to both the images. This is an easy approach, but we need to remind the designers that they should share the same speed, otherwise they won't scroll seamlessly. Even if it is good practice to enforce this by code, for simplicity's sake we will delegate the responsibility of matching the two speeds to the designers.

Drag and drop the background image of the package, and then duplicate it. Place one in such a way that it fills the screen completely, and the other one just above, as shown in the following screenshot:

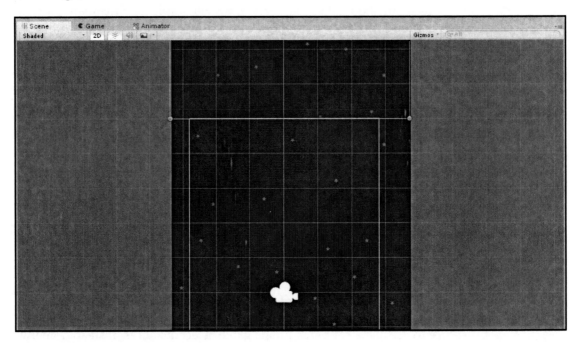

Now, create a C# script and name it `RepeatingBackground`. Attach the script to both the images, and open it.

As usual, we can define the speed as a public variable, so it can be easily set by designers:

```
public float speed = 1.3f;
```

Next, we need to use a couple of private variables to store the initial position and the offset, which is the y-length of the image, so we can write:

```
private Vector3 initialPos;
private float offset;
```

Then, we need to initialize these two variables at the `Start()` function. For the initial position, it is easy; for the offset, we have to retrieve the `SpriteRenderer` and extract the height, which can be found by retrieving the y-length from the size of the bounds:

```
void Start () {
    //Store the initial position
    initialPos = transform.position;

    //Store the y-length of the Sprite
    offset = GetComponent<SpriteRenderer>().bounds.size.y;
}
```

In the `Update()` function, we need to move the image downward. Why not use the `FixedUpdate()` function instead? For the first time with code, we need to move something in the `Update()` function because we don't have a **rigidbody** since the object/image doesn't have to interact (it's just a background, after all). As a result, not only can we use the `Update()` function, but we can move it by using its transform directly. Thus, let's write:

```
void Update () {
    //Scroll the background
    transform.position += new Vector3(0, -Time.deltaTime, 0);
}
```

Lastly, after the object has passed the offset, it has to be repositioned. Hence, we can check whether the absolute value of the difference between the current y position and the original one (which is a measure of the distance it has moved from the initial position, or in other terms the offset) is greater than the offset variable. If so, set the position for the initial one:

```
void Update () {
    //Scroll the background
    transform.position += new Vector3(0, -Time.deltaTime, 0);

    //Check if the scrolling has passed the offset, if so, reposition the image
    if(Mathf.Abs(transform.position.y - initialPos.y) > offset) {
        //Reposition the image
        transform.position = initialPos;
    }
}
```

Save the script, and remember to assign the same speed to both your background images. As a result, if you hit play, we have the background repeating indefinitely.

Falling stars and planets

Aside from the background, other "decorations" might fall from the sky, such as planets, satellites, or stars. In this section, we are going to implement a quick script that makes an object fall. Again, we are going to use the Update() function to move, instead of the FixedUpdate(), for the same reasons of the repeating background.

Create a new script and name it FallingScript. Open it, and add the speed variable as usual:

```
public float speed = 1.3f;
```

Then, since we don't want the object falling indefinitely, as we did for BulletController in Chapter 6, *No One Is Alone Forever*, we need a variable to store the time before the auto-destruction:

```
public float timeBeforeDestruction = 10.0f;
```

In the Start() function, we need to trigger the countdown for the auto-destruction, like we did for BulletController:

```
void Start () {
    //Destroy the falling object after timeBeforeDestruction
    Destroy(gameObject, timeBeforeDestruction);
}
```

Then, in the Update() function, we can just move the object downwards, as follows:

```
void Update () {
    //Move the object downwards
    transform.position += new Vector3(0, -speed * Time.deltaTime, 0);
}
```

Save the script, and attach it to any object you want to make fall (of course, remember to create a prefab first and to place the ordering layer, or the z coordinate, in such a way that the object is still rendered below spaceships, enemies, and bullets).

Rotating satellites

If you have noticed, in our package we have some planets with some circles around them. Even if the whole planet can be driven by `FallingScript`, we can create satellites as children of the planet, rotating around it. So, create a prefab for the planet with the circle, and attach `FallingScript`. Then, as a child (or children if you want more than one) attach satellites to the `RotatingSatellite` script we are going to create. As a result, we will have a planet with satellites orbiting around, as shown in the following image:

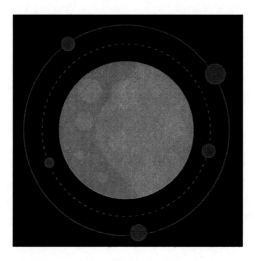

Now, let's create the aforementioned script (`RotatingSatellite`), and open it. Once again, we need the `speed` variable:

```
public float speed = 3f;
```

Then, we need a variable to store the radius of the orbit. By adjusting this value, designers are able to tweak how far the satellite orbits around it (or adjusting to the circle's radiuses):

```
public float radius = 1f;
```

For the motion, we just need to follow a circular path. If you are familiar with trigonometry, this is just having a cosine on the x and the sine on the y; as arguments of these trigonometry functions, we need the time scaled by the speed. Then, it's just a matter of assigning the variables to the new position. Of course, the position needs to be in local space, since we are assigning the new position with respect to the planet:

```
void Update () {
    //Calculate the new x and y of the circular motion
    var x = radius * Mathf.Cos(speed * Time.time);
    var y = radius * Mathf.Sin(speed * Time.time);

    //Assign the new position to the object transform
    transform.localPosition =  new Vector3(x, y, 0f);
}
```

Save the script, and enjoy satellites orbiting around your planets.

Creating the prefabs

In case you didn't do this during the last two chapters, it's time to prepare all the prefabs for the game. This small section will guide you through, but I invite you to try to do this by yourself. In fact, we did the bullet prefab, but you should do it also for the player, the different types of enemies, and the decorations we have seen in the previous section.

For both the player and the enemies, remember to attach `Collider2D` and `Rigidbody2D`. As we did for the bullet, we need to zero `Gravity Scale` on `Rigidbody2D`, but you can leave `isTrigger` unchecked on the collider. Also, remember to adjust the z coordinate or the ordering layer to make them always appear in the foreground. Needless to say, remember to attach the respective scripts to each one of them and set their values. Pay particular attention to the `BoundX` variable, which should be tweaked depending on the map you built.

As far as decoration elements are concerned, you just need to attach the scripts, and parenting satellites, and make sure they are always shown in the background.

Including power-ups

In *Angel Cakes*, we developed a pretty basic collection system. In this game, we're going to be using the same principles for collecting items such as health and stars. Here is how they look in the game:

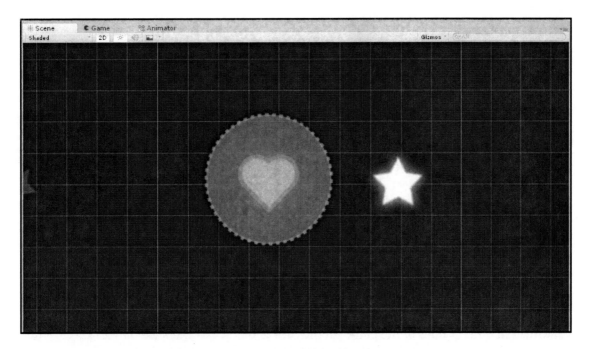

Actually, let's just take the script we used in *Angel Cakes*—if you recall, CollectableCake, and modify it.

For the stars, we should change the cakeValue variable to something such as starValue. Then, change the IncreaseScore() function call to the script you built before.

For the health, instead, we can erase the cakeValue variable, since each heart will grant just one life. Then, everything remains the same, just change the IncreaseScore() function call with this line:

```
FindObjectOfType<LivesCounter>().AddLife();
```

Save the script in another file, and you are good to go.

The next step is to create the prefabs for such collectables and make sure that the **Audio Source** component, as well as a **Collider 2D** with **is Trigger**, checked.

Spawning system

If we place an enemy and the player against each other, the fight is interesting. But, after the player has defeated the enemies, the game becomes infinitely boring. As such, you should create a spawning system that allows you to generate waves of enemies. Also, the spawning system should be able to generate power-ups and background decoration at random. This is, in general, is not an easy task. As a result, here we will implement a simple spawning system and explore the concept of coroutines. However, I suggest you read *Chapter 7, Trading Cupcakes and the Ultimate Battle for the Cake – Gameplay Programming*, of *Getting Started with Unity 5.x 2D Game Development* (`https://www.packtpub.com/game-development/getting-started-unity-5x-2d-game-development`). In particular, the section titled *Panda invasion - spawning pandas*, which explains coroutines in more detail, and how to create a good and simple spawning system.

Coroutines

Coroutines are a special structure in Unity that allows functions to be interrupted and continued in other frames of the game. In the case of our spawning system, we don't want to spawn all the enemies or decorations at the same time, but a little at a time. This, over time, can be controlled with coroutines. You can learn more and see some examples in the official documentation at `https://docs.unity3d.com/Manual/Coroutines.html`.

Creating spawning points

The basic idea behind a spawning system is that there are special points in which things are spawned. In scrolling games, such as this one, the spawning points are just beyond the visible part of the screen, so the player doesn't see the enemy or the decoration popping out of nowhere.

In Unity, the best things we can use to represent these points are just empty game objects, which we can place just above the camera, as shown in the following screenshot:

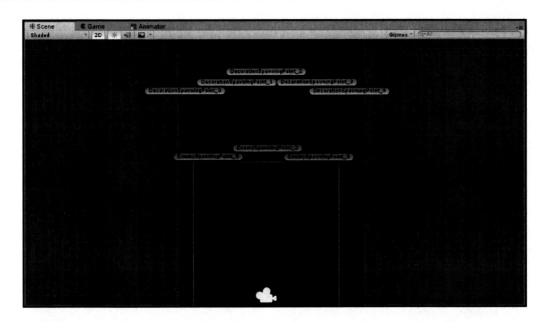

 Usually, it's hard to see empty game objects, because you need to select them. However, if you click on the icon next to their name in the **Inspector**, you can choose a label color. As a result, their name appears on the **Scene** view, and it is easy to identify them. The preceding screenshot shows exactly this process. Also, from there, you can deduce the name.

As you can see, we have created three spawning points for enemies just above the border of our camera and five spawning points for our decorations that are further away. Because they might be big objects and we want them to appear out of nowhere, you should check that in those points, the object is not visible on the camera.

 As a pro-tip, you can move the pivot point of such big objects so that when they are in those positions, they are not visible. As a result, you will be able to use closer spawning points; if not, use the same of the enemies if you wish.

Scripting the spawning system

Now that we have our points, it's time to create a script to handle the spawning. In this case, we will spawn random enemies after a random amount of time. Same for the decorations, but they will be on a different coroutine.

Create the script and name it SpawningSystem. First of all, we need two arrays to store the two different spawning points. We can store them as transforms so that we can easily retrieve their position. Of course, these should be set manually from the **Inspector** by designers, since this might depend on the different levels you want to implement:

```
public Transform[] enemiesSpawningPoints;
public Transform[] decorationSpawningPoints;
```

Then, we need two arrays for storing all the prefabs that we would like to randomly spawn. This goes both for decorations and enemies:

```
public GameObject[] enemies;
public GameObject[] decorations;
```

Then, we need to implement the two coroutines; they are very similar (which, if you want, to challenge yourself, you can transform the coroutines by adding parameters). Let's start with the enemies one. First, we need a loop that spawns a random enemy in a random spawning point. Then, we need to set a random timer before spawning again:

```
IEnumerator SpawnEnemies() {
    //Forever...
    while (true) {
        //...spawn a random enemy in a random location
        Instantiate(enemies[Random.Range(0,
enemies.Length)],enemiesSpawningPoints[Random.Range(0,
        enemiesSpawningPoints.Length)].position, Quaternion.identity);

        //Set a random ammount of time between 8 and 16 seconds before
to spawn another enemy
        yield return new WaitForSeconds(Random.Range(8, 16));
    }
}
```

It's similar with the decorations, but with decorations rather than enemies:

```
IEnumerator SpawnDecorations() {
    //Forever...
    while (true) {
        //...spawn a random decoration in a random location
        Instantiate(decorations[Random.Range(0, decorations.Length)],
        decorationSpawningPoints[Random.Range(0,
decorationSpawningPoints.Length)].position,
        Quaternion.identity);
        //Set a random amout of time between 4 and 9 before to spawn
another enemy
        yield return new WaitForSeconds(Random.Range(4, 9));
    }
```

}

Lastly, we need to start these two coroutines at the `Start()` function, so you can write:

```
void Start () {
    //Start the two coroutines
    StartCoroutine(SpawnEnemies());
    StartCoroutine(SpawnDecorations());
}
```

Save the script, create a new game object named `SpawningSystem`, and attach this script to it. Set all the variables in the **Inspector**, as shown in the following screenshot:

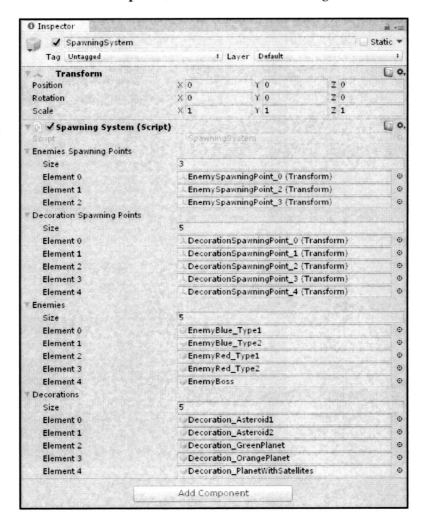

Of course, this is not the best solution for a spawning system, but at least you can get your feet wet with coroutines. Once again, you are free to experiment to improve on what this book teaches you because that is where the real improvement happens.

Testing the game

Now, we need to test the game so that everything runs smoothly.

If we hit play, the game looks cool, but there are things we could adjust. For instance, there is neither audio nor background music! Now, if you remember the content that we covered in the last chapter, you can definitely implement it. If not, I suggest going through the steps again to learn how.

Another thing that you might see is that your player is shooting too fast, or moves too slowly. In other instances, enemies might be too challenging, extremely fast, and so on. As a result, you should revise all the variables you exposed in the **Inspector**, and try to tweak them in such a way that the game becomes balanced.

In any case, you might end up discovering that the game is too simple to be fun; then, you can try to do the exercises in the next section, or draw some new ideas on how to develop your game further.

Exercises

Like we did in the previous chapter, here is a series of exercises you can do to not only improve your skills but also improve the overall quality of the game:

- As anticipated in the previous section, audio is missing in this game. But, since you learned how to implement it when working with *Angel Cakes*, here is your chance to test what you have learned.
- For the lives counter, the player can have a maximum of three lives because there are only three hearts. You can increase the number of hearts, but they would fill the UI up quickly. So, what about having a number next to the first heart in case the player has more than three lives? In this way, from zero to three lives the player has a visual feedback, and if the player has more than four lives they are represented by a number. Modify the `LivesCounter` script to include this modification.

- Alternatively, if you don't like the idea of giving the player more than three lives, you should still consider rewarding the player for collecting a heart. So, you can modify `LivesCounter` so that in the event that a life is added, but the player already has the maximum amount of lives, then the player's score is increased by five.
- Now that you have enough knowledge of the UI, you can improve the overall look, maybe by integrating your own graphics. For instance, try to head for something that looks like the following:

- In the spawning system, we have two coroutines. As anticipated, you can merge them to create a unique coroutine with parameters. As a result, you will be able to launch the same coroutine twice in the `Start()` function, just with different parameters (such as which array is taking the object to spawn).
- Our spawning system is great, but it doesn't take into consideration power-ups! Although you can place power-ups in the `decorations` array, you might want to implement another coroutine (or launch the same coroutine with different parameters if you did the previous exercises), to spawn power-ups as well.
- The spawning system works, especially after the previous two exercise, but it can be improved. What about spawning two enemies at the same time once in a while? Or even spawning a special unit such as a boss? Try modifying the spawning system.
- Our game has many decorations, a couple of power-ups, and enemies. Use your imagination, creativity, and skill to create more. Maybe create different levels, and design your own characters or backgrounds. Take inspiration from the next section, and make the most out of your game!

Other things you could consider adding to the game

If the previous section gave you an understanding of how it's possible to improve your game, here are more ideas to make your game more pleasant and challenge your skills.

Timer

What's a shooter without a little bit of excitement? Nothing says excitement more than a countdown. For instance, you can implement different modes, in which the player is invincible and has to get as many points as possible in a small amount of time. Maybe, instead of losing lives, if the player is hit, the score is decreased by five.

Increase the speed

Who doesn't like a little bit of fast-paced action? As the player gets better at the game, instead of increasing the strength of the enemy, you could make the game get faster. One way to do this, especially with top-down games, is to have the environment scroll faster as well as increasing your enemies' speed.

Combos

You may have kept to what we have discussed so far, you may have also added other characters and enemies. In either case, you will need to make sure that the game is and feels balanced. One way that you can manage issues with balancing can be by implementing combos. Combos offer you a way to reward players who improve their skills and encourage those who perhaps are not so good. In each instance, combos can help to facilitate a level playing field when given appropriately.

Bosses and waves

As anticipated in Chapter 6, *No One Is Alone Forever,* you can create bosses. If you follow the suggestion to read the book quoted in the *Spawning system* section, you will be able to count how many enemies are left for a wave, and at the end spawn a big boss!

Summary

In this chapter, we have explored how to integrate the UI—in particular, how to create lives counter that doesn't show the number of lives numerically, but visually.

Then, we explored the construction of an infinite scrolling environment by providing three useful scripts: one for scrolling the background, another to make objects fall, and the third to make satellites orbit their planets.

Finally, we included power-ups and did testing and balancing. We concluded with exercises and new ideas to bring your game to the next level.

Now, if you dare, let's jump into the last project of this book!

8
Building a Tilemap and Importing it into Unity

We are now on the home stretch with our third and final game for our book—RETROformer. In this chapter, you will learn all about more advanced map building. In particular, you will be introduced to a third-party tool for creating tiles named `Tiled`. In addition, you will learn how to incorporate these tiles into Unity to build 2D worlds. With this said, let's jump into it.

Throughout this chapter, we will cover the following topics:

- Creating tiles
- Introduction to the program – Tiled
- Importing TileSets into Unity with Tiled2Unity

We will also cover the basics of platformer-type games to provide you with some background information, ideas, and inspiration for creating the game in this section and in your own game projects.

Platforming games

Unlike collecting and shooting games, platformers require a bit more dexterity when it comes to creating gameplay and the player traversing the game's levels. Similar to the other game genres that we have explored, platforming games also have several variations. There are the more common ones like *Sonic* and *Mario*. In their essence, platforming games require you to traverse across platforms to navigate around the environment. Let's have a look at a few more detailed examples of the other types (subgenres) of platform games.

Side-scrolling

Side scrollers are a common type of platforming game. As the name suggests, the game is played through the perspective side-view camera angle, and the onscreen characters generally move from the left side of the screen to the right. Some popular examples include *Braid*, *Terraria*, and *Rayman*.

Infinite scrolling/endless runner

A game that just keeps going and going and going is an infinite side scroller or endless runner. The main aim of these games is to last as long as possible without dying or losing all your lives. In some instances, the game speeds up the longer the player goes, while encountering more objects requiring more dexterity to avoid them. Some popular examples include *Flappy Bird* and *Canabalt*, which you can play by visiting the following link:

```
http://adamatomic.com/canabalt/.
```

Now, let's get down to business and begin our third and final game.

Overview of the project for game #3 - RETROformer

Like the other projects, we will go through how to set up RETROformer.

We will be using two programs: Tiled and `Tiled2Unity` in conjunction with Unity to create RETROformer. Here is a brief overview of the roles that each will play in the development of RETROformer:

- **Tiled:** Where we will create the level environment that the player will navigate through
- **Tiled2Unity:** Where we will import the level created in Tiled into Unity
- **Unity:** Where we will implement player controls, a save system, various other interactive, decorative (for example, trees, background effects, and so on), and UI elements

At this stage you should be used to the file structures for creating games from the last 2. So for the third game, you can use the same folder structure that you have for the previous games.

Creating tiles

One of the most iconic things about 2D games is the use of tiles. Just like tiles within your house, combining tiles together can create patterns, and those patterns, within a game's context, can result in its levels. In this chapter, we will learn just how we can use tiles in a third-party program called Tiled, and how to then take the levels that we build and import them into Unity using the program `Tiled2Unity`. These are discussed more in just a moment.

Like the other games in this book, you can find the graphics package for this by visiting the following link:
`http://player26.com/product/retroformer/`.

Introduction to the program - Tiled and Tiled2Unity

Essentially, tiled is a free 2D map editor that will save you a lot of time working on your levels and creating TileSets. It is a tool that makes it much easier to create a 2D level, instead of doing it within Unity by duplicating game objects. You can download Tiled by visiting the following link here: `http://www.mapeditor.org/download.html`.

As the title suggests, we will also need to get another program called `Tiled2Unity`, which allows us to import levels that are made with Tiled. You can download the program by visiting the following link:
`http://www.seanba.com/tiled2unity`

Overall, the workflow follows this path: **Tiled** | **Tiled2Unity** | **Unity**.

Therefore, once you have installed both programs, you can begin first by opening up **Tiled**. In doing so, you should be greeted by the following screenshot:

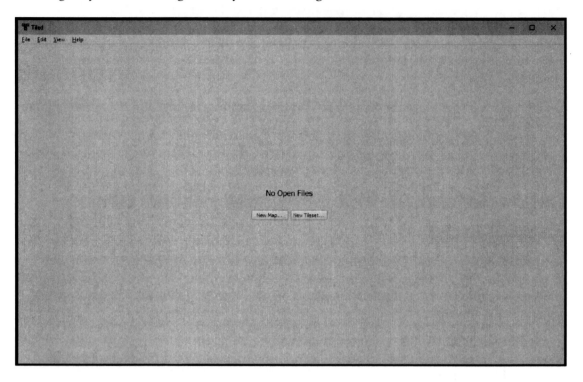

As you can see, there are two options: **New Map** and **New Tileset**.

- **New Map**: This will allow you to create a new space to create your game environment. This will be the space where we will be placing our tiles.
- **New Tileset**: This will allow you to create a set of different tiles based on an image that has been made for use as a Tileset. What this means is that the tiles themselves have been placed in such a way that they conform to a grid. Therefore, when you import a Tileset into Tiled, the image will be automatically sliced based on a grid size that you specify. We will explore this in a little bit.

As the name suggests, Tilesets could be described as a group of themed images, each one of them being a building block for a map. By using them all together, it's possible to easily create many maps based on the same theme, hence reducing the workload.

For now, we want to create a **New Map**. You will see a screen like the following screenshot:

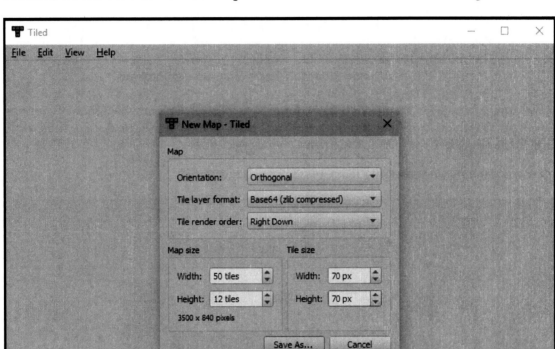

As you can see in this screenshot, there are a few different variables:

- **Orientation**: This setting tells us the type of map we will use. In this case, an **Orthogonal** map means that it is straight and not skewed like other maps, such as an isometric map would be.
- **Tile render order**: This is a setting for orthogonal maps only. What it does is it renders the tiles in a particular direction.
- **Map size**: This specifies how big the game map will be:
    - **Width** and **Height**: The size of the map will be dependent on the size that you set your Tiles to. The larger the tile size, typically, the larger your map will be.

- **Tile size**: This is how large each tile is on the tileset. These are generally determined by the tileset, as they will already have a set dimension for each tile. Don't worry if you have parts of a tileset that are made up of more than one tile. You will be able to combine multiple tiles later, once we have created the tileset. This will be discussed later in this chapter.
  - **Width** and **Height**: These values are set in pixels.

Make sure that you pay attention to the settings here. We will be using the following for our new map. Once you have changed the following values (**Tile Layer Format, Map Size**, and **Tile Size**), click **Save As...** and save it with your project files.

Now, you should see something like the following screenshot:

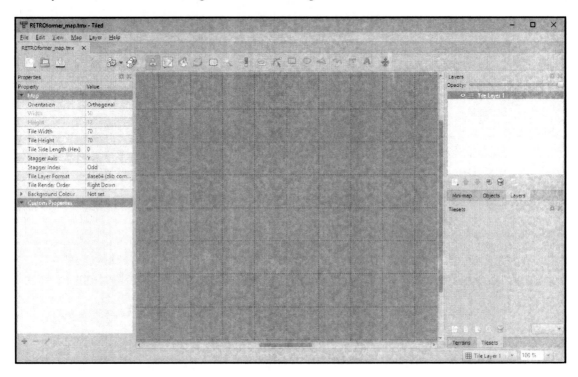

Looking at the bottom right-hand side of the window, you will see **Tilesets**. Here, we will need to create a new one. To do this, click on the new Tileset icon, as highlighted in the following screenshot:

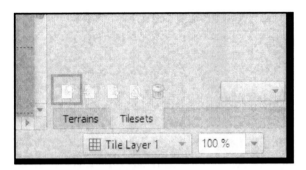

Once you have done this, you will see a pop-up like the one in the following screenshot:

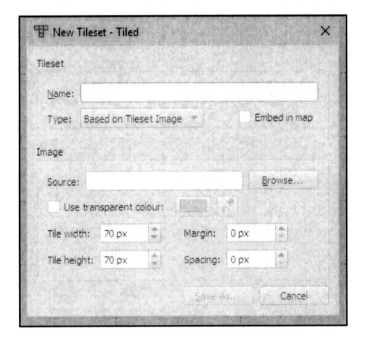

Before we start adding values, we will have a quick overview of each of the settings so that you can understand what each of them does:

- **Tileset**
  - **Name**: What you want your Tileset to be called. Remember to keep the naming conventions consistent with what you will or are using in Unity.
  - **Type**: The number of images that are used to create your Tileset, either a single image (Tileset Image) or a collection of images. For this tutorial, we will be using a single image.

- **Image**
  - **Source**: Location of the image on your computer.
  - **Use transparent color**: Specify a color that should always remain transparent. This is usually not an issue if your image is saved with a transparent (alpha) layer such as with a .png format. However, in some cases, it is also possible that an image will specify a transparent color that is highly contrasted to the colors within the Tileset as the key color for transparency.
  - **Tile width** and **Tile height**: As specified before, this is how large each tile will be, and is usually determined already by the Tileset.
  - **Margin**: This is any spacing that is around the tile.
  - **Spacing**: If there is space between the tiles, this is where you would specify it.

Here, we will need to give our Tileset a name and link it to the source image (where you saved the asset pack). Once you have named your Tileset and provided the Source, click **Save As...** to continue.

Now, you should see something like the following screenshot:

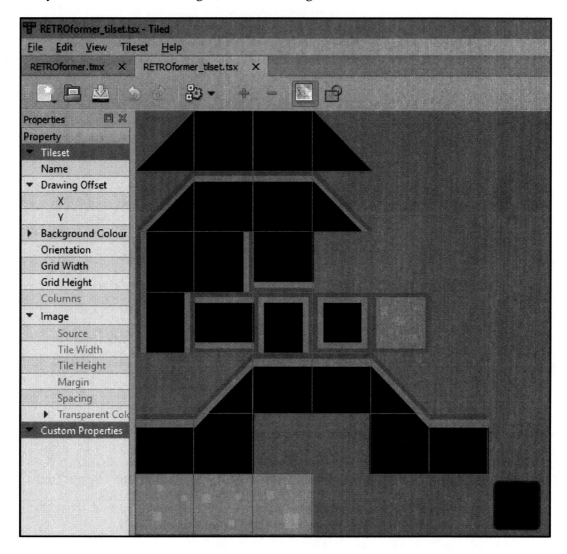

Just like you would when you're renovating your bathroom, you will want a guide or grid that will make sure each tile that is placed will align and be distributed evenly in conjunction with the other ones. To have such luxury within Tiled, go to **View** in the top navigation menu and in the drop-down list, make sure that **Snap to Grid** and **Snap to Fine Grid** are selected, like in the following screenshot:

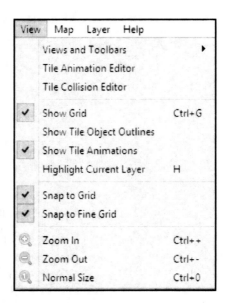

With this done, now comes the fun part... level construction!

The limitations of this process are only that of your imagination. Now, in the main screen in Tiled, you can begin to construct your level by selecting the tiles within the Tileset. To do this, simply:

1. Select which tile you wish to use from the **Tilesets** panel.
2. Inside the **TileMap** space, hold or click with the left mouse button where you want to position them within the map. You can think of this process like using a brush, and by selecting a specific tile it can be painted onto the level canvas.

After doing this, you can end up with something like the following screenshot. For now, just experiment:

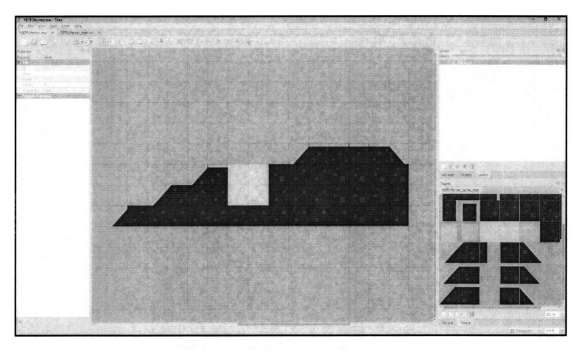

Above in an example of the level within Tiled using Sprites from the RETROformer Sprite Sheet.

If some objects are larger than a single tile, you can select multiple tiles at one time by holding down *Ctrl* and clicking on the tiles. They will be highlighted, like in the following screenshot:

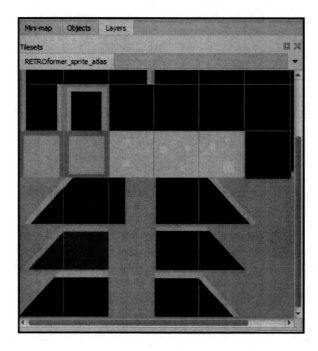

You can experiment with what you have just learned so that you can get used to the way Tiled works. Place them anywhere and everywhere as you please. Once you've got a feel for Tiled, let's move on to creating our first level.

If you have placed a tile(s) and wish to remove it, you can do so by clicking the eraser icon as highlighted in the following screenshot, or pressing *E* on the keyboard:

Once you are done, simply click the stamp icon, as highlighted in the following screenshot, or by pressing *B* on the keyboard:

Once you feel comfortable with using Tiled, we are ready to begin creating the level that we will use within our game. To begin, we will create a simple path with very few terrain features (hills, bottomless pits, for example). For now, this level will be simple so that we can learn how to implement it into Unity. Once we have this process down, you're more than welcome to spend a lot more time on refining your level and making it as detailed or complex as you wish.

In our game, we will have two different kinds of materials: Terrain and Water. At this stage, it is important to learn that we can separate the two types by placing them on different layers. If you look towards the top-right corner of Tiled, you will see the **Layers** panel, like in the following screenshot:

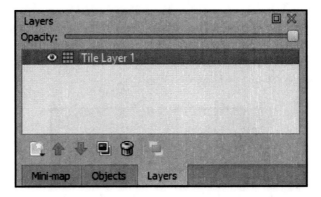

We will need to create a layer of both the water and the terrain. Since we already have one layer, let's create a second layer. We can do this by selecting the **New Layer** icon, and selecting **Tile Layer,** like in the following screenshot:

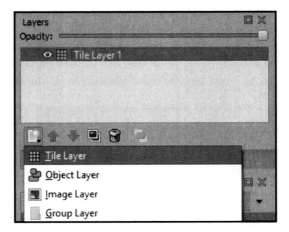

Now, we should have two layers, like the following screenshot. It is important to remember that the order of each layer plays a role in terms of rendering, which will also be the reason that the bottom layer **Tile Layer 1** will be the layer containing the water tiles:

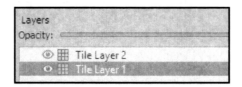

We need to rename them so that one is `Terrain` and one is `Water`. To do this:

- Right-click on **Tile Layer 1** and select **Layer Properties**.
- The **Layer Properties** panel should appear on the left-hand side of the screen (as seen in the following screenshot). Here, you can change the layer name. In this case, we will call it `Terrain`. Follow the same process for **Tile Layer 2**, and rename it `Water`:

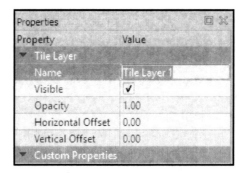

Once you're done, you will need to swap the layers so that the `Water` layer is under the `Terrain` one. You can do this by simply clicking on the layer that you want to move, and then dragging it above or below the others within the **Layers** panel. Once you have moved the `Water` layer to the bottom, your **Layers** panel should look like the following:

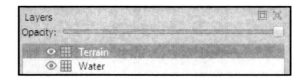

As you can see, there are also two other features in the **Layers** panel:

1. **Opacity**: This changes the level of transparency for the entire level. This is particularly helpful when you want to focus on a single layer, but want to know where the tiles are of another.
2. **Visible**: Next to the layer name, you will see an eye icon. Toggle this on and off to change the visibility of the layer.

Now, it's time to create our level. It is important to remember that when you drag any **Terrain** tiles, they are put onto the **Terrain** layer, and any **Water** tiles onto the **Water** layer. This will be important for later when we need to import it into Unity. The reason why it is important is that each layer has its own properties, which we can modify. That way, when we will use `Tiled2Unity` to import our maps into Unity, each layer's properties will then be applied to the game objects that will be automatically created. Essentially, this will save us a lot of time later from having to change each thing individually inside Unity. With this in mind, let's build our level. For our game, we will have a level that looks like the following screenshot. Feel free, though, to create something of your own as well:

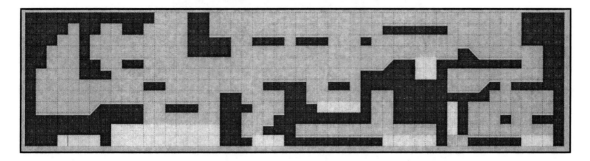

Mini-map

A useful feature of Tiled to remember is the Mini-map. When your levels begin to get larger, it can be difficult to navigate around them. If you click on the **Mini-map** panel, you can pan around your map to navigate to other areas quickly. You can also do this by holding down the Spacebar + right-click to pan around the environment:

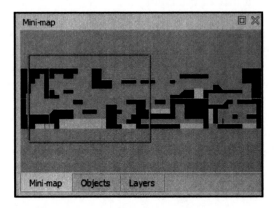

One thing to keep in mind, especially if you have found some issues with a tile map while building your maps, is editing it. In fact, if you make even some minor tweaks (for example, changing colors, image details, and so on) to the original image, it won't cause any issues. However, be very cautious if you move the location of tiles. This is because when you re-import the image after you have modified it, the image will update while maintaining the positions of the tiles. So, for instance, if you have used a tile then moved it within the Tilemap source image, when you update the Tilemap, whatever is in the original location will replace all instances of the tile that was in the map before you reimported it.

Changing level properties

With our level done, we have one last thing to complete before we're finished with Tiled. We need to now change the properties of our levels. To begin:

1. Select the **Terrain** layer.
2. Navigate to the **Properties** panel on the left-hand side of the screen.

2. Add the following **Custom Properties**:
   - unity:SortingLayerName
   - unity:SortingOrder
   - unity:isTrigger
   - unity:layer
   - unity:tagged

 The reason why we have added these custom properties is that later when you export the level with Tile2Unity, the software will read these custom properties to correctly import the map into Unity, with all the parameters you have specified. By doing this, you will avoid a lot of manual work in the later stages.

In the next screenshot, you can see an example of this along with the settings used for this project:

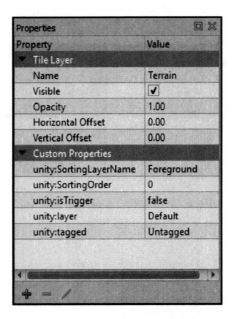

You will need to complete the above steps again for the **Water** layer if you have included water in your map. However, in this case, make sure that the **unity:isTrigger** is set to **True**. This is because, when the player is navigating around the map, we want to make sure that the game knows when the player falls into the water, and as a result, an action can occur, such as losing points or health.

To save time, especially if you are using the same Custom Properties, you can select all of the custom properties within the Terrain layer and copy them. Then, when you select the Water layer, you can paste them and adjust the values accordingly.

Adding colliders to our tiles

Once we have changed the properties of the **Terrain** and **Water** layers, we now need to add colliders to our tiles. To do this, you need to:

1. Select that tile from the **Tilesets** panel.
2. Then, navigate to **View | Tile Collision Editor**. You should now have a screen that looks like the following screenshot:

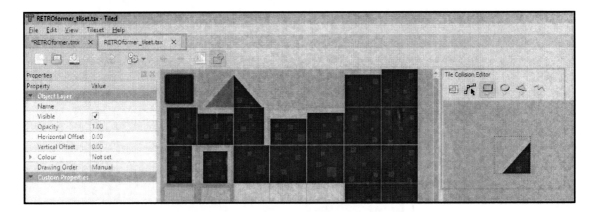

Lastly, in the **Tile Collision Editor**, select the rectangle tool (as highlighted in the following screenshot), and make sure that you draw a rectangle so that it is the same size as the tile, like so:

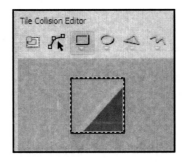

You will have to repeat the above steps for each tile that has been used within the map that the player will collide with. In our example, this isn't an issue because we will need to add colliders onto everything. But for Tilesets which have tiles that contain decorative assets such as various plants or other environmental adorations, you won't need to add a collider. Once you have finished adding colliders to all of the tiles, save it and open Unity.

There are many great features that Tiled offers, which we won't cover in this book. These features can help you to create more detailed and complex maps. Therefore, I encourage you to actively check out the documentation on their official website, by visiting the following link: `http://doc.mapeditor.org/en/latest/`.
Another place that I recommend checking out is this series of video tutorials: `http://www.gamefromscratch.com/post/2015/10/14/Tiled-Map-Editor-Tutorial-Series.aspx`. Even though they are a little old, they cover quite a few things about Tiled that are still relevant to the current builds.

Importing tilesets into Unity with Tiled2Unity

Now, this is where Tiled2Unity comes in handy. Once you have created your Tilemap in Tiled, we need to bring it into Unity so that the player will be able to interact with it.

Generally, most of the things that we have completed using third-party software can be done manually within Unity itself; however, third-party tools offer a way to increase efficiency, and in some cases, the output. In saying that, I do encourage you to explore the ways that you could complete these tasks within Unity, even if they are time-consuming. In the event that such programs are no longer available, it is useful to know the "manual" way to achieve the same results.

When you open Tiled2Unity, you will see a window like the following screenshot:

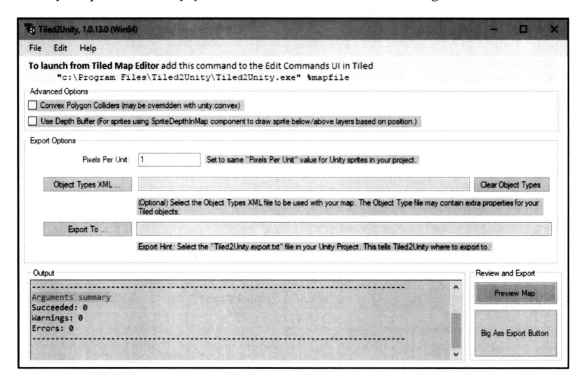

While initially this may be quite daunting, the whole process is very simple. To import our **Tilemap** from **Tiled**, simply:

1. Open/create your project Unity (if you haven't already).
2. In Tiled2Unity, navigate to **Help** | **Import Unity Package To Project**.

3. In Unity, a dialogue box will open. Now, click on **Import**. An example of this can be seen in the following screenshot. At this stage, all that is happening is **Tiled2Unity** is setting up the plugin within Unity. As a result, we can then use the `Tilemap` files (from **Tiled**) that we are about to import next:

4. In Tiled2Unity, navigate to **File | Open Tiled File...**.
5. Select your `Tiled` (`.tmx`) file and click **Open**.
6. Set your **Pixels per Unit** value in such a way that you are happy with your scale. Keep in mind that this value tells us how long a pixel is in the World Units of Unity. This might take some trial and error, especially when you are working on larger projects. However, once you have found an appropriate value to use, you should keep it consistent throughout your project, unless you have specific needs. In this book, we will go for a value equal to `0.02`.
7. Next, click **Export To...** and specify the location within your Unity project. This file should be inside the folder `Assets/Tiled2Unity` and called `Tiled2Unity.export`.

8. If necessary, click the **Preview Map** to make sure that you have the right Tilemap. You can see an example of this in the following screenshot:

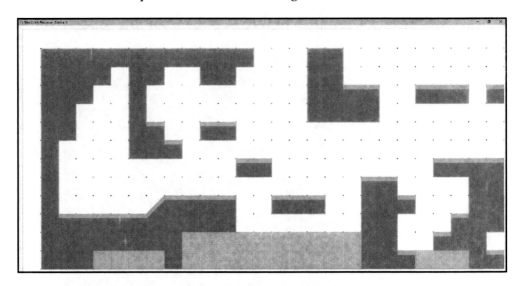

9. Lastly, click the **Export** button to export the Tilemap to Unity.

And voila. We are now finished with Tiled2Unity, so it's time to head back into Unity to continue making our game, which we will begin in Chapter 9, *Look, It Moves*.

Post-Tiled2Unity

Now, if we head back to Unity, you will see a new subfolder within Assets called Tiled2Unity, as shown in the following screenshot:

Within this folder, there is our map, which we created within `Tiled`. You can find it by navigating to `Tiled2Unity` | `Prefabs` | `RETROformer`, as demonstrated in the following screenshot:

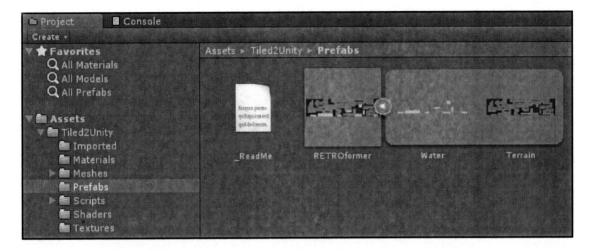

Here, you can also see the two layers that we created in `Tiled`: `Water` and `Terrain` as separate layers also within the prefab. Next, drag the `RETROformer` prefab into the scene. You will notice that it is quite large, but we can modify it easily within Unity.

Now, the level is ready for us to make it usable. For now, we'll finish here, and in `Chapter 9`, *Look, It Moves*, we'll begin to create some animations.

Summary

In this chapter, we have covered how to create tiles using the third-party program `Tiled`. We have learned how to set up different layers (such as Terrain and Water), so to better distinguish the different parts of the map once we import everything back into Unity. We used another tool named `Tiled2Unity` to export the map created in Tiled into Unity and learned how to set the environment up. We will continue with the environment in `Chapter 10`, *Let's Get Physical*. But for now, it's time to jump into `Chapter 9`, *Look, It Moves*, in which we will learn more about the Animation State machine, and we will build a more complex one.

9
Look, It Moves

Look, it moves! Well, not quite yet, but it soon will!

One of the most important aspects of any game is movement. Movement can be anything from a character moving within the environment, to the environment (and various parts of it) moving on its own. Animations breathe life into our environment, and take our static graphics and transform them into interactive worlds.

With this in mind, this chapter will cover the following topics:

- Explore how to build a more complex Animation State Machine than the one we did for the explosion in Space Shooter.
- We will do this by properly setting this State Machine up. We will be able to easily control the animations within the script in `Chapter 10`, *Let's Get Physical*, in which we will focus on building a controller for our main character.

Advanced animations

Back in `Chapter 5`, *Freeze! Creating an Intergalactic Shooter*, we saw a small introduction to the Unity Animation system. In this section, we will do a quick recap, and explain a little bit more about the system. Finally, we will implement an Animation State Machine for animating our main character. In fact, this will involve more than one state on the machine, thus it gives us the possibility to learn how to build a more complex state machine than the one we built for explosions.

A short recap of the animation system

Once again, feel free to explore the official documentation by visiting the following link: `https://docs.unity3d.com/Manual/AnimationSection.html`. Alternatively, follow the official video tutorial here: `https://unity3d.com/learn/tutorials/s/animation`

When it comes to the animation system in Unity, we can talk about State Machines. Each animation is a node, and the character can change animation according to certain variables of the State Machine. The character can stay only on one state per time and can change animation only to another node that it is linked to it by transitions (there are a few exceptions to this rule when you use nested animation machines, but we won't see them in this book). A transition is represented as an arrow that goes from one node into another. It contains different properties on how to perform the transitions, but more importantly, when to execute the transitions and change state in the animation machine.

In order to explain the process, let's take, for instance, the example in `Chapter 5`, *Freeze! Creating an Intergalactic Shooter* (which is similar to the state machine built in the book *Getting Started with Unity 5.x 2D Game Development*: `https://www.packtpub.com/game-development/getting-started-unity-5x-2d-game-development`). Despite the title, it's a book worth having a look at. In addition, you can also find an in-depth explanation of the animation system in *Chapter 4, No Longer Alone – Sweet-Toothed Pandas Strike*:

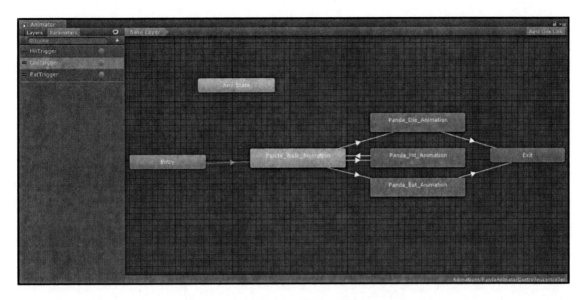

The **Entry** node is special because it indicates where the Animation State Machine starts and its transition fires immediately, leading the animation state machine into the **Panda_Walk_Animation** state. From this state, there are three transitions going outwards, in particular to **Panda_Die_Animation**, **Panda_Hit_Animation**, and **Panda_Eat_Animation**. These transitions are fired based on triggers that are defined on the left in the **Parameter** panel. Hence, when the script that controls the panda sends a trigger, the animation state machine changes state. This three animation state has only one transition, and it is fired automatically once the animation is finished. In particular, **Panda_Die_Animation** and **Panda_Eat_Animation** lead to the **Exit** state, which is another special state determining the end of the State Machine. On the other hand, the **Panda_Hit_Animation** state has the transition that goes back to the **Panda_Walk_Animation** state, in which the animation will loop until another trigger from script arrives.

Now that you should have a better understanding how state and transitions work, it's time to try on our own by building the animation for our character for this last project, which will be a... Panda!

Setting up the sprite sheet for the animations

If you recall what we did for the explosion, we had an animation sprite sheet with a single animation. Here instead, if you take `panda_animation_spritesheet.png` within our asset package, we have more than one animation:

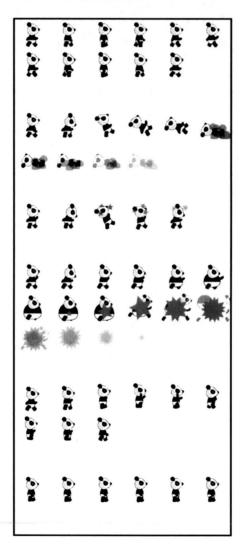

The image above is the Sprite Sheet that we will be using for our Panda animations. As you can see. there are many different types of animations for various situations.

So, let's go to the **panda_animation_spritesheet Import Settings**, and you should see something like the following:

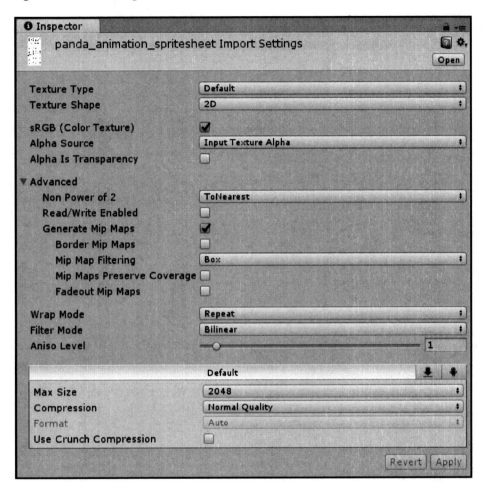

However, we need to set the **Texture Type** to **Sprite (2D and UI)**, as well as set the **Sprite Mode** to **Multiple**, as shown here:

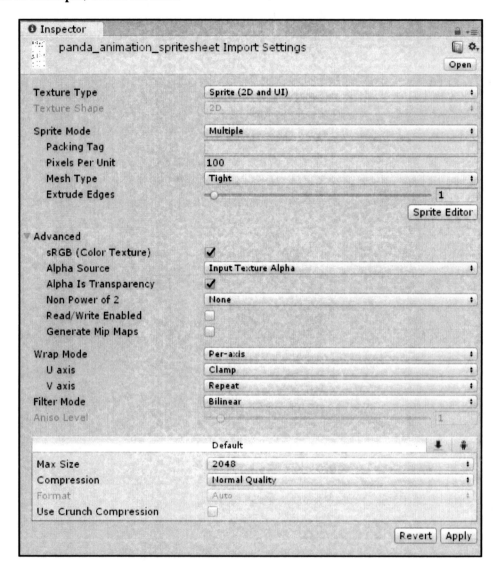

Then, open the **Sprite Editor**. In the **Slice** menu, select **Type** as **Grid by Cell Count** (since the sprite sheet has every animation frame in a specific cell). In particular, slice it into **6** columns by **17** rows. An example of this is shown in the following screenshot:

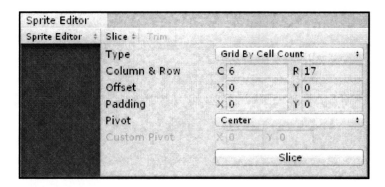

The following screenshot shows the end result. Here, you will faintly see a bounding box around each frame of the panda's animation:

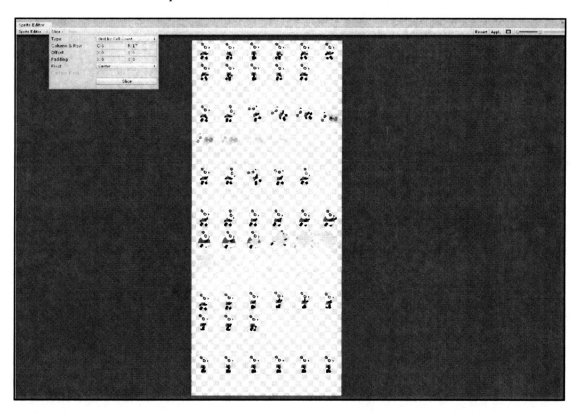

An example of the Panda animation Sprite Sheet after it has been sliced.

Now we have all the animations frames done, it's time to transform them into single animations.

Creating the animations from the sprite sheet

As you can see from the sprite sheet, we don't need all the frames; however, we need the following animations:

- **Idle**: When the character is not moving
- **Walk**: When the character is moving
- **Jump Start**: When the character starts to jump
- **Jump Air**: When the character is still in mid-air
- **Jump Landing**: When the character lands back

To create the preceding animations, we just need to drag the correct frames into the scene (ignore the size for now), and Unity will ask you where to save the single animations. Therefore, let's create a folder within our `Character` folder and call it `Animations`, in which we will save all the animations there.

For the single animations, here are the frames for each of them:

- **Idle animation:** Select and drag from frame 53 to frame 58; name the animation `Idle`.
- **Walk animation:** Select and drag from frame 0 to frame 10; name the animation `Walk`.
- **Jump Start animation**: Select and drag from frame 44 to frame 48; name the animation `Jump_Start`.
- **Jump Landing animation**: Select and drag from frame 48 to frame 52; name the animation `Jump_Landing`.
- **Jump Air:** This is a bit more tricky. In fact, the animation is made of a single frame (*frame 48*), and if we drag it into the **Scene** view, Unity will just place a sprite, without creating any animation. Thus, open the **Animation** window by navigating to **Window/Animation**. Then use the drop-down menu to select **Create New Clip**, as shown in the following screenshot. Then, just drag the single frame (*frame 48*) into the **Animation** window, and the trick is done:

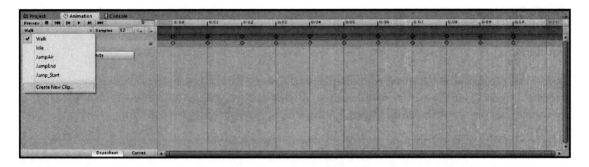

The image above is an example of the animation window within Unity.

Building the Animation State Machine

If you navigate to the `Animation` folder, you will not only find all your animations but also an Animator (in case you find more than one, delete them all but one). First of all, rename it `Panda_Animator`, and double-click to open it. You will end up in the **Animator** editor. You should have all the animations created in the previous sections as disconnected nodes. In case you don't have these animation nodes (if you had to delete the other animators), just drag the animations from the **Project** panel into the **Animator**. Feel free to rearrange them as you like; here is how I arranged them in order to not make transitions cross each other later on:

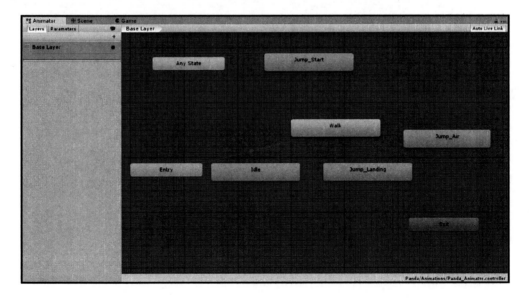

As you can see, there are all your animations already, but they are not connected by any transitions. Before we continue, think about how they should be connected, then continue to read here.

First of all, it's not fine that from the **Entry** node we go directly into the **Walk** node. In fact, we need to start with the **Idle** node. Hence, if **Idle** is not highlighted, then right-click on it and select **Set as Layer Default State**, as shown in the following screenshot:

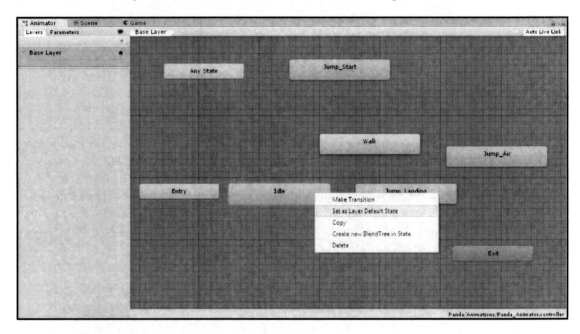

As a result, the **Idle** animation should be highlighted, and an arrow should go from the **Entry** node to the **Idle** one:

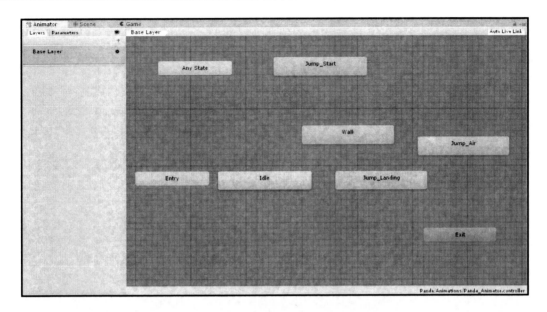

Next, from the **Idle** node, we can go both to the **Jump_Start** (because the character can jump when the player is not moving), or to the **Walk** node (because the character can start moving). As such, with the right-click and then **Make Transition**, create these two arrows. So far, you should have something similar to this:

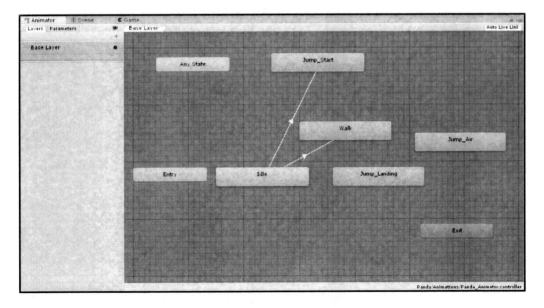

Now, it's time to connect the other nodes. From the **Walk** node, we can go back to **Idle**, in case we stop moving, or jumping, and thus go to **Jump_Start**. Make these other two transitions, and you will end up with the following:

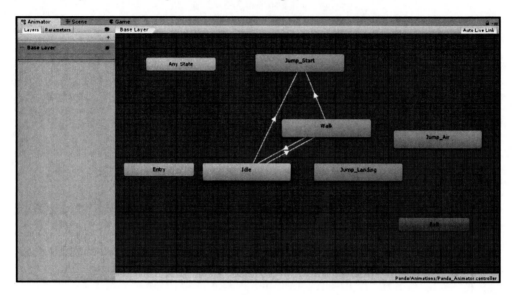

From the **Jump_Start** node, we cannot go back to **Idle** or **Walk** because we need to finish the Jump loop, so we need to go first to **Jump_Air** and then from there to **Jump_Landing**. This is the result so far:

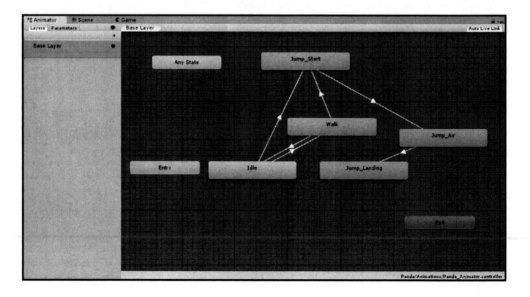

Finally, from the **Jump_Landing**, we need to go back to **Walk** or **Idle** (depending on whether the character is moving or not), and thus create two arrows towards them. This is the final result:

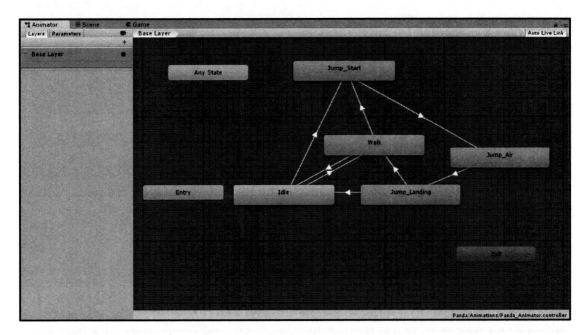

However, we haven't finished yet. In fact, we didn't establish any rule on how to fire the transitions. To do so, we need parameters. Go to the **Parameter** tab in the upper-left corner and create a couple of parameters. One parameter is of type **Float** and we will name it Speed; the other one is a **Boolean** and we will name it Jump. The idea is to have the Speed stored in the float parameter, to determine whether the character is moving or not, and in the Jump Boolean to determine whether the character is performing a jump or not.

Here is a screenshot of how the list of the parameters should appear:

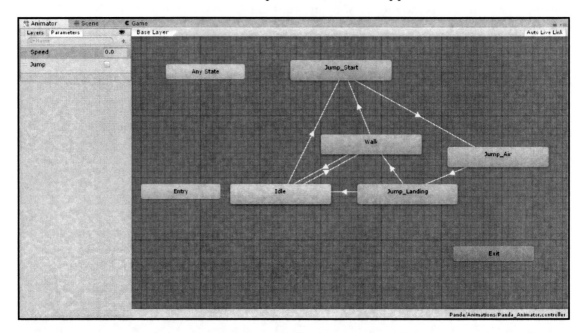

Now, we need to set all the transitions properly. If you select an arrow, in the **Inspector** you will see all the properties, and at the bottom, you can set conditions on when the transition is fired.

Following is the screenshot highlighting where to insert a condition on a transition:

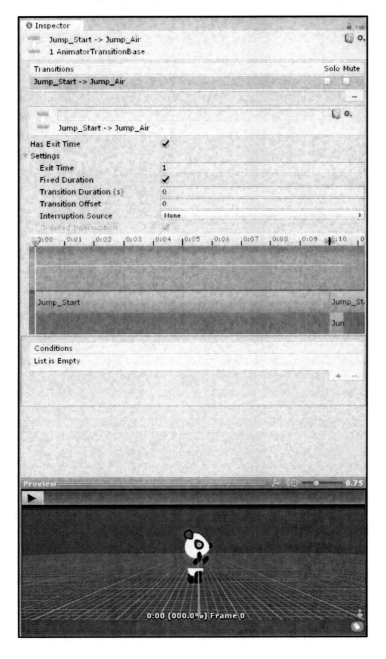

To properly set all the conditions for our Animation State Machine, follow these instructions, transition by transition:

- **Idle - > Walk**: Triggers if the **Speed** parameter is greater or equal than **0.01**.
- **Walk - > Idle**: Triggers if the **Speed** parameter goes below **0.01**.
- **Idle - > Jump_Start**: Triggers if the **Jump** Boolean becomes true.
- **Walk - > Jump_Start**: Triggers if the **Jump** Boolean becomes true.
- **Jump_Start - > Jump_Air**: Triggers as soon as the **Jump_Start** animation has finished, thus set the **Exit Time** to 1 and **Transition Duration** to 0, no further conditions.
- **Jump_Air - > Jump_Landing**: Triggers as soon as the **Jump** Boolean becomes false.
- **Jump_Landing - > Idle**: Triggers as soon as the **Jump_Landing** animation is finished (so set **Exit Time** to 1 and **Transition Duration** to 0, but on the condition that the **Speed** parameter is less than **0.01**).
- **Jump_Landing - > Walk**: Triggers as soon as the **Jump_Landing** animation is finished (so set **Exit Time** to 1 and **Transition Duration** to 0, but on the condition that the **Speed** parameter is greater or equal than **0.01**)

That was quite a lot of work, but we have finished with our state machine. The next step is to build a controller that is able to take care of this state machine, by setting the **Speed** and **Jump** parameters. But for now, take a rest and read the summary of this chapter, before we have fun in the next one.

Summary

Overall, this chapter has explained how to set up our third and final project—RETROformer. It's continued by explaining how to import all the assets for the project, as well as how to create some animations. Lastly, this chapter has explained how to implement a more advanced player controller that lets the character navigate through the environment in a more dynamic way.

Next, in Chapter 10, *Let's Get Physical*, we will continue to work on RETROformer. In addition, you will learn more about 2D physics in Unity, and how it can be applied to the platform game to create different Physics Material 2D. Lastly, we will learn and apply various physics to actions such as jumping or moving using forces.

10
Let's Get Physical

In this chapter, you continue to work on the third and final game in the book—RETROformer. You will learn all about 2D physics in Unity, and how it can be applied to the platform game. Here, we will learn this by applying physics to actions such as jumping and moving through forces. In particular, we will implement a **Movement Component** (which will take care of controlling the Animation State Machine of the previous chapter, as well as moving the character using physics) along with a **Player Controller** (which will send input based on the keyboard to the Movement Component). Keep in mind that if it is difficult to understand now, it will be much easier by the end of the chapter.

Throughout this chapter, we will cover the following topics:

- Physics Material 2D
- Finishing to set up the Environment
- Creating our Hero
- Movement Component for moving, jumping, and controlling the State Machine
- Player Controller for processing input based on the keyboard

With this said, let's begin.

Physics Material 2D

In 2D games, the concept of physics becomes a bit more, let's say, linear. By this, we don't have to worry about a ball bouncing off along the z-axis, or the trajectory of an arrow being dramatically affected by various environmental objects, other than those in plain view. For example, if there is a tree in the path of your character, chances are if you fire an arrow towards an enemy on the other side, the arrow will hit the tree first.

Don't worry if you didn't do too well in physics in school. This isn't a test, but rather an explanation about the physics behind the gameplay in a platformer. It is important to know these things for many reasons. For example, when you're trying to increase the difficulty within a level, it is important to remember and predict how certain elements within the game will behave. Parts of a game, such as an arc that a player jumps, gravity (or lack of), the velocity that a player can run, the amount of friction between the player and the ground beneath them, and so forth, are essential considerations that all have to do with physics. For this section, we are just going to consider Physics Materials 2D, which is the basic way to set some physics properties to a material.

You can create a Physics2D material with a right-click on the **Project** panel and then **Create | Physics Material 2D**. If you double-click on it, you can see its properties in the **Inspector**. When it comes to Physics2D material in Unity, there are only two parameters to take into consideration:

- **Friction**: Indicates the amount of friction; the less the friction, the more slippery the material. Try to create a new material with zero friction, then apply it to the terrain; you will end up with something very similar to ice.
- **Bounciness**: Indicates how much energy the material gives back when something hits the material. Try to create a new material with **Bounciness** to 1, and apply it to any sprite, and let it fall to the ground; you will see the sprite bounce. An example of this is shown as follows:

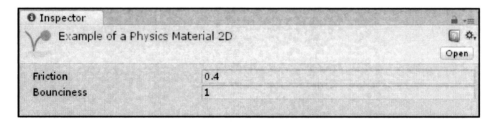

As far as the game we are creating goes, you can try to experiment with different materials for the different surfaces of your game. However, keep in mind that whether you're trying to outrun an enemy or beat the countdown to a massive explosion, sliding allows you to neatly glide across a large amount of space faster than you could run it. As a result, you can use this game mechanic if you wish.

Since our character will collide with the ground, we need to properly set it up.

First of all, as exported from **Tiled2Unity**, the **Terrain** comes already with a collider, which is great. However, we need to set a new layer for it, so when we do some checks to allow our character to jump, our system will go flawlessly.

Navigate to **Edit | Project Settings | Tags and Layers**. This is the screen that will open in the **Inspector**:

Open the **Layers** menu, and add a new one called **Ground**, as shown in this next screenshot:

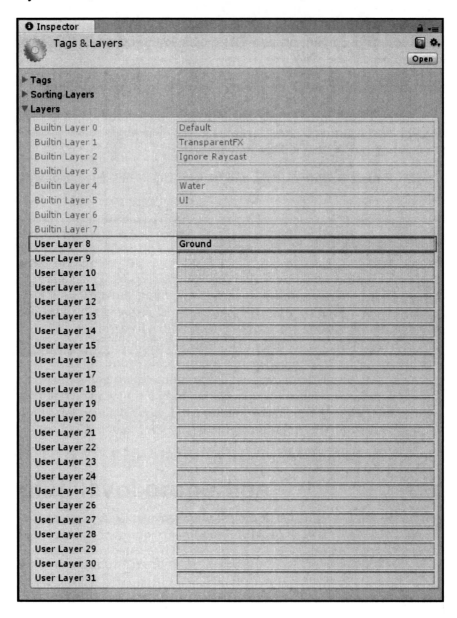

Also, later we will need a tag for implementing Jump Pads. Since we are already in the right menu, open the **Tag** menu, and add a **JumpPad** tag, as shown in the following screenshot:

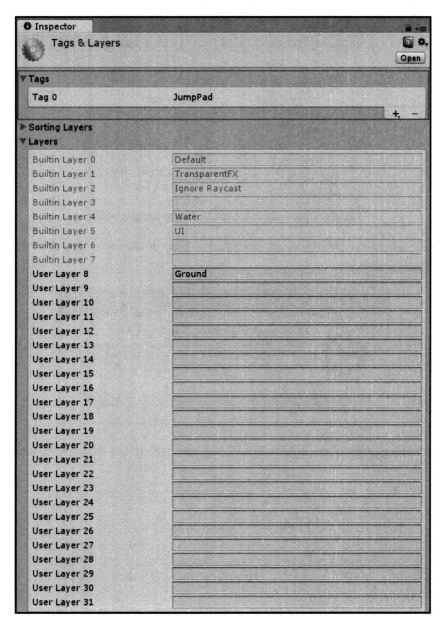

Finally, select our **Terrain** in the **Hierarchy** panel, and apply the **Ground** layer on it, like in the following screenshot:

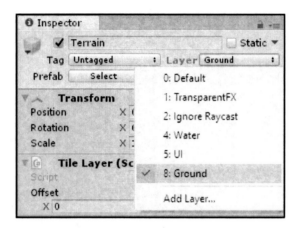

If it asks you to apply the change to all the children (like in the following screenshot), then click **Yes, change children**:

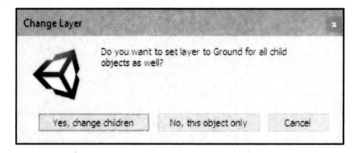

Now, our terrain is good to go, and it's time bring our hero to life in the next section.

Building the panda hero

In this section, we will go through the step to create our hero: an unstoppable panda! We will build it, keeping in mind how the Player Controller will act on the panda. If you have followed the steps in `Chapter 9`, *Look, It Moves*, you will already have a panda in the scene (which we can now rename `Panda Hero`), and the game object should already have, besides the **Transform**, a **Sprite Renderer** as well as an **Animator** component in which the **Controller** is the **Panda_Animator_Finished**:

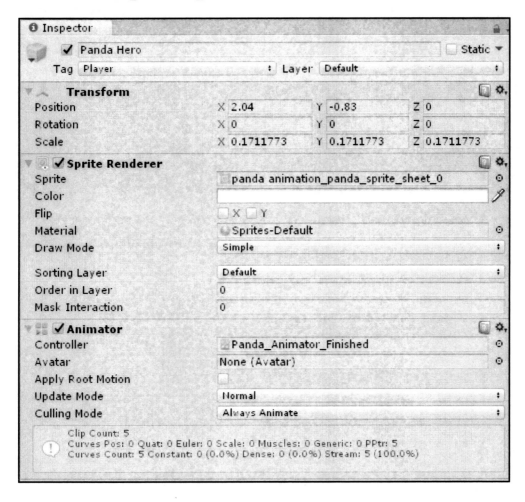

First of all, the character is definitely out of proportion (and possibly also rendered behind the terrain, which is not good). Unless we want to make a variant of Godzilla or King Kong that features a panda, we'd best change this:

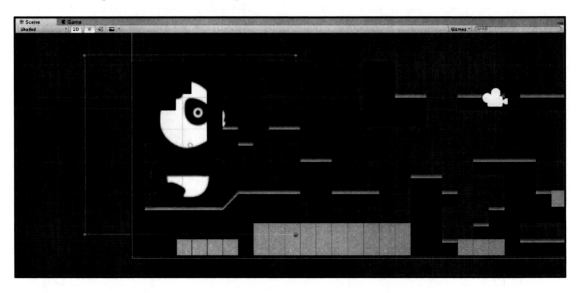

In order to fix the problem that the character is rendered behind the terrain, we need to change the sorting layer in its **Sprite Renderer**. We can, for instance, set the **Sorting Layer** to **1**, and the panda will be rendered on top:

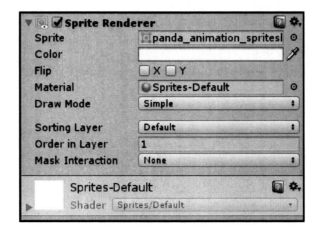

And this is how it appears in the **Scene** view now:

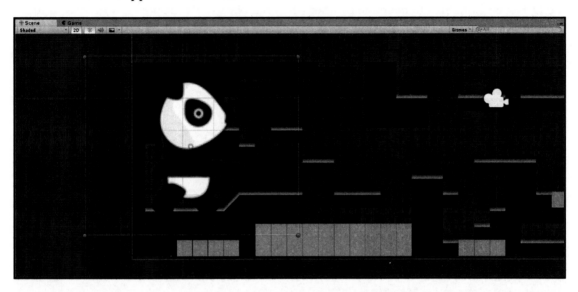

However, the character is still out of proportion. Thus, we need to scale it down uniformly, to fit the environment. You can either use the **Scale** in **Transform** or select the **Rect Tool** and while holding *Shift*, drag one of the corners to scale the character uniformly. The dimensions of our character should be reasonable with respect to the environment:

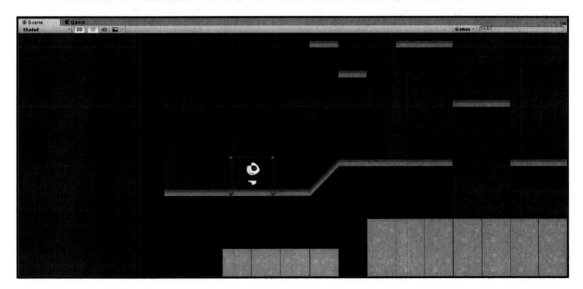

The next step is to add a collider, in particular, a `BoxCollider2D`. Here, we need to adjust the **Offset** and the **Size** to have the collider (the green box in the **Scene** view) just around the character without much space unoccupied by the character. The settings that work for me are **Offset = (0,0)** and **Size = (3.13,4.16)**. This is the result in the **Scene** view:

Also, it's good practice to set the **Tag** as **Player**. As a result, when you extend the game, you can check if a collision deals with the player, and/or locates the player's **game object** easier through code:

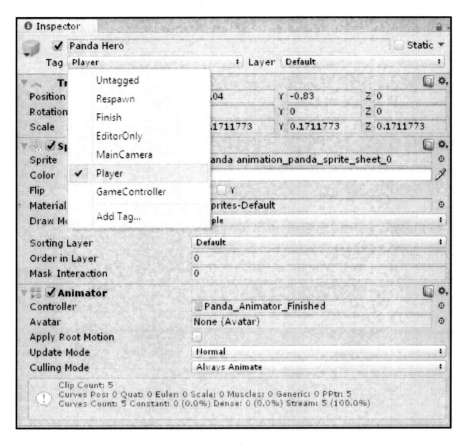

The next component is **Rigidbody2D**. This will allow the character to interact with the physical environment around it. Feel free to change the settings as you like. For instance, a value for the **Mass** equal to 3 should work pretty well. However, keep in mind that you absolutely need to check **Freeze Rotation Z** under the **Constraints** menu. Otherwise, we would end up with a rotating character, something we want to avoid:

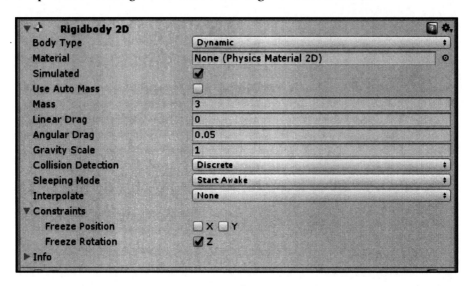

We need to create one more thing for our character: a **ground checker**. This is an empty game object attached to the character, which helps us to easily have another point to check whether the character is on the ground or not. Right-click on the **Panda Hero** in the **Hierarchy** panel, and select **Create Empty Game Object**. Rename the new object as Ground Checker. Now, in the **Inspector**, next to the name there is a cube: click on it, and the label menu shows up:

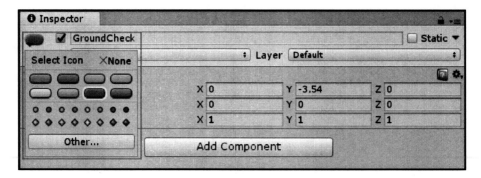

Click on any of that long bar. As a result, you will be able to see where the object is placed within the Scene view:

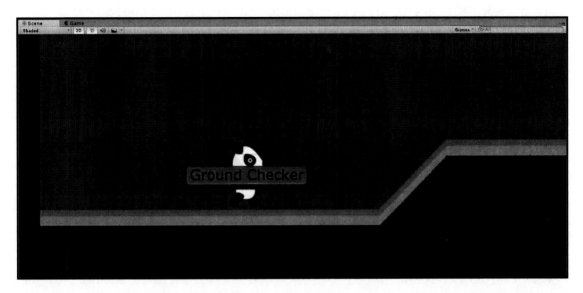

Use the *Moving Tool* to bring it beneath the character, as shown in the following screenshot:

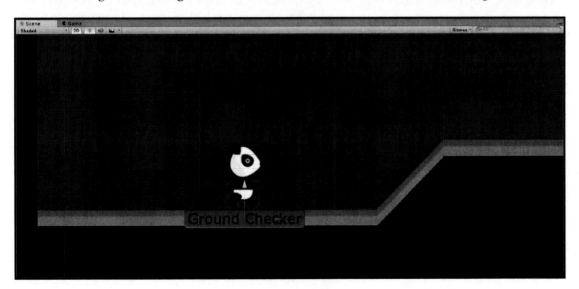

And with this, we have finished creating our character, and it's time to implement the movement of this panda.

Moving the panda

The controls in RETROformer are quite straightforward. We have just three actions:

- Move left
- Move right
- Jump

However, we need to sync these actions with the animation state machine created in the previous section. Moreover, in Chapter 9, *Look, It Moves*, we extended this controller so that it can be used by mobile devices as well. As a result, we need to build the controller in a modular way—we need a control scheme.

The control scheme

It's important to define a control scheme that allows us to control the character in different ways. Suppose that you want to ship the game both for (desktop) computers and mobile devices. One has a keyboard, the other one has a touchscreen. As a result, you need to write twice how the character should move based on the input. Now, imagine that you add also AI enemies; they need a script that not only makes them think but also move. However, all this repetition of the code can be avoided with a simple control scheme. We abstract the movement in a separate class, which doesn't care how the input arrives, but once it arrives, this class will make the character move. We can call this Movement Component, which we are going to implement in this section.

Have a look at the following figure of the control scheme:

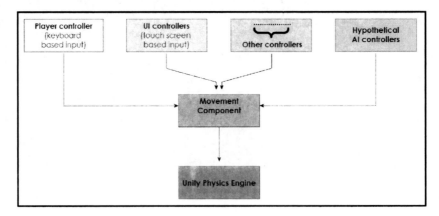

As you can see, the **Movement Component** can receive input from different sources. These sources don't have to worry about movement since the **Movement Component** will take care of that. The output of the **Movement Component** is to tell the physics engine which forces are applied to the character to make it move. Later, we will implement both the Player Controller (for input based on a keyboard) in Chapter 11, *Don't Forget to Save*, and the **UI Controllers** (for input based on the touchscreen) in Chapter 12, *The Nature of Export*. Here, in this chapter, we will focus only on the Movement Component.

The Movement Component

Let's start by creating a new C# Script and naming it MovementComponent. This class will contain all the logic that will allow our character to move (and to animate). In fact, it is a component that is attached to the panda character. In particular, it implements three functions, one for each action. Also, this component has to keep in consideration the animator, to show the right animation for the character.

Let's start by adding three private variables, one to store the Animator component, another one for the Rigidbody2D, and the last one for the SpriteRenderer:

```
private Animator anim;
private Rigidbody2D rb2d;
private SpriteRenderer spriteRenderer;
```

We can retrieve these three inside the Awake() function, by calling the GetComponent() function:

```
void Awake () {
    anim = GetComponent<Animator>();
    rb2d = GetComponent<Rigidbody2D>();
    spriteRenderer = GetComponent<SpriteRenderer>();
}
```

Since we want to avoid the case in which one of these three components is not found, we can force adding those every time we attach this script to a game object. We can achieve this using the `RequireComponent` before the class declaration, one for each of the components we want to enforce (for more information regarding this, you can check the official documentation here: `https://docs.unity3d.com/ScriptReference/RequireComponent.html`):

```
[RequireComponent(typeof(Animator))]
[RequireComponent(typeof(Rigidbody2D))]
[RequireComponent(typeof(SpriteRenderer))]
public class MovementComponent : MonoBehaviour {
        //[...]
}
```

Next, we still need some variables that define the settings of the `MovementComponent`. In particular, we need three variables. The first one is `moveForce`, which indicates with how much force the character is pushed when the player moves the character. The second is `maxSpeed`, which is the maximum speed along the x-axis at which the character can go, any force on the character that breaks this limit is ignored. Finally, the last one is `jumpForce`, which indicates the force applied to the character when the player jumps. Since all of them should be private (in the sense that they cannot be modified by external scripts) but at the same time tweakable from the **Inspector**, we need to insert the `SerializableField` attribute, as shown in the following code:

```
[SerializeField]
private float moveForce = 360f;
[SerializeField]
private float maxSpeed = 5f;
[SerializeField]
private float jumpForce = 1000f;
```

In a similar manner, we need to have another private variable, which needs to be set in the **Inspector**. The `groundCheck` is a variable storing the **Transform** of the `Ground Checker` game object we created before. This will allow us to correctly perform the jump:

```
[SerializeField]
private Transform groundCheck;
```

Also, we need to check in the `Awake()` function that the `groundCheck` variable has been correctly initialized, otherwise we launch a warning into the console and remove the `MovementComponent` from the character:

```
void Awake () {
    anim = GetComponent<Animator>();
    rb2d = GetComponent<Rigidbody2D>();
    spriteRenderer = GetComponent<SpriteRenderer>();

    //Check if the groundCheck variable is set
    if(groundCheck == null)
    {
        Debug.LogError("Ground Check missing from the MovementComponent,
        please set one.");
        Destroy(this);
    }
}
```

Now, we are ready to implement the two main functions to move our character.

The first one is `MoveCharacter()`, which takes as a parameter a normalized speed (a value between -1 and +1, where the sign indicates the direction, positive is right and negative is left). The function checks if the character isn't going faster than the maximum velocity specified in the `maxSpeed` variable, and if so, a force is applied to the **rigidbody** equal to the `moveForce`, scaled by the normalized speed facing the right direction:

```
public void MoveCharacter(float normalisedSpeed) {

    //If the max velocity is not reached, then...
    if(rb2d.velocity.x * normalisedSpeed < maxSpeed) {
        //... apply a force to the character
        rb2d.AddForce(Vector2.right * normalisedSpeed * moveForce);
    }
}
```

After having applied the force, the velocity is clamped to the maximum that the character can go, but only on the x-axis, while leaving invariant the y-axis:

```
public void MoveCharacter(float normalisedSpeed) {

    //If the max velocity is not reached, then...
    if(rb2d.velocity.x * normalisedSpeed < maxSpeed) {
        //... apply a force to the character
        rb2d.AddForce(Vector2.right * normalisedSpeed * moveForce);
    }
}
```

```
    //Set the velocity such as the x component is clamped,
    whereas the y component is the same
    float clampVelocityX = Mathf.Clamp(rb2d.velocity.x, -maxSpeed,
    maxSpeed);
    rb2d.velocity = new Vector2(clampVelocityX, rb2d.velocity.y);
}
```

As with jumping in any sense, jumping within a game is greatly affected by the strength of gravity. The less gravity, the more it is like you're walking on the moon, which can make things easier or more difficult, depending on what you're trying to do. Thus, the Jump() function, instead, is a little bit tricker, because, in order to perform a jump, we need to check whether the character is actually grounded (is touching the ground) or not. There are many ways in which we can do this. In this project, we are going to use a more classical approach. The character has a point attached to his base. Using a Linecast, we check whether there is terrain between the center of the character and this groundCheck point. If there is terrain, then the panda can jump and we can add a force toward the up direction:

```
public void Jump() {
    //Check if the character can jump
    if (Physics2D.Linecast(transform.position, groundCheck.position, 1
    <<LayerMask.NameToLayer("Ground"))) {
        if (rb2d.velocity.y <= 0) {
            //Perform the jump
            rb2d.AddForce(new Vector2(0f, jumpForce));
        }
    }
}
```

If the preceding code seems a bit complicated at first because of the LineCast() function within the *if-statement*, you may want to have a look to the following code, which does exactly the same, but the comments guide you step by step:

```
public void Jump() {
    // Get the index for the Ground layer mask.
    int layerMaskIndex = LayerMask.NameToLayer("Ground");

    // Calculate the layer mask value that can be used in the following
    // Physics2D.Linecast() method call. We use a bitwise left shift
    // operation to find the correct value which is 256 because we
    // use the 8th User Layer in our example: 1 << 8 = 256.
    int groundCheckLayerMask = 1 << layerMaskIndex;

    //Check if the character can jump
    if (Physics2D.Linecast(transform.position,
        groundCheck.position,
        groundCheckLayerMask))
```

```
    {
    if (rb2d.velocity.y <= 0) {
        //Perform the jump
        rb2d.AddForce(new Vector2(0f, jumpForce));
    }
    }
}
```

This is enough for the logic; however, we still need to animate the character. Thus, let's fill the Update() function so we can have control over the animation frame after frame. In particular, we need to set the Speed parameter of the animation state machine as the velocity along the x-axis. Likewise, we can use the velocity along the y-axis to set whether the character is grounded or not in the state machine, by setting the Jump parameter:

```
void Update () {
        //Set the Speed parameter in the Animation State Machine
        anim.SetFloat("Speed", Mathf.Abs(rb2d.velocity.x));

        //Set the Jump parameter in the Animation State Machine
        anim.SetBool("Jump", rb2d.velocity.y != 0);
}
```

Finally, depending on the sign of the velocity along the x-axis, we can flip the character through the **Sprite Renderer** to make the character face the correct direction:

```
void Update () {
        //Set the Speed parameter in the Animation State Machine
        anim.SetFloat("Speed", Mathf.Abs(rb2d.velocity.x));

        //Set the Jump parameter in the Animation State Machine
        anim.SetBool("Jump", rb2d.velocity.y != 0);

      //Check in which direction the sprite should face and flip
          accordingly
    if (rb2d.velocity.x != 0)
        spriteRenderer.flipX = rb2d.velocity.x < 0;
}
```

Save the script because it's ready to be added to the character.

Setting up the Movement Component

Now that we have finished creating the Movement Component, we need to attach it to the **Panda Hero Object**. The required components won't add anything new because we already have all the components that we need.

Besides tweaking the values for your game, the important setting is the `groundCheck` transform variable, which needs to be properly initialized. As such, take the **Ground Check** (which is attached to the **Panda Hero**), and drag it into the `groundCheck` variable. As a result, the component should appear in the **Inspector** as this:

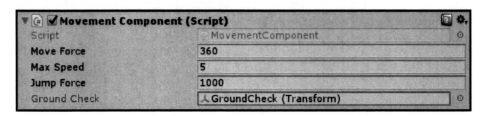

Player Controller

In the previous section, we implemented a script to move the character. However, if we hit Play, the character won't move, aside from idling. The reason lies in the fact that we have two functions to move the character, but no script calls them. If you go back to the *Control Scheme* section, you see that we need a Player Controller (or a UI interface in case of mobile games, but we will explore that later in `Chapter 12`, *The Nature of Export*), which sends the input to the **Player**. In this section, we are going to implement that script.

Create a new C# script and name it `PlayerController`. The script per se is very simple; however, we want to compile it only if the game is running either in the Editor or on a standalone version of the game (such as on Windows or macOS). As a result, we need to use compiler directives. So, after the name of the class, let's open the **Compile Directive**, which will compile all the code we are going to write if, and only if, we are running either in the **Editor** or in a standalone version of the game:

```
public class PlayerController : MonoBehaviour {
    #if UNITY_STANDALONE || UNITY_EDITOR
    //[...]
}
```

Now, it's time to think what the script should do. First of all, we need to retrieve the `MovementComponent` attached to the character. To do so, let's create a new variable of the type `MovementComponent`:

```
MovementComponent movementComponent;
```

Then, in order to initialize the variable, we can set its value in the `Awake()` function. We can achieve that by using `GetComponent()` to retrieve the `MovementComponent`. Furthermore, we need to launch a warning in case the `MovementComponent` is missing, and remove this very script from the **Panda Hero:**

```
void Awake () {
    //Retrieve reference to the Movement Component
    movementComponent = GetComponent<MovementComponent>();

    //Disable this script in case the Movement Component is not found,
      and leave an error message.
    if(movementComponent == null) {
        Debug.LogError("Missing MovementComponent on "
        + gameObject.name + " to run PlayerController.
        Please add one.");
        Destroy(this);
    }
    }
```

Next, we need to send the input to the `MovementComponent`. If you recall, the character needs to move left and right as well as jump. For the first two, we can just gather the value of the `Horizontal` axis value and use it as a normalized speed for the `MoveCharacter()` function. As a result, we will be able to use the arrows on our keyboard to move the character. As for the jump, we can use the up arrow to make the character jump. This is great, but we need to keep in mind that the `MovementComponent` uses `Rigidbody2D`. Hence, as we have seen for the previous projects, we need to use the `LateUpdate()` function. Here is how the code should be:

```
void FixedUpdate() {
    //Send input to the Movement Component in order to move the
  character
    movementComponent.MoveCharacter(Input.GetAxis("Horizontal"));

    //Check if the Up Arrow has been pressed, and if so,
      send the Jump input to the Movement Component
    if (Input.GetKeyDown(KeyCode.UpArrow)) {
        movementComponent.Jump();
    }
    }
```

Finally, we need to close the compiler directive by closing the if-statement, shown as follows:

```
public class PlayerController : MonoBehaviour {

    #if UNITY_STANDALONE || UNITY_EDITOR
    //[...]
    #endif
}
```

Save the script and attach it to the **Panda Hero**. There are no settings to set here, so we are good to go.

Summary

We started this chapter by learning how Physics Materials 2D works. From here, we added a new layer for properly identifying our ground, and we added a tag for Jump pads. Then, we moved on to building our Panda Hero by setting up all the components required. Next, we moved to exploring how we can create a Movement Component to allow our hero to move, and we designed it in such a way that it is modular. This means that how the input is received to the Movement Component is not important for the movement itself. As such, we have implemented a Player Controller to send input with a keyboard to the Movement Component.

In Chapter 11, *Don't Forget to Save!*, we will refine even further the Movement Component to implement jump pads, as well as exploring how we can save game data. In addition, you will learn how to script gameplay for this last game, and you will be provided with hints on how to enhance the overall quality of the game. With that said, turn the page!

11
Don't Forget to Save!

In this chapter, we continue building the game by giving suggestions about how to script gameplay. In addition, you will learn how to create and implement a basic save and load system into your game. Before concluding the chapter, we will extend the Movement Component to include Jump pads, to add a bit more pizzazz to your game. Lastly, this chapter covers some general topics for testing platformer games, which includes what to look for to ensure that everything is running correctly.

In particular, the chapter will cover:

- Save and load systems
- Jump pads
- Suggestions on how to finish up the gameplay of the game

Save and load systems

What is a game if it doesn't have a save and load system? It would be a nightmare... well, for some.

It is essential that in games which require you to progress through levels that gradually increase in difficulty, you have an option to save—unless, of course, you're a masochist and/or enjoy putting your players through the perils of permadeath and starting over. Then, by all means, skip this section.

There are different reasons, and consequently, ways with which you can implement a save option for players. For example, your game may allow a player to save any time and anywhere. Games like *Tomb Raider II* and *Abe's Oddysee* offer such approaches to saving. Typically, this option is provided via the pause menu, and the player is allocated a set number of slots that they can use to save. Alternatively, you may also have checkpoints that automatically save at specific locations, such as before and/or after an important event during gameplay. Games like *Army of Two* offer this to players. Other options can include specific locations or save points that a player can save, which are like checkpoints, located at specific points that a player will reach within the environment during gameplay. Games like *Final Fantasy X* offer this, as shown in the following screenshot:

Save Orb is located on the right-hand side of the screenshot taken during gameplay of Final Fantasy X

Creating a save/load system in Unity

There are different ways to save and load your game in Unity. For instance, you can encode your data into a file, and this gives you maximum freedom. In fact, you can allow players to save on your server, encrypt the file, and decide exactly how this file is structured. However, for beginners, this might not be the easiest approach, since Unity already offers a basic save system called **PlayerPrefs**. This system is great because it supports all the platforms, meaning you won't have to change code depending on which platform (Computer, Android, and more) you are going to ship in. Also, the system is very intuitive. With this said, let's dive into it.

PlayerPrefs

PlayerPrefs, as the name suggests, has been created with the purpose to save and store the player's preferences. In fact, this data is not sensitive, meaning that if the player can change those externally from the game, it's not a big deal. As a result, PlayerPrefs is very simple, and it works with a key-value system. However, often it is used to store game data as well, due to its simplicity and the built-in support in Unity. Although you can extend their functionalities with some plugins that you find in the Asset Store (for example, in order to encrypt the data), I suggest using a custom save/load system if you are planning to ship the game.

PlayerPrefs is useful also to debug functionalities when the save/load system is under construction, or just to store (as they are meant to be) your player preferences.

How do they work in practice? You can imagine that each PlayerPrefs is a pair containing a key, which has to be unique across all the PlayerPrefs, and a value. While the key is always a string, the value can be of different types. In particular, the basic types that Unity supports are:

- Integers (`int`)
- Decimal numbers (`float`)
- Strings (`string`)

However, these types can be extended with wrappers around these basic types. For instance, a Vector3 can be stored as three PlayerPrefs, one for each axis. The wrapper then creates three keys by appending to the passed key a suffix indicating the axis. In any case, we will stick to these basic types, which are more than enough for what we need. Here are some examples of possible key-value pairs, and in brackets, the type of the value:

- `<Score, 10>` (`int`)
- `<Time, 12,5>` (`float`)
- `<PlayerName, "John">` (`string`)

PlayerPrefs functions

From a code point of view, there are functions that allow us to interact with the system. They are all within the `PlayerPrefs` class, and they are static functions, so you don't need to instantiate a `PlayerPref` object. Rather, in your code, type PlayerPrefs followed by the name of the function you want to call: `PlayerPrefs.NameOfTheFunction()`. Obviously, the previous function doesn't exist, but it was an example of a function call.

Since these functions are not so many, let's see them all. The following three functions (one for each value type) set the pair `<key, value>`:

- `void SetInt(string key, int value)`: Stores (or overrides, in case it already exists) an integer value type associated with the key
- `void SetFloat(string key, float value)`: Stores (or overrides, in case it already exists) a decimal number value type associated with the key
- `void SetString(string key, string value)`: Stores (or overrides, in case it already exists) a string value type associated with the key

Similar to the preceding three functions, we have the three twin functions that instead of storing, retrieve the values based on the key. Keep in mind that if the key doesn't exist, they return the default value of the type:

- `int GetInt(string key)`: Retrieves (if it exists) the integer value associated with the key passed as a parameter
- `float GetFloat(string key)`: Retrieves (if it exists) the decimal number value associated with the key passed as a parameter
- `string GetString(string key)`: Retrieves (if it exists) the string value associated with the key passed as a parameter

Since we have said that the value might not exist, we have a function to check whether a specific key has an association within a pair:

- `bool HasKey(string key)`: Returns a Boolean, indicating whether the key passed as the parameter exists or not

Finally, here are a couple of functions to delete the pairs of values:

- `void DeleteKey(string key)`: Deletes (if it exists) the pair with the key specified as the parameter
- `void DeleteAll()`: Erases all the `<key, value>` pairs, thus erasing all the saved data

There is also a special function that forces the saving of memory. In fact, when we use a set, the save happens only within the context of the application/game, thus improving performance. Although when you close the game, Unity flushes everything in memory and thus saves. However, sometimes you want to force this process to happen before the game is closed (maybe after have saved important data, for example). This can be done with the following function:

- `void Save()`: Saves all the `<key, value>` pairs into the permanent memory

Variables to save in RETROformer

When you think about a save/load system, you want to save the variables that describe the player's progress or the game world state. In general, this might not be an easy step.

In the case of RETROformer, let's list what we would like to store to *save* the game. First of all, we may want to store the level (in case we have implemented more than one level), as well as the player's location in the world. Moreover, we want to save the score, and the time elapsed since the game started. This last piece of information is useful for players to understand how long they have been playing the game. Here is an example of saved games that contain the time elapsed (taken from *Horizon Zero Dawn* for PS4):

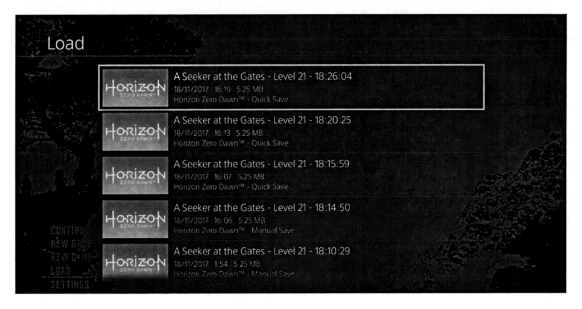

So, let's recap the variables we want to store for our game, and associate to each one of them a type:

- **Level**: We can store the level either as a string or as an integer. For simplicity's sake, we will go for the integer.
- **Position**: We cannot store this as a single PlayerPref, thus we will need two `<key, value>` pairs, one for each axis, both of type float.
- **Time Elapsed** so far: Clearly, this is a float type.
- **Score**: This depends on how you implement the score. If you followed the scoring system made for the other two projects, then the score will be an integer type.
- **Player's name**: This is a string, so we can showcase the use of this type as well.

Finally, we need to assign a unique key to each of these values, and then we will be ready to go. For the association, let's have a look to the following table:

What	Key	Value Type
Last level the player has played	Level	Integer
Last position of the player along the x-axis	PositionX	Float
Last position of the player along the y-axis	PositionY	Float
Time elapsed since the beginning of the game	Time	Float
The score that the player has reached	Score	Integer
The player's name	PlayerName	String

Building the save/load system for our game

In order to integrate the save/load system, we need to create a static class that will take care of saving and loading for us. Here, we need to take an important decision: whether this class will retrieve the information that it requires to save (such as level, score, and so on), or whether we pass them as parameters and rely on other scripts to do that.

In our case, we have a simple game so we can choose either. As a rule of thumb, you want to decouple the save system as much as possible. However, you should still have a central script that manages to do the saving, such as the **GameManager**, which is responsible for retrieving all the data needed for saving. Thus, we will go in passing as parameters the data to our save/load script, even if the system we are going to build is not generic but specific to our game. In particular, we will create a struct within the save/load script, which will hold the data to save. As a result, it will be easier to pass data as well as return it back, and you will have a chance to learn something new.

Furthermore, since we want our save/load system to support different save slots, we can add in front of any key (a prefix) the name of the slot in which the player wants to save. If you let the player decide the slot name, then you should also include the name of the slot in the save data. Otherwise, if the player can choose between just a finite set of slots, such as three, then the GameManager can handle this information based on which slot the player has clicked on the UI. Of course, this part will be left as an exercise since this chapter will focus only on the save/load system. However, later in the chapter, some suggestions are given to enhance the gameplay of this last game. Lastly, some hits are provided on where to use this system.

Let's start by creating a new C# Script and name it `SaveLoadSystem`, and you can remove the inheritance from MonoBehaviour and set is as static class since it will contain only static methods. First of all, we need to create the `struct`, so below the last }, we need to add the following struct:

```
using System.Collections;
using System.Collections.Generic;
using UnityEngine;

public static class SaveLoadSystem {
            //[...]
}

public struct SavingData {

    public int level;
    public float positionX, positionY;
    public int score;
    public float timeElapsed;
    public string playerName;

}
```

A `struct` is not much different than a class in C#, and this struct doesn't have any methods, just the data fields we have seen in the previous table.

 Although it's good practice to have a class and a struct per file, here, due to the very simple structure and the dependency with the main class of the file, we chose to keep it within the same file.

Now, we can start writing our script. In particular, we need two functions: one to save and another one to load. Let's start with the first one.

The `Save()` function will receive a `SavingData` structure as a parameter, as well as the string denoting the save slot. The function goes through all the data in the structure, builds new keys based on the save slot string, and sets all the data within PlayerPrefs. At the end, it calls the `Save()` function to actually save all the data on the permanent memory (for example, the hard drive):

```
public static void Save(string slotKey, SavingData data) {
        //Save into PlayerPrefs for each data item within the SavingData
structure
        PlayerPrefs.SetInt(slotKey + "_level", data.level);
        PlayerPrefs.SetFloat(slotKey + "_positionX", data.positionX);
        PlayerPrefs.SetFloat(slotKey + "_positionY", data.positionY);
        PlayerPrefs.SetInt(slotKey + "_score", data.score);
        PlayerPrefs.SetFloat(slotKey + "_time", data.timeElapsed);
        PlayerPrefs.SetString(slotKey + "_playerName", data.playerName);

        //Save into permanent memory
        PlayerPrefs.Save();
    }
```

On the other hand, we have the `Load()` function, which gives back a `SavingData` structure and takes as input the save slot key. As a result, the function is able to query the `PlayerPrefs` with the get-functions and store all the data within a newly created `SavingData` structure. At the end, it just returns the structure:

```
public static SavingData Load(string slotKey) {
        //Create a new SavingData structure
        SavingData data = new SavingData();

        //Load from memory each item to fill up the data structure
        data.level = PlayerPrefs.GetInt(slotKey + "_level");
        data.positionX = PlayerPrefs.GetFloat(slotKey + "_positionX");
        data.positionY = PlayerPrefs.GetFloat(slotKey + "_positionY");
        data.score = PlayerPrefs.GetInt(slotKey + "_score");
```

```
data.timeElapsed = PlayerPrefs.GetFloat(slotKey + "_time");
data.playerName = PlayerPrefs.GetString(slotKey + "_playerName");

//return the data structure
return data;
}
```

Refining the save and load system

If you want to be more sophisticated with your save and load system, then you will need three more functions.

The first one checks whether a save slot is available in the memory or not. Although you can implement this functionality within the load function (for example, returning null), for the sake of simplicity, we will create a separate function that returns a Boolean indicating whether the slot is available or not. This is useful when you need to show to the player which slots are empty or which ones are taken. The function is really simple, it just needs to check whether the key passed as a parameter exists. We can do this by checking only one of the data, which we have prefixed with the key.. In fact, if we do things right, we should have incomplete saving slots in which just partial information is available. Thus, here is the function:

```
public static bool HasSlot(string slotKey) {
    //Check whether the slotkey exist
    return PlayerPrefs.HasKey(slotKey + "_level");
}
```

Another useful function deletes a specific save slot. This can be done by taking in input the key and erasing all the items related to that slot. Here, you need to be sure to erase them all, especially if you don't want to have a problem with the function HasSlot():

```
public static void DeleteSlot(string slotKey) {
    //Delete the whole slot, item by item
    PlayerPrefs.DeleteKey(slotKey + "_level");
    PlayerPrefs.DeleteKey(slotKey + "_positionX");
    PlayerPrefs.DeleteKey(slotKey + "_positionY");
    PlayerPrefs.DeleteKey(slotKey + "_score");
    PlayerPrefs.DeleteKey(slotKey + "_time");
    PlayerPrefs.DeleteKey(slotKey + "_playerName");
}
```

Finally, a function that clears all the slots might be useful. In this case, the only things you save with PlayerPrefs are the slots. Therefore, we can easily use `DeleteAll()`, as we are about to do. Otherwise, you need a loop that calls the `DeleteSlot()` function on each one of the slots. In our case, the function is just a wrapper for the `DeleteAll()` function:

```
public static void DeleteAllSlots() {
    //Delete all the PlayerPrefs
    PlayerPrefs.DeleteAll();
}
```

Save the script and congratulate yourself, since now you have a working save and load system.

Jump pads

Up, up, and away with jump pads. These beautiful things give you that extra lift in precarious situations or when you can't quite reach that ledge with the golden key. But how can we implement them?

If you are trying to simulate a material that has a lot of bounciness, such as the trampolines that you went on when you were a kid, then just create a material with a lot of bounciness. However, often in games, jump pads are more platforms in which if you jump from them, your jumping boost is enhanced. So, let's implement the possibility to place Jump Pads in our level.

Creating the Jump Pad

First of all, we need to create the Jump Pad. Our Graphical package comes with a very nice jump pad sprite:

First, drag one of them into the map. We need to add a collider in order to prevent the player from going on the Jump Pad. Then, create a child **gameobject** and name it **Jump Pad Trigger Collider**. Next, set as a **Tag** for this second game object **Jump Pad**. Add a collider as well, and adjust the **Size** and **Offset** in such a way that the collider is just above the Jump Pad. Also, check the **isTrigger** variable, as shown in the following screenshot:

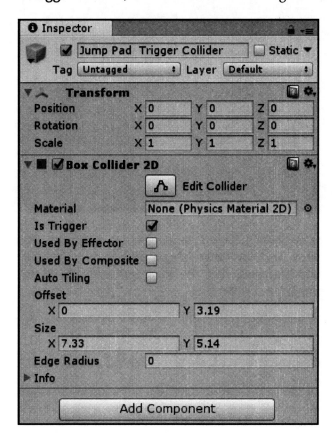

This is how it should look in the game:

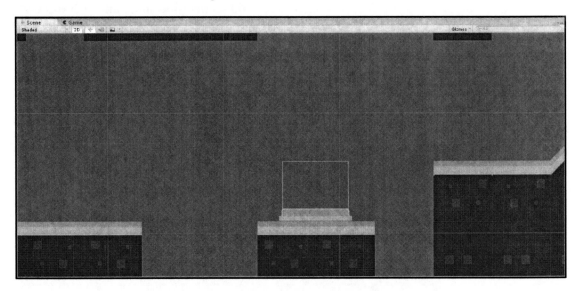

If you remember from the *Angel Cakes* collecting system, when the player comes in contact with a cake, it is collected. This was done using a special Unity function named **OnTriggerEnter2D**, which detects when the player entered the collider of the cake. Here, we are going to do something similar.

Open the **Movement Component** script, and let's add a variable called `onJumpPad` of type bool:

```
private bool onJumpPad = false;
```

Another variable is needed to determine how much the Jump Pad should push our hero up in the sky. A **serialized private float variable** will do the trick:

```
[SerializeField]
private float jumpPadMultiplier = 2;
```

Then, we create the `OnTriggerEnter2D()` function, in which we check whether the new collider has the tag **JumpPad**, and if so, we set `onJumpPad` to true:

```
public void OnTriggerEnter2D(Collider2D collision) {
    if (collision.gameObject.CompareTag("JumpPad")) {
        onJumpPad = true;
    }
}
```

Similarly, we need a `OnTriggerExit2D()` function to disable the `onJumpPad` variable by setting it to `false`:

```
public void OnTriggerExit2D(Collider2D collision) {
    if (collision.gameObject.CompareTag("JumpPad")) {
        onJumpPad = false;
    }
}
```

Finally, in the `Jump()` function, we need to modify the code. If the `onJumpPad` variable is `true`, then the `JumpForce` is multiplied by the `JumpPadMultiplier` variable. As a result, if `onJumpPad` is true, then the force of the jump will be much more:

```
public void Jump() {
    //Check if the character can jump
    Debug.Log(Physics2D.Linecast(transform.position,
    groundCheck.position, 1
    << LayerMask.NameToLayer("Ground")).collider);
    if (Physics2D.Linecast(transform.position, groundCheck.position, 1
    << LayerMask.NameToLayer("Ground"))) {
        if (rb2d.velocity.y <= 0) {
            //Perform the jump (multiply by jumpPadMultiplier if
                onJumpPad is true)
                rb2d.AddForce(new Vector2
        (0f, onJumpPad ? jumpForce*jumpPadMultiplier : jumpForce));
        }
    }
}
```

Of course, the function will look a bit different if in the previous chapter you used the alternative version. In any case, it's not a problem, since you just need to substitute the highlighted code from the function you wrote. However, the way that we have written the modified `AddForce()` function above might still be confusing, due to the ternary operator `?`. Again, below is shown a simplified version, which does not use the ternary operator. Feel free to choose whatever version makes more sense to you:

```
public void Jump() {
    //Check if the character can jump
    Debug.Log(Physics2D.Linecast(transform.position,
    groundCheck.position, 1
    << LayerMask.NameToLayer("Ground")).collider);
    if (Physics2D.Linecast(transform.position, groundCheck.position, 1
    << LayerMask.NameToLayer("Ground"))) {
        if (rb2d.velocity.y <= 0) {
            //Set the finalJumpForce to the current one
            float finalJumpForce = jumpForce;
```

```
                      // Multiply the final jump force by jumpPadMultiplier
                      // if player is on a jump pad.
                      if (onJumpPad) finalJumpForce *= jumpPadMultiplier;

                      //Perform the jump
                      rb2d.AddForce(new Vector2(0f, finalJumpForce));
                  }
              }
          }
```

Save the script, and create a prefab of the Jump Pad you have just created. Place them in your level, and test that everything works as it should. Lastly, pat yourself on the back for your hard work.

Wrapping up gameplay

To efficiently complete our game, we still need to insert a couple of gameplay components. This section will quickly go through them, to guide you. In fact, you have already seen most of this stuff in previous chapters and with the previous projects, so for an in-depth explanation, you can revise your work on the other projects.

Creating the user interface

We have seen a lot of user interface in the past two projects. Thus, I won't bother repeating how to create a score or a lives counter along with their respective scripts. Rather, this is left as an exercise for you. In particular, you can challenge yourself with the following:

- **Game Over Screen**: When the player falls in the water, a screen message should appear to the player saying that it's game over. Once you have created this screen, you can integrate it with the **WaterZone** script of the next section.
- **Winning Screen**: Very similar to the *Game Over Screen*, this message appears to the player when he or she finishes the game (reaches the end of the level). Prepare this message, so you can integrate it with the **WinningZone** script a couple of sections ahead.
- **Score System**: Create a scoring system in which the player collects objects around the map and earns points doing so. The scoring system should have the following features:
    - Show the score on-screen
    - Save the score with the Save System we created before

- Keep between levels (meaning that the score needs to be loaded at the beginning of each level, or put into a persistent scene)
- **Main Menu**: Create a main menu for your game, in which the player can load a previous save so the player can choose a slot. Otherwise, the player can choose a new slot and start a new game. However, before the game starts, the system should ask the player for the name.
- **Leaderboard**: If you are in the mood for a challenge, why not try implementing a leaderboard? Order the different players that you have for the slots in a leaderboard, showing first who has the highest score.

Keep in mind that we're not yet done completely with the user interface. If you recall from Chapter 10, *Let's Get Physical*, the Movement Component can take input also from UI controllers, to adapt the game to run on mobile devices. This is something that we are going to explore and learn in the next chapter.

As for the moment, let's finish up our gameplay!

Water zones

In our level, like in the following screenshot, there is water. Therefore we need to decide what happens when the player falls into the water.

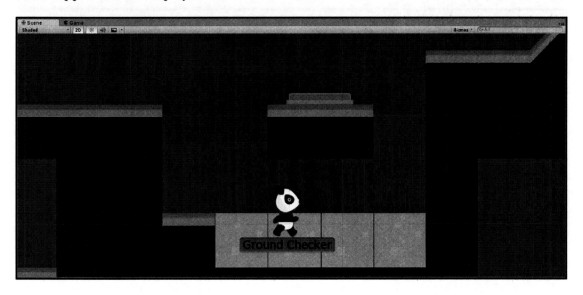

First of all, we need to adjust the water **Sorting Layer**, so that it appears preceding the player. So, select the child of **Water** from the **Hierarchy** panel, and change the **Sorting Layer** to **2** in the **Sorting Layer Exposed (Script)** component, shown as follows:

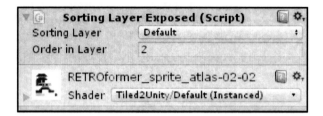

This is how it now appears in the game:

Water already has a collider, but we need to set it as **Is Trigger**, if it is not already:

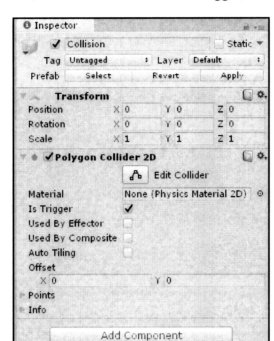

Also, Unity comes with a **Water** layer as default, so we can just set it as **Water** for good practice, and so change all its children as well:

Now, we need to create a script to restart the level once the player falls in the water (in our case, touches the water).

Let's start by creating a new C# script and naming it `WaterZone`. Let's add the requirement for a collider at the beginning of the class:

```
[RequireComponent(typeof(Collider2D))]
public class WaterZone : MonoBehaviour {
        //[...]
}
```

Next, we need to add the *using-statement* to use the Scene Manager (otherwise, as we did in our Space Shooter game, when we implement the lives counter, we can reference it directly within the line of code):

```
using UnityEngine.SceneManagement;

[RequireComponent(typeof(Collider2D))]
public class WaterZone : MonoBehaviour {
        //[...]
}
```

Afterwards, we can use the `OnTriggerEnter2D()` function to detect when the player touches the water. However, we don't want to immediately restart the scene as soon as the player touches the water, we need to insert a delay. To do so, let's implement a coroutine. Add a new variable to set how much delay should pass before restarting the level:

```
[SerializeField]
private float timeDelay = 1.0f;
```

Then, implement the coroutine. The first thing shown is a **Game Over** message (which is left as an exercise), then the script waits for `timeDelay` before restarting the scene:

```
private IEnumerator restartScene() {
    //Show a gameover message (left as exercise)

    //Wait timeDelay
    yield return new WaitForSeconds(timeDelay);

    //Restart Scene
    SceneManager.LoadScene("level1"); //substitute "level1" with
    the name of your level,
    also be sure to add the scene to the build settings
}
```

If you don't want to hardcode the name of your scene into the script, you can reload the same scene which is currently active in the `SceneManager`. Here is the code you need:

```
//Get the name of the current scene (i.e. level)
string sceneName = SceneManager.GetActiveScene().name;
//(Re-)load the same scene / level.
SceneManager.LoadScene(sceneName);
```

Finally, implement the `OnTriggerEnter2D()` function by starting the `restartScene()` coroutine:

```
private void OnTriggerEnter2D(Collider2D collision) {
    //If the player enters within the Water Zone,
    then restart the scene
    if (collision.CompareTag("Player")) {
        StartCoroutine(restartScene());
    }
}
```

Save the script and add it to the **Water** game object. From now on, every time the player touches the water, the game will restart after a small delay.

Winning zone

Similar to what we did for the Water zone, we need to create an endpoint for our map. Once the player reaches the endpoint, the game will show a message (left as an exercise) and load the next level. Since the structure is so similar to the Water zone, here is the direct script, which should be self-explanatory:

```
using UnityEngine;
using UnityEngine.SceneManagement;

[RequireComponent(typeof(Collider2D))]
public class WinningZone : MonoBehaviour {

    [SerializeField]
    private float timeDelay = 1.0f;

    [SerializeField]
    private string nextLevelToLoad = "level2";
    //substitute with the next level to load.
    Be sure it is included in the build settings.

    private IEnumerator loadNextLevel() {
        //Show a winning message (left as exercise)
```

```
        //Wait timeDelay
        yield return new WaitForSeconds(timeDelay);

        //Restart Scene
        SceneManager.LoadScene(nextLevelToLoad);
        //load the level named as in the nextLevelToLoad variable.
    }

    private void OnTriggerEnter2D(Collider2D collision) {
        //If the player enters within the Water Zone,
        then restart the scene
        if (collision.CompareTag("Player")) {
            StartCoroutine(loadNextLevel());
        }
    }
}
```

Enhancing the environment

The environment that you have created in Tiled is great, but at the same time, it is a bit empty. Have a look at this portion of the environment now:

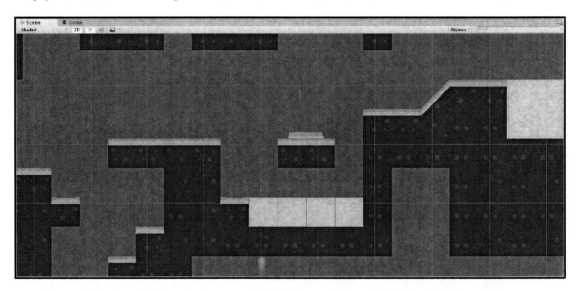

Thus, we need to bring decorative props into it! Thankfully, our package comes with great props, such as trees.

If you didn't, slice them with the **Sprite Editor**, to have all of them on different sprites. Then, drag them into the world and fill it as per your taste. Just remember to set the right **Sorting Layers** for it. In my case, I would go for a **Sorting Layer** of **0** or **-1** to be aligned with the terrain or behind it so the character will pass over it. In case you want to create an obstacle or a collectable, you can place it to a higher **Sorting Layer**, such as **2** or **3**. However, you need to remember to add a collider for it (and set isTrigger to true in the case of collectable, along with an appropriate script).

Here is one possible result in arranging props in the level:

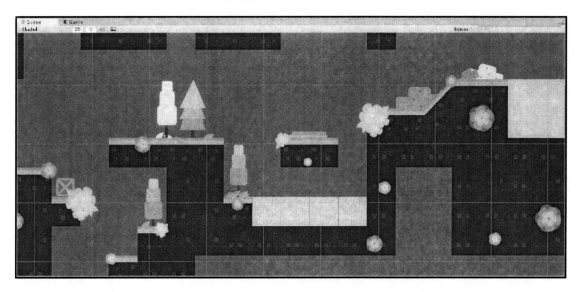

Finally, don't forget to share your creation, and to use your imagination and add props designed and drawn by you. Also, don't forget to add a nice background as well. You can find one in the graphics package you have downloaded.

Testing

Lastly, you should test your game. And after that, test again, and test again later on. Testing is an important phase during the development of your game, and you shouldn't ignore it.

Go through your game as an entirety, ask a friend or a relative to test your game, and observe any unwanted behavior. Write all the bugs down, and try to fix them one by one. After that, repeat the process and test your game again. When you are quite confident that there are no more "big" bugs, then you can continue with Chapter 12, *The Nature Of Export*, and export your game for publication.

Summary

So far, Chapter 11, *Don't Forget to Save!*, has covered how to create a save and load system for RETROformer. In particular, we explored the use of PlayerPrefs as an easy and built-in way for creating a save and load system. On the way, we learned a bit about structures and how they can be used to pass a large chunk of data between functions.

Lastly, this chapter concluded by suggesting to the reader how to implement some gameplay elements to enhance the gameplay.

Next, in Chapter 12, *The Nature Of Export*, we will learn how to export our game to various platforms (PC, iOS, Android). In addition, we will discuss how the input for the Movement Component can come from the UI so that touchscreen input can be used to move the character as well.

12
The Nature of Export

In this final chapter, we will learn about the final steps of producing a game. First of all, we will finish implementing our control scheme so that the game can also be played on mobile devices with touchscreens. We will use the Unity UI to achieve that.

Then, we will look at the very basics of the steps required to export the game. This will be enough to see your game running independently from Unity, either as a Standalone or on an Android device. However, building the game involves many other steps (optimizing the game, the content, the rendering, and so on) that are appropriate for more advanced users of Unity, and thus outside the scope of this book.

In particular, we will cover:

- Finishing the UI controller so that the player can control our Panda Hero from touchscreens.
- Exporting the game in general for Android devices.

With that said, let's get going!

Implementing mobile input for the game

One last step to conclude our game is to make it mobile friendly. So far, we can move the character only with a keyboard, but what about mobile devices with a touchscreen instead? If you remember the controls from Chapter 10, *Let's Get Physical*, we implemented the Movement Component independently from the input. As a result, the Player Controller script is responsible for gathering the input from the player to send it to the character. Also, we made the **Player Controller** inactive in the case of mobile devices, which is great. However, now it's time to implement the controller for the touchscreen. This will compile when the game runs neither in the Editor or in a standalone version.

To implement the system, we will use the UI system in Unity, which is already suitable for gathering input from touchscreens. Let's start by creating a UI image by right-clicking on the **Hierarchy** panel and then on **UI/Image**. We can use the graphics provided in our package. In this case, the graphic that we need looks like a triangular button. Using the knowledge we learned from Chapter 11, *Don't Forget to Save!*, let's scale it to the right size and place it well in the UI. Then, duplicate it and place another arrow next to it. Finally, use the up arrow from the other side of the screen, like in the following screenshot:

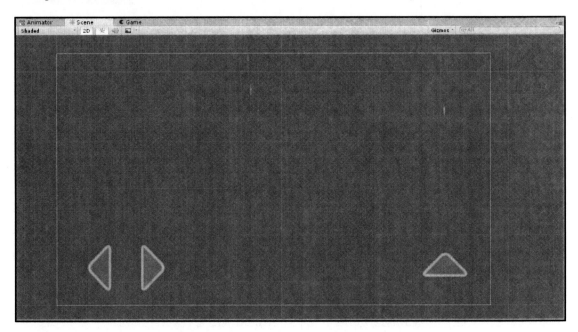

Wonderful! Now we can make them interactive with a bit of scripting.

MovingController

So, let's create a new C# script and name it `UI_MovingController`. First of all, we need to add a *using-statement* so we can use the Handlers for the Unity Event System. To do so, add this line before the declaration of the class:

```
using UnityEngine;
using UnityEngine.EventSystems;
public class UI_MovingController : MonoBehaviour {
    //[...]
}
```

Then, in the declaration of the class itself, we need to implement two interfaces to intercept every time that this button is pressed or released. As a result, we can determine when the button is held down. The first interface is IPointerDownHandler, whereas the second one is IPointerUpHandler. You can write them after the inheritance from MonoBehaviour, as shown in the following code:

```
public class UI_MovingController : MonoBehaviour, IPointerDownHandler,
IPointerUpHandler {
    //[...]
}
```

Before we implement the interface, we need to add a couple of variables. The first one is to store the reference to the **Movement Component** of our character. The second variable is the direction, which indicates if this is the button that goes right or left, respectively placing a value of +1 or −1. These must be private variables, but serializable so that they can be set in the **Inspector**:

```
[SerializeField]
private MovementComponent movementComponent;

[SerializeField]
private float direction = +1f;
```

Also, we need a third variable to store whether the button is held down, which needs to be private:

```
private bool isHolding;
```

Now, in the Awake() function, we need to check if we are running in a mobile environment. If not, we destroy the whole button from the interface, since we don't need to show it anymore:

```
void Awake() {
    //Destroy this script in case we are not running on mobile
    #if !(UNITY_STANDALONE || UNITY_EDITOR)
    Destroy(gameObject);
    #endif
}
```

In the `Awake()` function, we can also check that the reference to the Movement Component is properly set:

```
void Awake() {
    //Destroy this script in case we are not running on mobile
    #if !(UNITY_STANDALONE || UNITY_EDITOR)
    Destroy(gameObject);
    #endif

    //Disable this script in case the Movement Component reference is not
set and leave an error message.
    if (movementComponent == null) {
        Debug.LogError("Missing reference on MovementComponent on " +
gameObject.name + " to run the Controller. Please add the reference.");
        Destroy(this);
    }
}
```

Next, we can implement our interfaces. In the first one, with the `OnPointerDown()` function, we just need to set `isHolding` to `true`:

```
public void OnPointerDown(PointerEventData eventData) {
    isHolding = true;
}
```

Similarly, for the second interface with the function `OnPointerUp()`, we set `isHolding` to false:

```
public void OnPointerUp(PointerEventData eventData) {
    isHolding = false;
}
```

Finally, in the `LateUpdate()` function (`LateUpdate()` because the Movement Component uses Rigidbody2D; that's why we don't use the `Update()` function instead, we pass the direction to the Movement Component if `isHolding` is set to `true`:

```
private void LateUpdate() {
    if (isHolding) {
        movementComponent.MoveCharacter(direction);
    }
}
```

As you can see, we always pass a value of one. The axis implementation of the keyboard instead passes increasing values up to one (similarly when the key is released). This gives smoother movements. As an exercise, you can try to implement something similar for this button by taking into consideration for how long it has been pressed.

Save the script and add it to both the buttons. Remember to reference the Movement Component, as well as placing the right direction for the button (**+1** for right and **-1** for left). This is the setup for the left button:

JumpController

Create a new C# script and name it `UI_JumpController`. As we did for the `UI_MovementController`, we need to insert the using-statement for using the `EventSystems`:

```
using UnityEngine;
using UnityEngine.EventSystems;

public class UI_JumpController : MonoBehaviour {
    //[...]
}
```

Then, we need to implement just the `IPointerDownHandler`, because we don't need to check when the button is held, but rather jump every time the button is pressed:

```
public class UI_JumpController : MonoBehaviour, IPointerDownHandler {
//[...]
}
```

Again, the Movement Component variable is needed, but it's the only variable we need this time:

```
[SerializeField]
private MovementComponent movementComponent;
```

In the `Awake()` function, we still need to check if it's running in a mobile environment (if not, we can destroy the whole button from the interface):

```
void Awake() {
    //Destroy this script in case we are not running on mobile
    #if !(UNITY_STANDALONE || UNITY_EDITOR)
    Destroy(gameObject);
    #endif
}
```

We also need to check if we have the reference to the Movement Component:

```
void Awake() {
    //Destroy this script in case we are not running on mobile
    #if !(UNITY_STANDALONE || UNITY_EDITOR)
    Destroy(gameObject);
    #endif

    //Disable this script in case the Movement Component reference is not
set and leave an error message.
    if (movementComponent == null) {
        Debug.LogError("Missing reference on MovementComponent on " +
gameObject.name + " to run the Controller. Please add the reference.");
    Destroy(this);
    }
}
```

Finally, in the implementation of the interface, we can make the call directly to the `Jump()` function of the Movement Component:

```
public void OnPointerDown(PointerEventData eventData) {
    movementComponent.Jump();
}
```

Save the script and attach it to the **Jump** button. Then, set the reference to the **Movement Component**, and we are good to go. This is how it should look in the **Inspector**:

Exporting the game

Drum roll! The game is now finished and it's time to export. Unlike the other chapters, we'll also cover how to export the game to mobile devices such as iOS and Android. You can use the same approach for the other games, should you also wish to export them to mobile devices. In addition, we'll also cover some best practices for exporting to mobile devices. However, keep in mind that we didn't rearrange the input to work on a mobile device. In that case, it's better if you refer to a specific book about mobile game development.

For a standalone build, if you want to build your game as an executable to run on a PC or Mac, Unity offers a simple process to do so:

1. Open the **Build Settings**. You can find this by navigating to the top menu, **File | Build Settings**, or via the keyboard shortcut *Ctrl + Shift + B* (or *command + Shift + B* on a Mac).
2. Highlight the **PC, Mac & Linux Standalone** item from the **Platform** list.
3. Add the scenes by dragging them into the **Scenes In Build** list box.
   - Adjust more detailed settings by pressing the **Player Settings...** button; if you leave the default, the build will succeed (whereas for Android you will need to change at least the identifier, and be sure to have the right libraries installed—this will be explained later in the chapter).

4. Press **Build** and choose where to save the game:

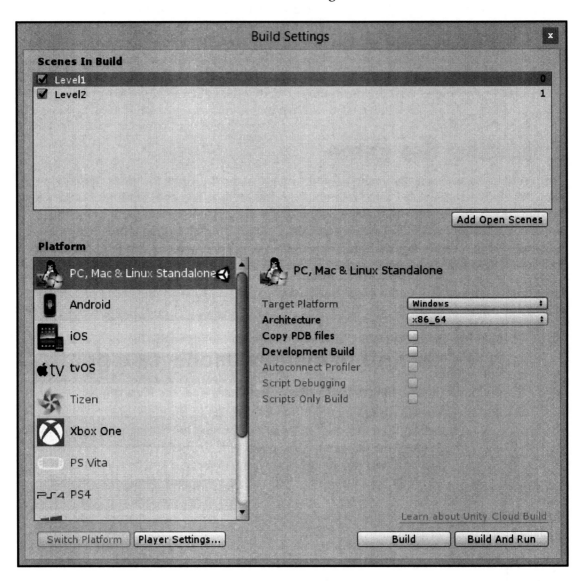

Navigate to the folder where you have exported your game, double-click on the `.exe` file, and your game will start.

For Android

Let's begin with Android. There are a few additional things that we will need to download and do before we can be completely ready to export anything from Unity to use on an Android device. We will cover what these things are, how to set them up, and how you can then export the projects in this book for Android (and later iOS) devices:

1. To begin, we first need to download and install Android Studio by visiting the following link: `https://developer.android.com/studio/index.html`. This is a pretty straightforward process, so for now, just follow the installation wizard and make sure that you install it in an ideal location (for example, the programs folder).

2. Next, make sure that you have enabled developer options on your Android device. The location of this setting may vary depending on the phone, so if you can't locate it, please consult your phone's manual. In general, you will be able to locate it here: **Settings | About phone | Build number**. In the developer options, you will also find the **Install from Unknown sources** option, which allows you to install your exported game for testing . We will discuss this later in the chapter.

   Here is an example of this process on a specific device: the Galaxy S7.

   You need to navigate to **Settings | About phone | Software info | Build number**. Tap several times on the **Build number** list item until there is a popup that tells you that the developer mode has been successfully unlocked.

   Usually, after having enabled the developer options, they will show up in the top-level menu of the settings dialog as a list menu item.

   Open the developer options and simply enable the first switch to permanently enable developer mode. Confirm the popup **Use development settings** with **OK** and close the settings menu.

3. Configure the Android SDK path in Unity.

   If you want to create a Google Play account so that you can publish your games and applications on the Google Play store, you can do so by visiting the following link: `https://play.google.com/apps/publish/signup/`.

   There is a one-time fee to get your account running, but then you are good to go and get publishing!

Preparing an Android Unity project

Now that we have the Android side of things taken care of, we need to get our project ready to build for an Android device.

To begin, we need to:

1. Open the **Build Settings**. You can find this by navigating to the top menu: **File | Build Settings** or via the keyboard shortcut *Ctrl + Shift + B* (or command + *Shift + B* on a Mac).
2. Highlight **Android** from the list of platforms on the left.
    - You will see, if you haven't already (as in the following image), that you need to install the *Android Module for Unity* (~116mb). Therefore, click **Open Download Page**, download it to an ideal location, and install it.
    - If you already have it installed, then click **Switch Platform**, located in the bottom left of the dialogue box:

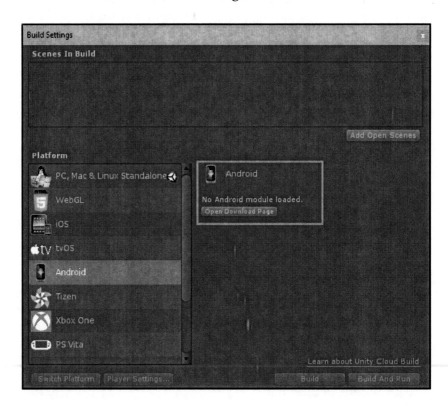

3. Once you have done that, you will need to restart Unity so that the module will load. After you have done this, you will see the following screen with an array of different options for building on an Android device:

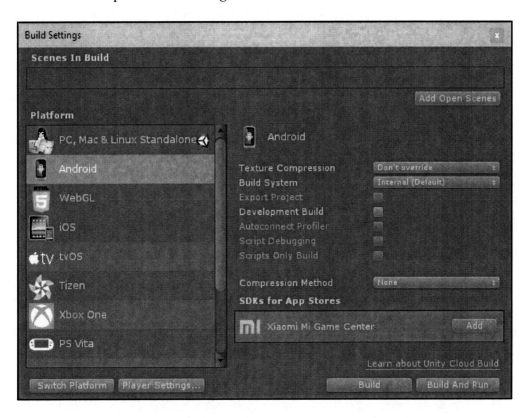

4. Then, you need to click on the **Player Settings...** button. You will have in the **Inspector** all the settings to export your game and to build it on a specific platform. You can set the name of your company, and the name of the game, as well as an icon. In particular, if you select the **Android** tab, you will have four sub-tabs, as shown in the following screenshot:

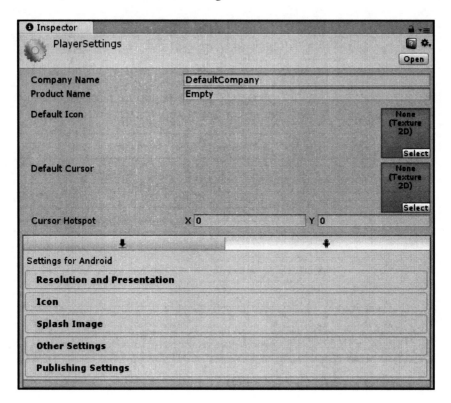

5. If you open the **Other Settings** tab, you will have many options. The most important ones, at least to have a successful build, are under the **Identification** label. These settings allow you to uniquely identify your game and set the requirements to make it run. The **Package Name** should be in the form com.YourCompany.YourGameName, a unique identifier. Be sure to change it before you do any builds:

Other Settings

Rendering

Color Space*	Gamma
Auto Graphics API	☑
Multithreaded Rendering*	☐
Static Batching	☑
Dynamic Batching	☑
GPU Skinning*	☐
Graphics Jobs (Experimental)*	☐
Virtual Reality Supported	☐
Protect Graphics Memory	☐

Identification

Package Name	com.Company.ProductName
Version*	1.0
Bundle Version Code	1
Minimum API Level	Android 4.1 'Jelly Bean' (API level 16)
Target API Level	Automatic (highest installed)

Configuration

Scripting Runtime Version*	Stable (.NET 3.5 Equivalent)
Scripting Backend	Mono
Api Compatibility Level*	.NET 2.0 Subset
Mute Other Audio Sources*	☐
Disable HW Statistics*	☐
Device Filter	FAT (ARMv7+x86)
Install Location	Prefer External
Internet Access	Auto
Write Permission	Internal
Android TV Compatibility	☑
Android Game	☑
Android Gamepad Support Level	Works with D-pad
Scripting Define Symbols*	

Optimization

Prebake Collision Meshes*	☐
Keep Loaded Shaders Alive*	☐
▶ Preloaded Assets*	
Stripping Level*	Disabled
Enable Internal Profiler* (Deprec	☐
Vertex Compression*	Mixed ...
Optimize Mesh Data*	☐

The other options under **Identification** are pretty straightforward. Remember that it is important to change and/or update the version of your game every time you publish an update.

After you have finished that, you can come back to the build menu. If you click on the **Switch Platform** button, the Unity Logo will move next to **Android,** as shown in the screenshot. Keep in mind that the process might take several minutes, depending on the size of your project:

Finally, you will need to add scenes into the build by dragging and dropping them to the preceding space. In the following screenshot, I'll insert **Level1** and **Level2** (which I created):

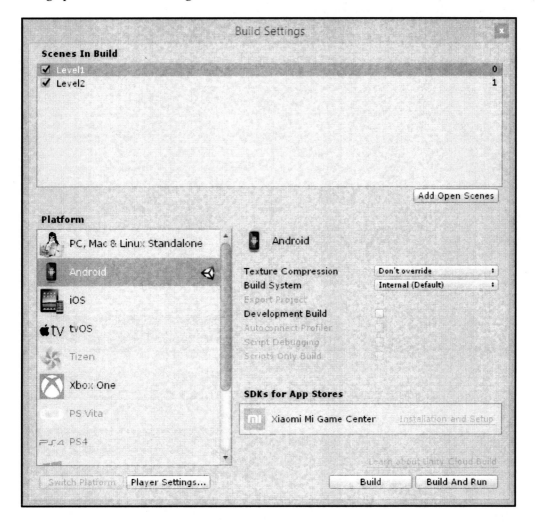

One last thing before we export the game. We need to decide if this is a **Development Build** or not. Since our game has just two levels, and we want to add more to it before we release it, we can check the **Development Build** checkbox. This way, not only will the **Development Build** appear, but you will have access to a series of debug tools (outside of the scope of this book) that were otherwise not available. In fact, once checked, you will have another three checkboxes for these debug tools:

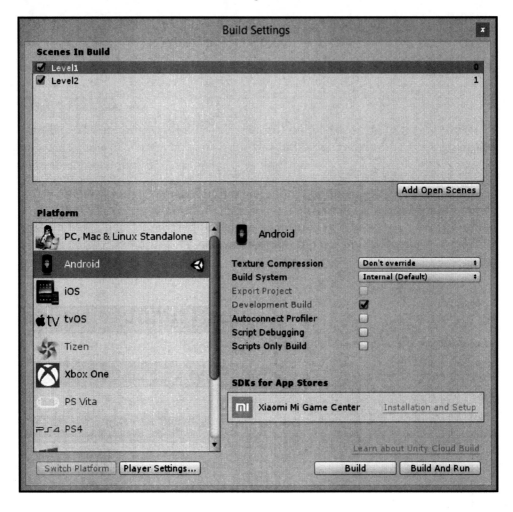

Now, you are ready to export by pressing the **Build** button. Unity will ask you where to export the .apk file to. Once you do this, you can import it to your phone in any location and install it.

 If this is the first time you've developed for an Android phone, you might want to enable **Install from Unknown sources** in the developer options on your phone. Modern Android systems might redirect on that option when you try to install a .apk, such as the game you have just built. However, on older Android systems, you need to enable the developer mode. How to enable it might depend on your phone, but usually, you do it by tapping seven times on the build version in your system info (as explained earlier in the chapter).

Summary

We started the chapter by using UI elements to interact with touchscreens so that our game could work on mobile devices.

Then, we moved onto describing how to export the game, with a particular focus on Android builds. We have covered many of the basic topics when it comes to learning about 2D game development in Unity. Congratulations!

If there is one important thing that you should continue to do on your journey as a game developer, it is to never stop learning. Technology changes so quickly, and therefore software and hardware are always advancing and quickly becoming obsolete. In saying that, to stay above and beyond and to ensure that your skills today are as strong as those needed for tomorrow, never stop learning.

Other Books You May Enjoy

If you enjoyed this book, you may be interested in these other books by Packt:

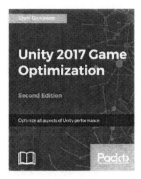

Unity 2017 Game Optimization - Second Edition
Chris Dickinson

ISBN: 978-1-78839-236-5

- Use the Unity Profiler to find bottlenecks anywhere in your application, and discover how to resolve them
- Implement best practices for C# scripting to avoid common pitfalls
- Develop a solid understanding of the rendering pipeline, and maximize its performance by reducing draw calls and avoiding fill rate bottlenecks
- Enhance shaders in a way that is accessible to most developers, optimizing them through subtle yet effective performance tweaks
- Keep your scenes as dynamic as possible by making the most of the Physics engine
- Organize, filter, and compress your art assets to maximize performance while maintaining high quality
- Discover different kinds of performance problems that are critical for VR projects and how to tackle them
- Use the Mono Framework and C# to implement low-level enhancements that maximize memory usage and avoid garbage collection
- Get to know the best practices for project organization to save time through an improved workflow

Mastering Unity 2017 Game Development with C#
Alan Thorn

ISBN: 978-1-78847-983-7

- Explore hands-on tasks and real-world scenarios to make a Unity horror adventure game
- Create enemy characters that act intelligently and make reasoned decisions
- Use data files to save and restore game data in a way that is platform-agnostic
- Get started with VR development
- Use navigation meshes, occlusion culling, and Profiler tools
- Work confidently with GameObjects, rotations, and transformations
- Understand specific gameplay features such as AI enemies, inventory systems, and level design

Leave a review - let other readers know what you think

Please share your thoughts on this book with others by leaving a review on the site that you bought it from. If you purchased the book from Amazon, please leave us an honest review on this book's Amazon page. This is vital so that other potential readers can see and use your unbiased opinion to make purchasing decisions, we can understand what our customers think about our products, and our authors can see your feedback on the title that they have worked with Packt to create. It will only take a few minutes of your time, but is valuable to other potential customers, our authors, and Packt. Thank you!

Index

2

2.5D games 18
2D game development
  about 15
  reference 23
  X-axis 16
  Y-axis 16
  Z-axis 16
2D games
  about 19
  best practices 85
  with perspective camera 21
2D project
  creating, in Unity 26

3

3D environment 17
3DStudioMax 155

9

9-slicing Sprites 77, 79, 81, 83, 84

A

A-Team 14
Adobe Color CC
  reference 130
advanced animations 236
Android Unity project
  preparing 304, 306, 308, 310, 311
Android
  game, exporting 303
Angel Cakes project
  9-slicing Sprites 77, 79, 81, 83, 84
  about 49
  assets, configuring for game 68, 69, 71, 73, 75

assets, importing into engine 67
  folder setup 67
  reference 49
  setting up 65
Angel
  assembling 100
  components, enforcing 104
  creating 97
  player input, retrieving 106
  player, tagging 101
  script, creating 102, 103
  variables, exposing in inspector 104
Animation State Machine
  building 243, 244, 245, 246, 247, 248, 250
animation system
  about 154, 236, 237
  references 154
animations
  creating, from sprite sheet 242
  explosion, saving as prefab 163
  generating, from sprites 158, 160
  reference 236
  sprite sheet, setting up for 238, 239, 240, 241
  state behavior, adding for destroying explosion 160
assets, Unity
  3D model files 40
  animations 40
  audio files 41
  images 39
  importing 41
  meshes 40
  naming conventions 41
  placeholder objects 38
  primitive objects 38
Audio Listener 92
Audio Source

reference 93
audio
    about 90
    happy track, selecting 94
    importing 92
    references 94
    retro track, selecting 96
    sad track, selecting 95
    sounds, selecting for background 94
    sounds, selecting for FX 94

B

background music
    integrating, in game 96
best practices, 2D game
    naming 87
    scaling 87
    textures 85
Blender 155
bullet controller
    components, enforcing 181
    hit spaceships 184
    reference, obtaining to rigidbody 182
    variables, exposing in Inspector 181
bullet
    auto-destroying 183
    moving 183

C

Canabalt
    reference 212
collectable system
    about 108
    Angel Cakes, setting up 108
    cake, testing 113
    cake, triggering 111, 113
    components, enforcing 110
colliders
    about 99
    adding, to tiles 228
components, Unity User Interface (UI)
    Console window 33
    Game View 31
    Hierarchy Window 28, 29
    Inspector window 31
    Project window 34
    Scene View 30
control scheme
    defining 264
coroutines
    about 202
    reference 202

D

diegetic UIs 124
Doppler Effect 91

E

endless runner 212
enemy controller
    about 174
    aiming system, modifying 178
    alternative enemy controller 177
    creating 174
    movement, modifying 175
    requisites 174
    second enemy controller, creating 178
    shooting deadly bullets 177
    variables 175
environment
    enhancing 292

F

First-Person Shooter (FPS) 149

G

game #2
    designing 151
    overview 148
game design 8
game design process
    A-team 14
    about 10
    workflow 10
Game Objects
    prefab, creating for cake 114
    prefabs 114
    prefabs, creating for player 114

Game Over Screen
  creating 140
  scripting 141
gameplay
  user interface, creating 286
  water zones 287, 289, 290
  winning zone 291
  wrapping up 286
games
  Android Unity project, preparing 304, 306, 308,
    310, 311
  approaches 9
  collecting concept 53, 54
  elements 8
  exporting 301, 302
  exporting, on Android 303
  improving, ideas 208
  mobile input, implementing for 295
  platforming 211
  testing 206
Gizmos 45

H

hotkeys, Unity
  reference 37

I

infinite scrolling 212
infinite scrolling map
  background, repeating 195, 196
  building 195
  falling stars 198
  planets 198
  rotating satellites 199
Is Kinematic 98

J

jump pads
  about 282
  creating 282, 284, 285
JumpController
  creating 299, 301

K

kinematic motion 98

L

level properties
  modifying 226

M

map
  building 115, 117
Maya 155
Mecanim animation system 154
Mesh Renderer 55
Meta UIs 126
Mini-map 226
mobile input
  implementing, for game 295
  JumpController, creating 299, 301
  MovingController, creating 296, 298, 299
Movement Component
  about 265, 266, 267, 269
  setting up 270
MovingController
  creating 296, 298, 299

N

non-diegetic UIs 125
Non-Power Of Two (NPOT) textures 85

O

orthographic 3D 17

P

panda hero
  building 257, 258, 259, 261, 262, 263
panda
  moving 264
parallax effect 21
Physics Material 2D
  about 252, 254, 255
  bounciness parameter 252
  friction parameter 252
physics system

colliders 99
overview 98
Rigidbody 98
player controller
about 166
requisites 166
script, creating 167
player
moving 168, 169
shooting possibility 170
PlayerController
about 98, 270, 271
character, moving to new position 107
creating 97
testing 108
PlayerPrefs
about 275
functions 276
Power Of Two (POT) textures 85
power-ups
including 200, 201
prefabs
creating 200
primitive objects
reference 39
project setup, for game #2
about 152
assets, importing for space shooter 152
organizing 153

Q

Quark
about 50
reference 50

R

RETROformer
about 50
overview 212
reference 50
variables, saving 277, 278
Rigidbody 98

S

save/load system
about 273
building, for game 278, 280
creating, in Unity 274
refining 281
shooting games
first person 149
overview 149
third person 150
top-down 150
shooting system
bullet controller, creating 181
bullet prefab, creating 180
creating 166
explosion, testing 172
side-scrolling 212
sound FX 90
Spatial Blend 91
spatial UI 126
spawning points
creating 202, 203
spawning system
about 202
scripting 204, 206
special folders, Unity
about 42
Assets 42
Editor 43
Editor default resources 44
Gizmos menu 45
Hidden Assets 49
plugins 44
Resources 48
Standard Assets package 46
StreamingAssets folder 48
sprite animations 155, 156
Sprite Creator 55, 60, 62, 63
Sprite Editor
about 55, 56
using 56, 57
Sprite Packer 55, 59, 60
Sprite Render
about 56

parameters 56
Sprite Renderer 55
sprite sheet
  animations, creating from 242
  setting up, for animations 238, 239, 240, 241
Sprites 55
sprites
  animations, generating from 158, 160

T

TexturePacker 86
Textures 55
Third-Person Shooters (TPS) 150
Tiled2Unity
  about 213, 232
  download link 213
  tilesets, importing into Unity 229, 230
Tiled
  about 213, 214, 217
  download link 213
tiles
  colliders, adding to 228
  creating 213
tilesets
  importing, into Unity 229, 230
Trigger 108

U

UI system
  in Unity 133
Unity Engine 22
Unity User Interface (UI)
  components 28
  overview 27
Unity
  2D project, creating 26
  assets 38
  built-in features 25
  download link 22
  downloading 22
  hotkeys 37
  save/load system, creating 274
  special folders 42
  tilesets, importing into 229, 230

workspace, customizing 34
User Experience (UX) 128
User Interface (UI), for games
  color 130, 131
  consistent 132
  designing 128
  ergonomics 132
  feedback 128, 130
  focused 132
  goals 133
  integrity 133
  multi-device design 132
  simple 132
  test 133
User Interface (UI), in Angel Cakes
  building 134
  challenges, adding 144
  collection systems 134
  font, importing 134
  functionality, adding 142
  score increasing function 139
  scoring system, programming 138
  setting up 135, 136, 137
  testing 143
  UI, scripting 134
User Interface (UI)
  building 188
  designing 121, 122
  diegetic UIs 124
  function 127
  lives counter, creating 190, 191, 192
  Meta UIs 126
  non-diegetic UIs 125
  overview 120, 121
  programming 123
  setting up 188, 189, 190
  spatial UI 126
  star score counter, creating 194
  types 123
  usability 127

V

Virtual Reality (VR) 126

W

workflow process, game design
 about 10
 concept development 11, 12
 design and prototyping 12
 finalizing 14
 implementation 13
 iteration 14
 testing 13
workspace

customizing, in Unity 34

X

X-axis 16

Y

Y-axis 16

Z

Z-axis 16

CPSIA information can be obtained
at www.ICGtesting.com
Printed in the USA
FFOW01n2344080518
46518453-48488FF

9 781786 460271